Trade, Industrial Policy and
International Competition

This is Volume 13 in the series of studies commissioned as part of the research program of the Royal Commission on the Economic Union and Development Prospects for Canada.

This volume reflects the views of the author and does not imply endorsement by the Chairman or Commissioners.

Trade, Industrial Policy and International Competition

RICHARD G. HARRIS

Published by the University of Toronto Press in cooperation with
the Royal Commission on the Economic Union and Development
Prospects for Canada and the Canadian Government Publishing
Centre, Supply and Services Canada

University of Toronto Press
Toronto   Buffalo   London

Grateful acknowledgment is made to the following for permission to reprint previously published and unpublished material: Minister of Supply and Services Canada; Massachusetts Institute of Technology (Technology Review).

©Minister of Supply and Services Canada 1985

Printed in Canada
ISBN 0-8020-7255-0
ISSN 0829-2396
Cat. No. Z1-1983/1-41-13E

CANADIAN CATALOGUING IN PUBLICATION DATA

Harris, Richard G.
Trade, industrial policy and international competition

(*The Collected research studies / Royal Commission on the Economic Union and Development Prospects for Canada*,
ISSN 0829-2396 ; 13)
Includes bibiliographical references.
ISBN 0-8020-7255-0

1. Canada — Economic policy — 1971– 2. Canada — Commercial policy. 3. Canada — Industries. I. Royal Commission on the Economic Union and Development Prospects for Canada. II. Title. III.Series: The Collected research studies (Royal Commission on the Economic Union and Development Prospects for Canada) ; 13.

HC115.H37 1985   330.971'064   C85-099289-3

PUBLISHING COORDINATION: Ampersand Communications Services Inc.
COVER DESIGN: Will Rueter
INTERIOR DESIGN: Brant Cowie/Artplus Limited

CONTENTS

FOREWORD *ix*
INTRODUCTION *xi*
PREFACE *xv*
ACKNOWLEDGMENTS *xvii*

CHAPTER 1.
The Dilemma of Canadian Economic Development in the 1980s *1*
Introduction *1*
Trade and Economic Development, 1946–82 *4*
The Technological Revolution *7*
Strategies for Canadian Economic Development *8*
The Paradigm Problem *12*
An Outline of the Study *14*

CHAPTER 2.
Trade and the World Economy *17*
Introduction *17*
Alternative Theories of International Trade *18*
International Trade, 1945–74 *20*
The Product Cycle Theory of International Trade *21*
Trade and Investment in the 1970s: Post Product Cycle *24*
World Trade and the Industrial Innovation Races *26*
Conclusion *35*

CHAPTER 3.
**The Classic Theory of Comparative Advantage and
Its Implications for Canada** *37*
Introduction *37*
The Factor Proportions Theory of Comparative Advantage *37*
Challenges to the FP Theory *40*
Policy Implications of the FP-CAV Theory *43*
Problems and Prospects with an FP-CAV Perspective on
   Industrial   Structure and Trade *46*
      Renewable and Non-Renewable Resources *46*
      Savings and Capital Accumulation *47*
      Human Capital and FP Theory *51*
      Public Infrastructure and Regional Diversity *52*
Conclusion *55*

CHAPTER 4.
Economic Integration *57*
Introduction *57*
Transactions Costs, Markets and Trade Between Spacially
   Separated Markets *58*
External Scale Economies: Firms and Markets *61*
Firms: Location and Market Strategy *64*
Trade and Income Determination *68*
Policy Implications *71*

CHAPTER 5.
Entry Barriers and Competition in the Small Open Economy *75*
Introduction *75*
Static Entry Barriers *76*
   Scale Economies *76*
   Product Differentiation *80*
   Absolute Capital Requirements *81*
   Barriers to Export from the Small Open Economy *82*
Dynamic Theories of Competition *85*
   Pre-emptive Large-Scale Investment *86*
   Competition on the Learning Curve *88*
   Dynamic Protection Arguments *88*
Summary *91*

CHAPTER 6.
Schumpeterian Competition and the Small Open Economy *93*
Introduction *93*
The Schumpeterian Hypotheses: The Evidence *95*
Schumpeterian Competition and Market Failure in R&D *99*

The Open Economy   *100*
   The Open Economy Policy Perspective   *103*
   The Large Country Perspective   *104*
   The Small Country Perspective   *105*
Technology Transfer versus R&D   *107*
Conclusion   *109*

CHAPTER 7.
Industrial Policy in the Small Open Economy   *111*
Introduction   *111*
Economists and the Theory of Policy   *113*
Public-Private Sector Interaction: Planning and Targetting   *116*
Free Trade Versus Protection   *118*
Strategic Posture of Industrial Policy   *121*
Mega-Projects and the Resource Sector   *125*
Education and Job Retraining Policy   *127*
Adjustment Policy and the Losing Industries   *129*
The Problem in the Basic Industries   *131*
High Tech Industries, Industrial R&D and Technology Transfer   *136*
Industry Location and Policy Coordination   *141*
Non-traded Goods Sector   *143*
Conclusion   *143*

CHAPTER 8.
Conclusion and Summary   *145*

NOTES   *154*

BIBLIOGRAPHY   *161*

FOREWORD

When the members of the Rowell-Sirois Commission began their collective task in 1937, very little was known about the evolution of the Canadian economy. What was known, moreover, had not been extensively analyzed by the slender cadre of social scientists of the day.

When we set out upon our task nearly 50 years later, we enjoyed a substantial advantage over our predecessors; we had a wealth of information. We inherited the work of scholars at universities across Canada and we had the benefit of the work of experts from private research institutes and publicly sponsored organizations such as the Ontario Economic Council and the Economic Council of Canada. Although there were still important gaps, our problem was not a shortage of information; it was to interrelate and integrate — to synthesize — the results of much of the information we already had.

The mandate of this Commission is unusually broad. It encompasses many of the fundamental policy issues expected to confront the people of Canada and their governments for the next several decades. The nature of the mandate also identified, in advance, the subject matter for much of the research and suggested the scope of enquiry and the need for vigorous efforts to interrelate and integrate the research disciplines. The resulting research program, therefore, is particularly noteworthy in three respects: along with original research studies, it includes survey papers which synthesize work already done in specialized fields; it avoids duplication of work which, in the judgment of the Canadian research community, has already been well done; and, considered as a whole, it is the most thorough examination of the Canadian economic, political and legal systems ever undertaken by an independent agency.

The Commission's research program was carried out under the joint direction of three prominent and highly respected Canadian scholars: Dr. Ivan Bernier (*Law and Constitutional Issues*), Dr. Alan Cairns (*Politics and Institutions of Government*) and Dr. David C. Smith (*Economics*).

Dr. Ivan Bernier is Dean of the Faculty of Law at Laval University. Dr. Alan Cairns is former Head of the Department of Political Science at the University of British Columbia and, prior to joining the Commission, was William Lyon Mackenzie King Visiting Professor of Canadian Studies at Harvard University. Dr. David C. Smith, former Head of the Department of Economics at Queen's University in Kingston, is now Principal of that University. When Dr. Smith assumed his new responsibilities at Queen's in September, 1984, he was succeeded by Dr. Kenneth Norrie of the University of Alberta and John Sargent of the federal Department of Finance, who together acted as Co-directors of Research for the concluding phase of the Economics research program.

I am confident that the efforts of the Research Directors, research coordinators and authors whose work appears in this and other volumes, have provided the community of Canadian scholars and policy makers with a series of publications that will continue to be of value for many years to come. And I hope that the value of the research program to Canadian scholarship will be enhanced by the fact that Commission research is being made available to interested readers in both English and French.

I extend my personal thanks, and that of my fellow Commissioners, to the Research Directors and those immediately associated with them in the Commission's research program. I also want to thank the members of the many research advisory groups whose counsel contributed so substantially to this undertaking.

DONALD S. MACDONALD

At its most general level, the Royal Commission's research program has examined how the Canadian political economy can better adapt to change. As a basis of enquiry, this question reflects our belief that the future will always take us partly by surprise. Our political, legal and economic institutions should therefore be flexible enough to accommodate surprises and yet solid enough to ensure that they help us meet our future goals. This theme of an adaptive political economy led us to explore the interdependencies between political, legal and economic systems and drew our research efforts in an interdisciplinary direction.

The sheer magnitude of the research output (more than 280 separate studies in 72 volumes) as well as its disciplinary and ideological diversity have, however, made complete integration impossible and, we have concluded, undesirable. The research output as a whole brings varying perspectives and methodologies to the study of common problems and we therefore urge readers to look beyond their particular field of interest and to explore topics across disciplines.

The three research areas, — *Law and Constitutional Issues*, under Ivan Bernier; *Politics and Institutions of Government*, under Alan Cairns; and *Economics*, under David C. Smith (co-directed with Kenneth Norrie and John Sargent for the concluding phase of the research program) — were further divided into 19 sections headed by research coordinators.

The area *Law and Constitutional Issues* has been organized into five major sections headed by the research coordinators identified below.

- Law, Society and the Economy — *Ivan Bernier and Andrée Lajoie*
- The International Legal Environment — *John J. Quinn*
- The Canadian Economic Union — *Mark Krasnick*

- Harmonization of Laws in Canada — *Ronald C.C. Cuming*
- Institutional and Constitutional Arrangements — *Clare F. Beckton and A. Wayne MacKay*

Since law in its numerous manifestations is the most fundamental means of implementing state policy, it was necessary to investigate how and when law could be mobilized most effectively to address the problems raised by the Commission's mandate. Adopting a broad perspective, researchers examined Canada's legal system from the standpoint of how law evolves as a result of social, economic and political changes and how, in turn, law brings about changes in our social, economic and political conduct.

Within *Politics and Institutions of Government*, research has been organized into seven major sections.

- Canada and the International Political Economy — *Denis Stairs and Gilbert Winham*
- State and Society in the Modern Era — *Keith Banting*
- Constitutionalism, Citizenship and Society — *Alan Cairns and Cynthia Williams*
- The Politics of Canadian Federalism — *Richard Simeon*
- Representative Institutions — *Peter Aucoin*
- The Politics of Economic Policy — *G. Bruce Doern*
- Industrial Policy — *André Blais*

This area examines a number of developments which have led Canadians to question their ability to govern themselves wisely and effectively. Many of these developments are not unique to Canada and a number of comparative studies canvass and assess how others have coped with similar problems. Within the context of the Canadian heritage of parliamentary government, federalism, a mixed economy, and a bilingual and multicultural society, the research also explores ways of rearranging the relationships of power and influence among institutions to restore and enhance the fundamental democratic principles of representativeness, responsiveness and accountability.

Economics research was organized into seven major sections.

- Macroeconomics — *John Sargent*
- Federalism and the Economic Union — *Kenneth Norrie*
- Industrial Structure — *Donald G. McFetridge*
- International Trade — *John Whalley*
- Income Distribution and Economic Security — *François Vaillancourt*
- Labour Markets and Labour Relations — *Craig Riddell*
- Economic Ideas and Social Issues — *David Laidler*

Economics research examines the allocation of Canada's human and other resources, the ways in which institutions and policies affect this allocation, and the distribution of the gains from their use. It also considers the nature of economic development, the forces that shape our regional and industrial structure, and our economic interdependence with other countries. The thrust of the research in economics is to increase our comprehension of what determines our economic potential and how instruments of economic policy may move us closer to our future goals.

One section from each of the three research areas — The Canadian Economic Union, The Politics of Canadian Federalism, and Federalism and the Economic Union — have been blended into one unified research effort. Consequently, the volumes on Federalism and the Economic Union as well as the volume on The North are the results of an interdisciplinary research effort.

We owe a special debt to the research coordinators. Not only did they organize, assemble and analyze the many research studies and combine their major findings in overviews, but they also made substantial contributions to the Final Report. We wish to thank them for their performance, often under heavy pressure.

Unfortunately, space does not permit us to thank all members of the Commission staff individually. However, we are particularly grateful to the Chairman, The Hon. Donald S. Macdonald; the Commission's Executive Director, J. Gerald Godsoe; and the Director of Policy, Alan Nymark, all of whom were closely involved with the Research Program and played key roles in the contribution of Research to the Final Report. We wish to express our appreciation to the Commission's Administrative Advisor, Harry Stewart, for his guidance and advice, and to the Director of Publishing, Ed Matheson, who managed the research publication process. A special thanks to Jamie Benidickson, Policy Coordinator and Special Assistant to the Chairman, who played a valuable liaison role between Research and the Chairman and Commissioners. We are also grateful to our office administrator, Donna Stebbing, and to our secretarial staff, Monique Carpentier, Barbara Cowtan, Tina DeLuca, Françoise Guilbault and Marilyn Sheldon.

Finally, a well deserved thank you to our closest assistants: Jacques J.M. Shore, *Law and Constitutional Issues*; Cynthia Williams and her successor Karen Jackson, *Politics and Institutions of Government*; and I. Lilla Connidis, *Economics*. We appreciate not only their individual contribution to each research area, but also their cooperative contribution to the research program and the Commission.

IVAN BERNIER
ALAN CAIRNS
DAVID C. SMITH

In this volume Richard Harris discusses how new theories of international trade which stress the role of industrial structures relate to Canada's policy options toward her external environment. Professor Harris represents a new generation of Canadian economists who are blending their strong analytical skills with a commitment to policy-relevant research, and this volume is further evidence of their work. Richard Harris has already received praise in Canada and abroad for his work on applied general equilibrium analysis incorporating both scale economy and industrial organization.

In this volume, he argues that a coherent industrial policy, based on selected and limited forms of government action, is crucial to sustained long-term growth and employment in Canada, while at the same time keeping the social risks of such a policy within acceptable limits. Some of his conclusions — that free trade and an active industrial policy are complements, not substitutes, and that picking winning industries to promote is both viable and desirable — will be controversial. However, the importance of his closely reasoned arguments to the policy debate will be acknowledged by all. The research effort at the Commission is indeed fortunate to have his latest work on these issues made available in this way.

JOHN WHALLEY

ACKNOWLEDGMENTS

In preparing this monograph, I have benefited from discussions and comments of numerous people involved in the research part of the Royal Commission's activities. Specifically, I should like to thank Gerry Helleiner, Jim Markusen, Ed Safarian, Ron Shearer, John Whalley, Bruce Wilkinson and Ron Wonnacott. I would also like to thank Ruth Crow, who edited the manuscript. Finally, thanks to my wife Nancy, who suffered with my preoccupations while the study was being prepared.

RICHARD G. HARRIS

Chapter 1

The Dilemma of Canadian Economic Development in the 1980s

Introduction

From 1960 until 1983, world national product grew at the unprecedented rate of about 5.5 percent per annum. Over the same period world trade grew at an average annual rate of about 8 percent. In 1946, the United States was the single major economic power in the world. By 1982, Japan, the European Economic Community and the Communist bloc countries all constituted economically integrated regions which rivalled the United States in terms of economic power. The developing nations, which were pre-industrial colonial outposts in the 1950s, emerged as the fastest growing nations in the world by the middle of the 1970s. Technical change, as indicated by economic innovations, proceeded at a fairly fast but uneven pace throughout most of the postwar decades; recently, it has literally taken off with the development and application of micro-electronic technology. The "computer on the chip" promises, according to some, the emergence of the post-industrial society.[1]

While there were significant economic changes within Canada in the postwar decades, notably the decline of agriculture and growth in the service sector, these were minor developments compared to the changes in the world economy during the same period. Canada continued to develop both its resource and manufacturing sectors at a relatively even pace, matching the growth of the neighbouring U.S. economy. Canadians enjoyed a rising standard of living throughout the period, particularly in the 1960s and early 1970s.

For these reasons, public policy with respect to economic development in Canada, while attracting attention from social scientists and politicians, was not a controversial issue in the postwar period. There was a social consensus that the resource and manufacturing sectors should develop simultaneously, and a general commitment by Canada to fostering improvement in the world trading system through multilateral negotiation on tariff reductions. The closest thing to a national debate on economic development in this period was the ongoing argument about foreign investment and the possible costs and benefits of economic integration with the United States. Even this debate attracted remarkably little public attention. Regional tensions between Central and Western Canada were mollified by growth in the resource exports of the West and development of the manufacturing sector in Central Canada through special policies such as the Canada–U.S. Auto Pact. Tariff barriers were reduced in Canada and throughout the world, and Canadians shared widely in the benefits through lower prices for imported goods, and increased wages and profits from the sale of exports.

Since the mid-1970s, however, public concern about economic issues has steadily increased. Developments in the world economy have become more noticeable to the average Canadian. The first hint of this was the 1974 OPEC oil shock, but that was slight in comparison to what followed. Rapid technological change, the discovery of raw material supplies around the world, intense international competition in industrial goods from the Japanese and, more recently, from the developing countries, have generated a new sense of urgency in addressing fundamental questions of Canadian economic development. The concern in the large industrial countries with "de-industrialization" of the basic manufacturing sector is now shared by most Canadians living in Central Canada. Where will the jobs be generated that are lost to the new technologies and foreign competitors? In the resource-based regions of Canada, the fall in raw material prices and decline in the quality of Canadian resource supplies have led to serious doubts about the future export potential of these sectors.

For the first time since John A. Macdonald set out a strategy for economic development in the National Policy of 1879, there is general recognition among informed Canadians that changes in the economic structure of Canadian industry are inevitable and that the policy issues concerned with these changes are difficult and pressing. What type of economic structure should be encouraged? How should it be encouraged? What is the role for the market system and international trade? Is there a case for an "industrial strategy" involving protection and promotion of selected industries? These are some of the questions which led to the creation of the Royal Commission for which this study was prepared.

The purpose of this study is to address the questions posed for trade and industrial policy by the developments referred to in the preceding paragraphs. The study provides a review of Canadian and international literature on the subject and a critical synthesis of this literature within a common theoretical framework. It includes studies in international trade, labour economics, industrial organization, international business, and development economics. Public policy literature on industrial policy, most of it written for U.S. audiences, also bears on many of these questions, although much of it is of little relevance to Canada in other respects. The objective of this synthesis of the literature has been to draw out the implications for Canadian trade and industrial policy with respect to economic development and structural change in the economy.

Limitations of time meant that some important issues related to structural change and the course of economic development within Canada were left untouched. These include the causes of and policies toward technological unemployment; labour-business relations as an evolving institution in the economy and their impact on adjustment to structural change; and the integration of macroeconomic and microeconomic policy toward structural change and economic development. The study is concerned solely with the microeconomic international trade aspects of structural policies. Hence, the focus throughout the study on trade and industrial policy.

The study does not provide a detailed treatment of the regional aspects of Canadian trade and industrial policy, although many of the issues it deals with have an implicit regional connotation because of the industries involved. It gives little attention to coordination and competition between different levels of government because the federal government is the dominant participant in forming trade and industrial policy.

There is a wide divergence of views about many trade and industrial policy issues discussed in the study. This divergence is due in part to the fact that those addressing the issues represent various disciplines, but even more significant are the differences in underlying political ideology. The viewpoint generally taken here is that of mainstream neoclassical economics. This means a predisposition toward free markets and a view that government intervention should be limited to clearly identifiable market failures or be motivated by concerns for social and economic distributive justice. However, conventional theory is viewed as unsuited for some of the problems, and the economic case for government policy directed toward facilitating structural change is stronger than the neoclassical synthesis of contemporary economic theory would suggest.

While the economic case for enlightened government intervention may be strong, the political case is less certain. The experience of many economies with a wide variety of interventionist microeconomic policies in the 1960s and 1970s was not uniformly successful and in some cases an outright disaster. Our National Energy Program would be high on the list. On the other hand, there have been some quite successful economic development policies.

The policy recommendations made here are economic arguments made without reference to many of the political realities of policy intervention by governments in Canada. Carrying them forward into practical terms would require further analysis of their political and bureaucratic feasibility.

Trade and Economic Development, 1946–82

This section summarizes the relevant facts about Canadian trade and economic development over the last three decades. An excellent discussion of many of these developments is provided in Bruce Wilkinson's *Canada in the Changing World Economy* (1980). Changes in trade patterns are described in External Affairs, *A Review of Canadian Trade Policy* (1983) and the Economic Council of Canada, *The Bottom Line* (1983).

Table 1-1 gives a breakdown of employment by sector for the years 1946, 1966 and 1982. There are three striking trends: the relatively rapid decline of the agricultural sector; the long-term decline of the manufacturing sector from 25 percent of the labour force in 1946 to just over 18 percent in 1982; and the increase in the size of the services sector. The resource sector remains a small employer on a national scale. These trends are common in other industrialized countries, particularly the growth in the services sector. The growth in services, together with a

TABLE 1-1 Employment by Sector, 1946–82

Industry	1946	1966	1982
	(percent)		
Goods:			
Agriculture	24.8	7.6	4.4
Fishing, trapping and forestry	2.3	1.4	2.5
Mines, quarries and oil wells	1.5	1.7	
Manufacturing	25.3	24.4	18.2
Construction	4.7	7.0	5.6
	58.6	42.1	30.7
Services:			
Transportation, storage and communications	7.2	7.6	8.2
Trade	12.0	16.5	17.4
Finance, insurance and real estate	2.6	4.2	5.7
Community, business and personal services	19.6	23.9	30.8
Public administration	n.a.	5.7	7.2
	41.4	57.9	69.3
	100.0	100.0	100.0

Sources: B.W. Wilkinson, *Canada in a Changing World Economy* (Montreal: C.D. Howe Research Institute, 1980), Table 3; and Department of Finance, *Economic Review, April 1983* (Ottawa: Minister of Supply and Services Canada), Table 5.1.

shift in industrial production to some of the developing countries, has contributed to the belief that the economy is "de-industrializing."

The Canadian economy is small in absolute terms and relatively open in comparison with the large economies. In Table 1-2, this is noted in terms of exports as a percentage of GDP. From 1965 to 1980, this percentage grew from 15.6 to 25.6 percent. In the large industrial countries, the percentage was much smaller but also grew.

TABLE 1-2 Ratio of Merchandise Exports to Gross Domestic Product

	1965	1974	1980
		(percent)	
Canada	15.6	21.6	25.6
United States	3.9	7.0	8.4
Japan	9.5	12.2	12.4
EEC	8.2	11.7	11.1

Source: Canada, Department of External Affairs, *A Review of Canadian Trade Policy* (Ottawa. Minister of Supply and Services Canada, 1983), Table 3.

Note: Excludes intra-community trade.

In general, the world economy is becoming much more dependent on trade. The particular relationship between Canada and the United States is well known. In 1981, 68.7 percent of Canadian imports were from the United States and 66.2 percent of Canadian exports went to the United States. Growth in Canada–U.S. trade has been concentrated in end products, due partly to the Auto Pact. The newly industrialized countries (NICs) account for less than 8 percent of Canadian imports. Canada has significant levels of protection against these imports.

A major feature of world economic development in the twentieth century was the considerable growth of all countries between 1960 and 1973. Canada was no exception. However, the world slowdown in growth after 1973 affected Canada dramatically, as shown in Table 1-3. Canadian exports grew at an annual rate of 10 percent over the 1963–73 decade and slowed to 2.5 percent over the 1973–83 decade. Japan's performance was spectacular in contrast to the other industrial countries. Over this period of productivity slowdown, growth of the underdeveloped countries exceeded growth of the industrialized countries.

Changes in Canada's trade patterns are revealed in Table 1-4. The general trend has been a decline in exports of raw and semiprocessed material and an increase in exports of finished manufactured goods. From 1960 to 1981, finished manufactured exports grew from 7.8 to 31.2 percent of merchandise exports. This trend has continued in the recent recovery, creating dramatic increases in Canada's trade surplus. The trade data, unlike the employment data, support a fairly optimistic

TABLE 1-3 Growth in Economic Activity and Trade
        of Industrialized Countries
        (annual rate of change in volume)

Region	GNP or GDP		Exports		Imports	
	1963–73	1973–80	1963–73	1973–80	1963–73	1973–80
Industrialized countries (total)	5.0	2.5	9.0	5.0	9.0	3.0
United States	4.0	2.0	7.5	6.0	9.5	2.5
Canada	5.5	1.5	10.0	2.5	11.0	3.0
Japan	10.5	4.0	16.0	9.0	14.5	1.0
EEC (9)	4.5	2.0	8.5	4.5	8.0	3.5

Source: Canada, Department of External Affairs, *A Review of Canadian Trade Policy* (Ottawa: Minister of Supply and Services Canada, 1983), Table 5.

TABLE 1-4 Distribution of Domestic Merchandise Exports
        among Major Commodity Group (1960–81)

	1960	1974	1981
	(percent)		
Food, feed, beverages and tobacco	18.8	12.2	11.6
Inedible crude materials	21.2	24.6	18.7
Inedible fabricated materials	51.9	33.8	37.6
Finished manufactured goods (inedible end products)	7.8	29.2	31.2

Source: Canada, Department of External Affairs, *A Review of Canadian Trade Policy* (Ottawa: Minister of Supply and Services Canada, 1983), Table 6.

view of the absence of "de-industrialization" in the Canadian economy. Manufacturing is gaining in importance as a traded goods sector of the economy.

Services have yet to play an important role in Canadian trade. Currently, Canada is in a deficit position in services trade. However, trade in services is growing in international importance. Services now account for about 25 percent of world trade in goods and services. This worldwide growth of the services sector may prove to be the major development in trade patterns over the next decade. Related to trade in services is the transfer of "invisibles" by multinational corporations through transfers between the parent and foreign subsidiaries. Given the extensive degree of foreign ownership in Canadian industry, this trade is important to the Canadian economy. The statistics on intracorporate trade are generally not as good as other trade statistics, but an often-cited Statistics Canada study found that 72 percent of imports into

Canada in 1978 were to foreign-controlled firms, and estimated that a large part of this trade consisted of intrafirm transfers (see External Affairs, 1983, p. 31). The study found that imports were highly concentrated. Fifty enterprises accounted for almost 50 percent of all imports and 35 of the 50 were foreign-controlled.

The Technological Revolution

A fundamental assumption of this study is that developments in microelectronic technology are going to change dramatically the nature of manufacturing industries and consequently of world trade in industrial products. While this assumption seems self-evident to many, there are skeptics. After all, we have yet to provide an adequate explanation of the productivity slowdown of the 1970s and many believe productivity growth is unlikely to accelerate. This view, however, fails to recognize the fundamental changes microprocessor technology has brought to numerous industries over a short time. The value of time series studies on 1960s and 1970s data in predicting either technological innovation or productivity changes into the 1980s and 1990s is questionable.

The current "revolution" is of recent origin and is just beginning to have a noticeable impact in many industries. The use of industrial robots is an interesting example because robots change the way existing industrial products can be produced and are also an emerging growth industry based on the new technology. From 1970 to 1982, robot use in the United States grew from 200 to 4,500. Most of that growth occurred in 1981–82 with the installation of many robots in U.S. auto plants. The United States was substantially behind Japan, however, where 14,000 robots were in use by 1981. Some estimates predict that over 100,000 robots will be in use in the United States by the end of 1985.

Robots have been used primarily in industries within the metalworking sector, including fabricated metal products, machinery, electrical and electronic equipment, and transportation equipment. Improvements in software and in sensor technology, which allow robots to both "see" and "feel" with extraordinary accuracy, are extending the range of tasks that they can perform in both the manufacturing and service sectors. In some industries the cost incentive to adopt robots is overwhelming. The robots installed by General Motors in many of its U.S. plants in 1983 had an hourly cost of $6 (including maintenance and depreciation), while the worker they replaced was paid $23 to $24 per hour. The wage-robotics trade-off was noted by GM Chairman Roger B. Smith, quoted as saying that "every time the cost of labour goes up $1.00 an hour, 1,000 robots become more economical."[2]

Surprisingly little work has been done by economists to assess the longer-term impact of robots. One study, headed by Robert Ayres at Carnegie-Mellon, reports results of a 1981 survey of firms in the metalworking sector.[3] Firms were asked to estimate the number of jobs in a particular occupational category which could be eliminated by robots. Some results, reported in Ayres and Miller (1982), are given in Table 1-5. Ayres and Miller estimate that 40 percent of the jobs in the metalworking sector could be replaced by robots existing today and an even greater number over the longer term.

Robotics is just one example of the way production methods and products are being transformed by applications of microprocessor technology. There are countless others, most of them post-1980. The revolution in technology has two major effects on industry: low-skilled jobs may be displaced by computer-based machines as the relative cost of labour to machine rises; and a host of new products and process innovations may be developed, altering the structure of existing industries and creating a large number of new industries. Both factors figure prominently in the analysis of Canadian trade and industrial policy.

Strategies for Canadian Economic Development

A review of the historical pattern of economic development strategies in Canada and their relation to trade policy may help to put the rest of the study in perspective. The emphasis will necessarily be on the more recent period. Much economic history literature is available which deals with the early period of economic development following Confederation.[4]

Basic economic development strategy in Canada was simple until the post–World War II period. First, it was based on the export of Canada's relatively abundant primary products — wheat, furs, fish, lumber, minerals and, more recently, oil and gas. Second, it used tariffs and other restrictions on imported manufactured goods to encourage the development of an indigenous manufacturing sector within Central Canada. Heavy public sector investment in transportation and communications networks that connected the geographically dispersed markets in Canada allowed the export of the primary commodities, and provided access for Canadian manufacturers throughout the domestic market.

Both promotion of primary commodity exports and import substitution in manufacturing have been and continue to be common policies throughout the world. In most countries one or the other of these policies tends to be favoured. Canada and a few other small resource-based economies were unique among the many small industrializing countries in maintaining high levels of income which were broadly shared by all citizens, and in promoting economic development relatively evenly across all sectors.

Throughout this period, the problems stemming from proximity to the United States were primarily political, although some economic difficulties with protection were noted in studies done in the 1920s and 1930s.

TABLE 1-5 Occupational Tasks Suitable for Robotization

Occupation	Level I Robots		Level II Robots	
	Range of Response	Average Weighted Response	Range of Response	Average Weighted Response
		(percent)		
Production painter	30–100	44	50–100	66
Welder/flamecutter	10–60	27	10–90	49
Machine operator		20		50
Machine operators (NC)	10–90	20	30–90	49
Drill press operators	25–50	30	60–75	65
Grinding/abrading operators	10–20	18	20–100	50
Lath/turning operators	10–20	18	40–60	50
Milling/planning operators	10–20	18	40–60	50
Machine operators (Non-NC)	10–30	15	5–60	30

Source: Robert Ayres and Steven Miller, "Industrial Robots on the Line," *Technology Review* (May/June 1982), Table 1.

Notes: Level I robots refers to those on the market in 1981. Level II robots refers to those with rudimentary sensing capabilities; these are currently in use in a number of industrial applications. NC refers to numerically controlled operators; Non-NC refers to non-numerically controlled operators. Machine tool operators include the separate types of machinists listed below. These estimates are used as an average to approximate the percentage of all categories of machinists listed below which could be robotized.

The tariff was widely recognized as a reason for the large amount of U.S. direct investment in Canada, as U.S. firms set up subsidiaries in Canada so as to jump the tariff barriers.

Aside from the 1911 election, in which reciprocity with the United States was a major issue, the general question of free trade played little part in Canadian economic policy until after World War II. The development of the International Monetary Fund and the General Agreement on Tariffs and Trade (GATT) by the industrialized countries of the Western Bloc after World War II was a response to the disastrous levels of protection and "beggar-thy-neighbour" policies of the Depression period. Canada shared in the commitment by all industrialized countries to promote "freer" trade in both goods and investment, although it had some of the highest tariff barriers among the industrialized countries. The growing significance of scale in modern production processes meant that if the Canadian manufacturing sector was going to develop further, it had to look beyond the domestic market. The commitment to the GATT was, at least in part, a recognition of this need.

Concern about access to foreign markets became prevalent in policy discussion in the 1960s. A number of studies detailed the "miniature replica" effect of Canadian industry, with its attendant inefficiencies.[5] The Automotive Products Trade Agreement of 1965 was an arrangement for explicit industry rationalization of particular firms within the North American auto industry, to reduce the obvious inefficiencies of excessive product diversification induced by tariff protection. Discussion about the general merits of free trade for Canada in the 1960s may be viewed as a debate between "nationalists" and "continentalists." The continentalists viewed as natural the tendency for Canada's manufacturing sector to become integrated within the North American industrial structure. The nationalists were pessimistic about the economic benefits of such a policy and believed that its political and cultural consequences would be negative. They favoured an economic strategy of protection, government rationalization of industry, and reduction in the degree of foreign ownership of industry.

In the 1970s, the issue of dependency on foreign industry and technology was highlighted by the Gray Report (1972), which resulted in establishment of the Foreign Investment Review Agency. During the early 1970s, there were renewed calls for an industrial strategy for Canada, although there was much opposition among both federal bureaucrats and the Canadian business community. The seeds of an idea had been sown but what the strategy might be was never made clear.

The jump in energy prices in 1974 led to renewed emphasis on the resource sectors of the economy. This change in relative prices, together with the growing political power of the western provinces, gave impetus to an industrial policy explicitly focussed on the resource sectors. After the second oil price shock, in 1979, such an industrial policy was implemented in the National Energy Program. In hindsight, it is remarkable how economic policy became so single-tracked in this period. Other important developments were rapidly emerging in the world economy but received far less attention. The infamous federal white paper on economic development,[6] which clearly was a stab at industrial strategy by the federal government, paid little attention to many of these developments. There is currently a perception that economic development policy is at a crossroads, in that no clear direction is being articulated by government.

Canada's current situation poses some difficult questions for economic development policy. Some proponents of the post-industrial society question the need for an industrial base in a modern economy. This is an extreme view, but the importance of trade in services as a viable base for economic development cannot be dismissed. The strategy called for with respect to manufacturing is quite different from that in 1967. Appropriate disinvestment is called for in the case of Canadian industries which are already developed but cannot compete without protection from low-wage competition from abroad. In many traditional industries, Canada's primary competitors have been other industrialized countries and in many instances Canada has been the high-cost supplier. Now the newly industrializing countries are emerging as important competitors, producing these traditional manufactured goods at costs far below those of any industrialized country. In the development of new industries, there is the classic nexus between export promotion and import substitution as alternative development strategies, compounded by uncertainty and disagreement as to which new industries should be developed. High technology seems to offer most opportunity for the future, but competition in these industries will be severe.

Appropriate investment and disinvestment policies must be made in circumstances which make the choices difficult and the risks substantial. Foremost among these is the rapidity with which capital moves about the globe in response to economic pressures. The "runaway plant," which is moved solely to get access to cheaper labour, is one manifestation of capital mobility. This movement imposes small costs on shareholders but large costs on the workers who lose their jobs and on their community. While capital has become more mobile, labour adjustment has become more difficult. The highly specialized skills of new industries require long training periods and substantial investment in human capital. Moving a farm worker from Saskatchewan to an auto assembly job in Windsor at the end of World War II was a far simpler matter than turning an unemployed auto worker into a computer programmer in the 1980s. The difficulty of making the adjustment, the long lead times required and the heavy investment have created a need for increased planning by firms, individuals and governments. At the same time, heavy investment and uncertainty about future developments create individual and social risk. Risk management and planning require sophisticated economic intelligence.

Recognizing the options and the risks in alternative courses of economic development strategy is only the beginning. Further issues concern the appropriate role of the market system, the extent and form of government interventions, and the way trade policy should be conducted during a period of such extensive change. These are some of the questions the study will attempt to address.

The Paradigm Problem

The standard view of most orthodox economists is that patterns of trade and investment are explained by the doctrine of comparative advantage, and that free markets are the most effective institutional device for exploiting comparative advantage and realizing the benefits of trade. Government intervention is regarded as useful only to the extent that it helps these "natural" forces. A substantial body of theoretical and empirical literature lends considerable weight to this paradigm of economic analysis, and Canadians have probably contributed more to it than to any other field of economics. This paradigm forms the basis for much of current trade policy throughout the industrial world, and for much of what passes for macroeconomic policy. Every economist, of whatever methodological bent, admits that the theoretical structure underlying the neoclassical theory of resource allocation and its open economy extensions do not give a fully accurate picture of the real world. Nevertheless, its defenders regard it as useful, approximately true, and both elegant and logically consistent in its internal structure. The latter feature is one which, in practice, receives the most attention from economic theorists.

In addressing the issues of global competition and Canadian economic development, it is my opinion that the strict paradigm of neoclassical trade theory is not useful or accurate in its description for a substantial part of world trade and investment patterns. There is another, more eclectic, view of the market system, including the functioning of world industrial markets, which is consistent with a large body of empirical evidence, is founded upon a reasonably consistent body of theory, and bears directly on Canadian concerns about international competition and Canada's role in the world economy. This view includes the conventional doctrine of comparative advantage, in a modified form, within its theoretical framework. It does, however, cast a different light on the manner in which the market allocates resources, and consequently the manner in which microeconomic policy, hereinafter referred to as industrial policy, impinges on the economy.

The intellectual underpinnings for this theory come from the field of industrial organization. Industrial organization is a sub-discipline of economics concerned with "imperfect" market structures or, more generally, the inner working of product markets, firms and industries. It has had little to do with the neoclassical conception of perfect competition so widely embraced elsewhere in economics. For many years it was a predominantly empirical discipline, studying the characteristics of firms and industries in great statistical detail. In recent years, the theoretical structure has become more elaborate, providing a deeper appreciation of the way resource allocation is conducted in product markets. The weakness of the industrial organization perspective is that it lacks the generality that economists like to invoke. This is particularly true in the discussion of trade patterns and the market forces which shape them.

Developments in the economics of information and exchange, including the study of non-market transactions, also offer some important insights on these issues. These are the modern equivalent of the popular 1960s literature on market failure. In loose terms, market failure refers to any set of structural conditions surrounding economic exchange which violate the assumptions underlying Adam Smith's famous "invisible hand" theorem on the efficiency of competitive markets. In the postwar period, market failure became the major economic doctrine justifying the intervention of government in the marketplace. Kenneth Arrow was perhaps the first prominent economist to recognize the possibilities for market failure, in a series of papers published in the 1960s.[7] The general concept, however, had been around for a considerable time before that.

Some ardent proponents of the capitalist system never accepted the market failure notion, because they denied the relevance of the formal model used by neoclassical economists in their description of "competitive capitalism."[8] In the 1970s the idea of market failure fell into some disrepute. The problem was that the alternatives involving bureaucratic decision making suffered from their own brand of administrative failures — in some cases considerably more dramatic than the market failures which motivated the intervention in the first place. Currently, most economists in North America subscribe to a view that may be described as the "practical optimality" of free markets. In this view, the free market may not be optimal relative to some ideal allocation system, but is often the best practical method of ensuring efficiency in resource allocation, certainly more efficient than bureaucratic administrative procedures, which are often not subject to the same "bottom line" considerations as private sector activity.

The idea of market failures, however, is of considerable intellectual importance. While caution is called for in using market failure analysis as an argument for government intervention, the failure itself is cause for social concern as to an appropriate institutional response. Pollution is perhaps the best known example of a bona fide market failure — no one expects free enterprise to resolve a significant pollution problem.

The foundations for the "alternative view" of the market system put forward in this study lie in recognition of the importance of market structures, including the many markets that are oligopolistic or monopolistic, and the importance of certain market failures in explaining trade, investment and their impact on the Canadian economy. This alternative view provides a framework within which to organize empirical analysis and evaluate the impact of economic policy.

These ideas have been circulating in the profession for many years. Some of the early work on trade and investment in Canada by Eastman and Stykolt (1967), for example, rested quite explicitly on the industrial organization view of resource allocation. Market failures, which are prominent in the "alternative view," have played an important role in numerous policy documents. However, these concepts were not integrated with a more unified, or general equilibrium, view of resource allocation and, in particular, were not applied to broad questions about trade and economic structure.

The study does not examine these questions exclusively from the "alternative" viewpoint. Some time is spent addressing the evidence on the conventional neoclassical theory of comparative advantage, both international and Canadian, to assure that what is useful and significant in the doctrine of comparative advantage is not discarded. Comparative advantage based on the abundance of certain natural factors of production must be recognized as important in a theory of trade and any system of resource allocation, market or non-market. The importance of natural resources in the Canadian economy must be accounted for in an approach toward resource allocation which lays claim to some generality.

An Outline of the Study

The study has two main objectives. It reviews the intellectual framework within which trade and industrial policy questions are examined by economists, and outlines the policy implications of different intellectual positions. It then looks at policy options for Canada and makes a number of recommendations. These recommendations are based on: assumptions about trends in the world economy; an intellectual position on how world industrial markets function, reflecting an "imperfect competition" view of these markets; and a basic political assumption that governments intervene in domestic and international markets through various industrial policies, including trade policies, on behalf of national factors of production. There are better and worse industrial policies to achieve the same political and economic ends. The study seeks to identify those which are better. It does not deal in detail with a complete free market position, because that is viewed as largely irrelevant in the current circumstances. Taking an ideological stand on free markets versus government-directed economic planning or industrial strategy is counter-productive and inhibits a realistic examination of economic policy. It is time to do better.

To anticipate what follows, the main conclusion is that a coherent industrial policy for Canada based on selected and limited forms of government action is crucial to sustaining long-term growth and employment while keeping the social risks of such a policy within acceptable limits. First and foremost, trade and investment policies must be aimed at assuring access to large markets for Canadian industrial goods. Free trade is absolutely crucial for a small open economy. Second, government must actively foster an adjustment out of those industries in which Canada has a competitive disadvantage and into those industries where there are potential export growth prospects. Neither policy is likely to be successful without the other, for both political and economic reasons. One major alternative to such a policy would be an industrial strategy based on import substitution. Some industrialized countries seem to be currently leaning in this direction and there are proponents of such a policy within Canada, particularly among those who are often identified as "nationalists," but under current circumstances nothing could be worse for the Canadian economy. In making the case for the type of export-oriented industrial policy that is most sensible for Canada, the study also examines the reasons why an industrial strategy based on import substitution is particularly unsuitable.

The study is organized into a sequence of topics based on the objectives outlined in the previous paragraphs. Chapter Two assesses past and current trends in the world economy. This provides the basis for assumptions as to what Canadian policy must treat as exogenous and be cognizant of. Chapter Three reviews the evidence on Canadian comparative advantage within the tradition of neoclassical trade theory; provides a critical evaluation of that evidence and theory; and considers the question of "engineering" a long-run comparative advantage within a classical framework. Chapter Four deals with the basic question of what economic integration between two countries or regions implies about the nature and efficiency of resource allocation within and between them. An understanding of this set of issues is of considerable importance because the world economy is becoming increasingly integrated and decisions about such issues as seeking a free trade arrangement with the United States would naturally change the degree of economic integration between the two countries. This chapter considers the role of the firm as a mechanism for internal resource allocation and the impact of the firm on market-conducted trade and investment. The location decision of the multinational enterprise is treated in detail, as is the issue of external economies to economic integration.

Chapters Five and Six return to the context of the small open industrial economy which is not integrated with a larger trading bloc. World market structure is explicitly treated as a determinant of national industrial structure and international trade. The emphasis in Chapter Five is on traditional static entry barriers. In Chapter Six, the focus is on technologically progressive or Schumpeterian industries. The chapter reviews both theoretical and empirical arguments and discusses incentives of large versus small economies in the use of alternative trade policy instruments. It also deals with the particular concerns raised by entry barriers in export markets, policy toward industrial research and development, and technology transfer.

Chapters Seven and Eight deal with general implications of the analysis for future patterns of Canadian economic development and trade and industrial policy. Chapter Seven details aspects of the current industrial policy debate that are relevant to Canada, addressing questions concerning the appropriate trade policy and industrial policy for basic industries and growth industries. Chapter Eight provides policy conclusions and a summary.

Chapter 2

Trade and the World Economy

Introduction

The world economy has gone through great changes in the twentieth century and the pace of change is unlikely to abate over the last two decades. It is vitally important to appreciate these developments because Canada's economy is strongly integrated with the world economy. In the past decade, Canada has exported 25 to 30 percent of GNP; large fractions of Canadian industry are controlled by foreign multinationals; and a large fraction of Canadian wealth is held abroad, much of it in the form of foreign direct investment in other countries. Consequently, international developments must be kept foremost in assessing domestic trade and industrial policy options.

This chapter provides an assessment of trends in the world economy over the last three decades; explains how they have been interpreted in the past; and considers the possible direction of current trends. The chapter provides a synthesis of descriptive and statistical work on international trade and discusses the major changes in economic thought about world trade over the same period. The ways in which events are interpreted is, in my opinion, as important as the events themselves in understanding how economic policy is made. International trade theory is the principal intellectual tool economists have used to assess structural change in the world economy.

In examining policy options, the economist must make assumptions about the set of variables taken as exogenous to the analysis. Canada is often viewed as a small open economy, not large enough to appreciably affect prices in the markets in which it buys and sells. This hypothesis has been accepted by most economists. Of course, no nation is indifferent about the prices of the goods it buys and sells. It is vital to understand how the prices of goods exported and imported by Canada are determined in the world economy and why a nation exports certain commodities and imports others. The pattern of trade between Canada and other nations depends upon developments in the rest of the world. The pattern of Canadian trade will be discussed in the next chapter. In this chapter the focus is on the world economy.

Alternative Theories of International Trade

Before looking at world trading patterns, a brief summary of alternative theories of trade is provided here to explain how certain positions come to be held by various policy makers and how empirical departures from orthodox theory have been incorporated within the standard paradigm of economic theory. In some cases the theory itself has been rejected in favour of an alternative.

The classic theory of international trade is based on the doctrine of comparative advantage associated with David Ricardo, who developed the theory in the early nineteenth century. In Ricardo's simplified framework, all commodities which can be traded are produced by a single factor of production, which may be referred to as labour, but countries need not have equal absolute advantage in producing the same commodity. What matters in explaining trade patterns are the relative, or comparative, labour costs, not the absolute costs. If, for example, in Canada one unit of labour can produce either two units of wheat or one unit of cloth and in Britain one unit of labour can produce two units of cloth or one unit of wheat, then the comparative cost of a unit of wheat in Canada is one-half a unit of cloth and the comparative cost of a unit of wheat in Britain is two units of cloth. Since Canada has a lower "cloth" price of wheat than Britain, it has a comparative advantage in the production of wheat, while Britain has a similar comparative advantage in the production of cloth. In such a case, Ricardo demonstrated, given similar demand conditions in Canada and Britain, each country would export the commodity in which it had a comparative advantage. The doctrine of comparative advantage was a major achievement of the classical economists.[1]

The theory was extended in a number of directions. Many economists felt that the assumption of a single factor of production and technology which can differ between countries was inappropriate for a static or long-run theory of trade. The Heckscher-Ohlin version of the theory drops both of these assumptions. It assumes identical technologies in all countries and ignores any significance in lags in the international transmission of technology. The major advantage of the theory is its ability to handle many factors of production, which gives the theory its major empirical content. We now think of countries as endowed with naturally given and exogenous quantities of various factors of production. Different countries may have different endowments of natural factors such as land and labour, and these factors cannot be transported across national boundaries, although they can be employed in varying quantities in industries within each country.

In the Heckscher-Ohlin model, the concept of relative factor proportions replaces the concept of comparative cost. For example, Canada has a relative abundance of land to labour over Britain, because it has a higher ratio of land to labour. The major prediction of the factor proportions version of the comparative advantage theory is that a country will export those commodities which use relatively more of its abundant factor. Thus, Canada would export agricultural products as opposed to cloth, because agriculture uses relatively more land.[2]

The doctrine of comparative advantage has had a powerful influence on economists since its introduction. It is still the principal model of international trade taught today, usually with emphasis on the factor proportions version. Actual empirical testing, however, did not begin until the 1950s. The theory received its first major test when Leontief attempted a test using his newly developed input-output analysis.[3] To the surprise of many, including Leontief, the theory was not confirmed by the data and produced the famous "Leontief paradox." Leontief found that American exports tended to be labour intensive rather than capital intensive. This contradicted the comparative advantage theory because most economists believed that the United States had a higher ratio of capital to labour than its major trading partners. Many attempts were made to explain the paradox, and some of these will be discussed later.[4]

During the 1960s there was a counter-development in the empirical analysis of international trade patterns by economists who were not content with the predictions of the comparative advantage doctrine. This development occurred mostly outside the mainstream analysis of international trade, where the emphasis remained upon the theoretical development of the traditional model. The basic empirical difficulty is fairly simple to explain. In observing trade between nations, no one disputed the ability of the factor proportions theory to explain trade in primary or natural resource products. After all, Canada exports wheat and Saudi Arabia exports oil. The difficulty was in explaining trade in manufactured products. In the 1960s there was no convincing theory that explained why the United States exported television sets and the Germans exported steel. By the late 1960s the Japanese case was even more puzzling from a comparative advantage perspective — why should Japan have a comparative advantage in the production of motorcycles and portable radios?

Some writers met these puzzles by focussing on what may be called technology factors. The propositions which emerged were not so much theories as empirical generalizations about the nature of world trade. The most widely cited, and perhaps the closest to a theory, was what became known as the "product cycle" theory of international trade. It may be useful to review the features of world trade as of the mid-1960s, when the theory was developed, before going into the details of the product cycle view of international trade.[5]

International Trade, 1945–74

At the end of World War II, the United States was the dominant economic and political force in the non-Communist world. Europe and Japan were rebuilding after the damage of the war. The developing nations were still largely non-industrial and served mainly as exporters of primary commodities to western economies. The United States was the major exporter of technologically sophisticated, capital-intensive products during the early postwar period. What it did not export directly, it exported indirectly through the establishment of branch plants of its major corporations in foreign countries. The growth of multinational enterprise was to lead to a major change in the conduct of international trade. The integration of international capital markets was also proceeding. With the development of the international monetary system,[6] there was an unparalleled growth in borrowing and lending between nations. The extensive development of the Eurodollar market is one example. The U.S. dollar served as the world's medium of exchange, and international trade and investment literally took off. Growth was fostered by the General Agreement on Tariffs and Trade (GATT), which was an organized attempt by the industrialized nations to bring down the high levels of tariffs erected in the years preceding World War II.

Between 1945 and 1974, Europe and Japan made dramatic economic recoveries. Germany and Japan experienced particularly high rates of economic growth. American multinational firms became a prominent feature on the European economic landscape but never penetrated Japanese markets, for a variety of reasons. Trade in primary commodities grew significantly. Many of the developing countries began building an industrial base, selling primary commodities in large volume to finance purchases of imported capital equipment. Energy was cheap and was generally regarded as unlimited for all practical purposes.

An important characteristic of this period was the extent to which the American free enterprise system and capitalist ethic were exported to much of the world. For almost two decades most economists viewed the free enterprise system as the most effective engine of economic growth. It was not until the middle 1960s that general concern with the environment, poverty, and other "market failures" began to receive serious attention by politicians and academics.

The achievement of the Soviet Union in launching the world's first space satellite had considerable influence on the study of trade patterns. Shortly after the launching of Sputnik in 1957, the American economics profession turned its efforts to the analysis of technological change as a force in economic growth. Studies of technological change by Solow (1957) and Denison (1962) confirmed the overwhelming importance of technology in explaining economic growth. A parallel development was the analysis of education in terms of "human capital."[7] These developments soon affected thinking about international trade. Several statistical studies conducted during the 1960s attempted to explain U.S. trade in manufactures by emphasis on the technology factor, including the human capital embodied in the labour input. The results of these studies all pointed to the same conclusions: U.S. exports tended on average to be technology-intensive relative to U.S. imports and the exports of other industrialized countries.[8]

Studies also pointed out the importance of U.S. multinationals as a vehicle by which these exports reached foreign markets.[9] During the 1950s and early 1960s, U.S. multinationals grew at a rapid pace. Products that the United States had previously exported were now produced abroad by U.S. subsidiaries. Furthermore, many of the components of these goods had been produced in the United States and shipped to the foreign-based subsidiary for assembly and marketing. Research and development and technologically intensive production continued to be performed in the United States. Later these trends were reversed, but this was the general pattern of international trade by the late 1960s when the product cycle theory was developed.

The Product Cycle Theory of International Trade

The product cycle theory was developed because the conventional theory of international trade could not satisfactorily explain economic developments in the postwar years. Raymond Vernon (1966) of the Harvard Business School developed the product cycle theory of international trade by applying a modification of the product cycle theory, which was popular in U.S. marketing literature of the time, to his observations of current trade patterns. His conception was not a full-blown microeconomic theory but a dynamic, "stylized" version of international trade theory based on historical facts. Nevertheless, its explanatory power was considerable. Many accounts of this theory are available, so only a brief description will be provided here.

The product cycle starts with the observation that in a dynamic economy new technology continually results in new products, which may be consumer goods or may incorporate new process innovations that change the methods by which existing goods are manufactured. In addition to these new manufactured goods, there are primary commodities whose production and supply are dictated to a large degree by nature, and there are the standard factors of production — labour and capital. Any manufactured good goes through a product cycle from the date of its introduction to its mature, mass-produced phase or to its ultimate demise. In the early phase of the product cycle, a new consumer good is produced in small volumes in specialized plants. Purchasers tend to be high income consumers, and the demand is relatively price inelastic. The product tends to be highly differentiated or even tailored to individual consumer needs, and production is generally done in small batch lots with considerable use of highly skilled labour. If the product is successful, more individuals will become potential consumers and larger scale methods of production will be adopted. These methods will be more capital intensive and yield lower unit costs, bringing down the price of the good. At lower prices, more consumers will adopt the good, and it will move from upper income to middle income users.

At this point, other firms will seek to imitate the technology of the original producer and competition will break out. This middle phase of the product cycle is also characterized by production differentiation as firms compete for different market segments by offering variety and quality differences. If the imitation lag is long, the initial innovating firm can earn substantial monopoly profits. The final stage of the product cycle is the mature phase in which the good is produced for the mass market. At this point product differentiation is reduced, product features are standardized, and the good is produced in large-scale plants which are highly capital intensive. The skill levels required of labour in these plants is generally low because of the extreme division of labour allowed by product standardization. The state of industry competition at this stage is either competitive or oligopolistic, and competition is based more on price than quality.

This is the standard product cycle theory. Vernon adapted it to international trade. He observed that the United States was responsible for most of the product innovation of the postwar period for a number of reasons. It was well endowed with capital, and R&D tended to be a capital-intensive process in many industries. It had one of the best educated work forces in the world and a high percentage of the world's skilled engineers and scientists. This was due mainly to high levels of education throughout the United States and also to training provided by the military during World War II and to U.S. immigration policies. For these reasons, Vernon noted, the innovation phase of the product cycle tended to occur within the United States.

The large high-income U.S. market also provided a natural testing ground for new products. Vernon traced the following developments as the product entered the middle phase of the cycle. International demand grew as world consumers became aware of the product and its uses. U.S. companies began to serve this market by exporting. However, as demand increased, it soon proved desirable to transfer production abroad by establishing foreign branch plants, given the tax and tariff policies of many of these countries and some reluctance by U.S. firms to transferring technology to third parties. This transfer tended to be concentrated in Europe and other industrialized countries where the market size and skill levels of the work force were commensurate with the middle phase of the product cycle. Much of the high technology end of the production of components stayed in the United States, as did the R&D process. Market structure at this stage tended to be oligopolistic, with competition among a few competing U.S. multinationals.

Technological know-how cannot be suppressed forever, and eventually imitators appeared both at home and abroad. In the mature phase, large-scale standardized production occurred worldwide. From the international perspective it was natural that, given the low skill requirements in this phase, production would be transferred increasingly to low wage/low skill countries. Ultimately, the product cycle theory of trade predicted that the United States would cease entirely to export the product, and would become an importer from the low wage countries.

An important part of the theory is its explanation of why the United States remains a high income country and other countries remain lower income countries, in relative although not absolute terms. Three factors are at work. First, the United States retains its role as world product innovator, which means that U.S. labour retains a high level of human capital and earns rents on its innovative capacity. Furthermore, natural market forces impel U.S. firms to do a large amount of industrial R&D and provide the technological opportunities which allow the stream of innovations to continue. Second, imitation lags by foreign competitors remain substantial, allowing U.S. innovators to earn some significant quasi-rents in the initial and middle phases of the product cycle. Third, natural market forces discourage firms in other countries from attempting to compete with U.S. firms in the technological race. Vernon gives a number of reasons why foreign firms did not compete. The necessary capital and human resources for R&D were simply not available in other countries. High industrial wage levels gave U.S. firms a greater incentive than foreign firms to develop and adopt labour-saving process innovations. The concentrated industrial structures of these industries in the early phases of the product cycle created substantial entry barriers both to domestic and foreign firms. Given that foreign firms faced less well-developed capital markets than U.S. firms, they faced higher costs than U.S. firms in raising the capital needed to enter the industry.

The mainstream economics profession never adopted the product cycle theory wholeheartedly. However, the theory provided a useful explanation of trade and investment patterns of the postwar period. It is probably the most insightful hypothesis on the determinants of international trade since the contributions of Heckscher and Ohlin. What is even more interesting is that the theory embraced those factors which were ultimately to explain why it would not work in the future. In 1979 Vernon wrote a paper explaining this. Multinational firms, key players in the product cycle theory, were one of the main elements in explaining why the pattern of trade predicted by the product cycle could not persist.

Trade and Investment in the 1970s: Post Product Cycle

A number of developments spelled the ultimate extinction of the product cycle theory trade pattern. Key developments in world trade and investment in the 1970s could not be accommodated in the theory as first expounded.

First and foremost, Japan and Germany had emerged as world economic powers with rates of economic growth well above that of the United States. The European Common Market provided a market size to rival that of the United States. Differences in income levels between the United States, Germany and Japan, once orders of magnitude apart, had narrowed rapidly and continued to do so.

A second development was OPEC. The 1974 oil price increase affected the world economy in two important ways. The relative price of energy rose dramatically, decreasing real income in all oil-importing nations and raising the cost of their industrial products. Wealth was transferred from the industrialized world to the oil-exporting countries, particularly those in the Middle East. From the vantage point of 1984, this transfer of wealth may not have been permanent, but most economists agree that the relative price of energy is unlikely to return to its pre-1974 levels in the near or medium term.

Another important development was the unprecedented integration of world capital markets which began in the 1960s. It is difficult to overstate the significance of this development. It meant, for example, that large multinational corporations and governments were not dependent upon the savings developed in their own countries. A large multinational could simply go to the New York or London Eurodollar market and borrow upon funds which represented the collective savings of a substantial portion of the non-Communist world. This meant that savings flowed to the country where investment was most productive and could earn its highest rate of return. Furthermore, the speed at which this occurred was astounding. It is worth noting that during this period the United States had one of the lowest savings rates among industrialized nations, but the largest outflow of investment.

Vernon (1979), observing the period from 1968 to 1978, emphasizes the important role played by multinationals. Multinational firms have traditionally been associated with a particular country, in most cases the United States but increasingly Germany, France and Japan. As the multinationals grew over this period and extended their production and sales around the globe, an inevitable change took place in the perceptions of their management. Instead of viewing themselves as belonging to a particular national market system, they came to view themselves as part of an integrated world economy. All decisions were taken with an eye to maximizing the overall economic efficiency of the global firm. This meant locating production, sales, R&D and management wherever profitable opportunity and the constraints of competition dictated. The development of the multidivision form of corporate organization and advances in information and communication technology made it possible to manage a global firm on a day-to-day basis.

This reorientation of the multinational firm had and continues to have profound effects. The firm was no longer subject to the wishes of any single government or bound by the constraints of any single national labour or capital market. Furthermore, because these firms were multi-plant and often horizontally diversified, a significant portion of international trade in goods was conducted entirely by non-market means, reducing the effectiveness of the traditional market-oriented tax and tariff instruments in controlling international trade.

These developments in the late 1960s and 1970s caused the preconditions of the product cycle to disappear. The growth of the European and Japanese markets made it possible for product introduction to take place there as well as in the United States. The high savings rates in Europe and Japan and the integration of world capital markets increased the access to capital for potential market entrants from these countries. Both Europe and Japan had fostered a highly skilled work force and a significant industrial R&D establishment. The U.S. multinationals also no longer followed the pattern assumed by the product cycle theory. With the global perspective of these firms, the transfer of technology to other countries proceeded much faster than in earlier decades. Both the introduction of the product and its production now jumped almost immediately to the European market, even if the original innovation had taken place in the United States. The Japanese proved to be remarkably able at adopting and improving on U.S. technology, and U.S. multinationals had never established much of a hold there. The Japanese, with their lower wage rates and skilled labour force, managed to compete with and beat U.S. industry in a number of the middle and higher technology products.

A very significant development during the 1970s was the emergence of high-growth developing nations. Taiwan, Singapore, South Korea, Hong Kong, Brazil, Mexico, India and others began to acquire "non-traditional" manufacturing capacity. Economic historians associate this development with the industrialization process.[10] These countries, referred to as newly industrializing countries (NICs) to distinguish them from the less developed countries (LDCs) and the industrialized countries (ICs), found their first manufacturing niche in a class of goods not conveniently covered by the product cycle. These were the highly labour-intensive industries characterized by low scale economies and hence low capital requirements, including textiles, clothing, shoes, toys, and manually assembled electronic products. Low wage rates and the availability of an organized and hard-working labour force made the NICs the natural location for these industries. Over time, with the growth in income and skill levels, and moderate degrees of political stability, the NICs also became natural candidates for some of the standardized goods with large-scale economies produced in the mature phase of the product cycle. Vernon (1979) argues that the multinationals will be increasingly drawn to these countries as the production site for goods in this phase unless raw material and transport cost problems dictate location elsewhere.

The changes outlined above are the reasons why the product cycle no longer explains U.S. and world trade patterns as well as it did in the 1950s and 1960s. The key ingredients of this theory — product and process innovation, technology transfer, multinational enterprise, scale economies and product differentiation — are clearly still important in understanding the world trade and investment scene.

World Trade and the Industrial Innovation Races

This section outlines a theory of world trade, investment and industrial competition for the 1980s which builds upon the insights of the product cycle theory and observations about current economic trends. It is not a theory in the traditional sense of having relevance beyond the current circumstances, but seeks to bring some cohesion to overall patterns of world trade. Continuing political and economic changes in the world economy will render this theory obsolete in the longer term but the general outline which follows should be valid for the next decade and possibly longer. Many of the issues and perspectives of this section are covered in greater detail in relation to Canada in subsequent chapters. The plausibility of the particular world trends offered here should be more apparent at the end of the study. The purpose at this point is to provide a general view of the context in which Canadian trade and industrial policy must be placed.

The theory looks at three sets of major national actors in the world economy: (a) the major industrialized trading blocs, consisting of Japan, the European Common Market (in particular Germany, France and Britain), and the United States; (b) the newly industrializing countries and some less developed countries which could make the jump to industrialization in the next decade; (c) the remaining less developed countries, which may be usefully divided into petroleum-exporting and non-petroleum-exporting countries. This scheme omits the Communist bloc countries and China, although trade with these countries, particularly China, may prove to be an important development of the next two decades.

The theory focusses on three features of the current economic scene. The first is the continuing pace of technological change, particularly in microelectronics. These developments provide the impetus for continued product and process innovation and also reduce the number of skilled and semi-skilled jobs in a wide variety of manufacturing and service industries. For example, the introduction of flexible computer-based manufacturing processes may simultaneously reduce the importance of scale economies in many industries and permit production of goods which are less standardized and more suited to individual user needs in a variety of industrial and consumer areas. It is difficult to assess claims about the potential of the microelectronics revolution, but the results so far are impressive. Although statistical studies of the impact of the new technology are not yet available, it would be unwise to understate its importance.

The second major feature of the current world economic situation is the change in the relative price structure of goods and factors since the early 1960s. Wage rates among the major industrialized nations are much closer than they were two decades ago. While there is still, for example, a significant gap between U.S. and Japanese real wages in similar industries, it is becoming steadily smaller. Wages in the NICs and LDCs, however, remain at dramatically lower levels in all skill categories. Given the extreme mobility of capital, this creates strong economic pressures to shift production toward low wage countries. These wage differences existed a quarter century ago as well, but at that time the level of economic development and political stability of these countries was so low and transport and communications costs were so high as to preclude them as viable bases for production. The other major change in relative prices is in energy and suggests continued emphasis on process and product innovations which economize on energy use. In the longer run, oil is only one of the world's major raw materials. If world economic growth continues, and in particular if the LDCs start to attain growth rates comparable to the NICs, there will be continued pressure on supplies of primary commodities. Prices of these commodities may increase, tempered by the pace of innovation to reduce the raw material demands of industrial production and to substitute non-material inputs.

The final feature of current world developments is a political one. All Western governments have been slightly shellshocked by events of the 1970s and early 1980s. Productivity slowdowns, energy crises, inflation, recession and international competition have led governments to become increasingly defensive with respect to external shocks. The level of world economic integration attained since World War II has considerably reduced the power of individual governments to control economic events within their own boundaries. One of the many types of political responses this has invoked is a trend toward increased government intervention in industrial development.[11] In many cases, this has put governments on a collision course with the multinationals. Governments would like to retain the employment base of existing industries, while multinationals would like to move the location of production in response to factor price differences. More problematic are the "mercantilist" or competitive aspects of industrial development policies. Intervention in the industrial markets of their own country puts governments in direct confrontation with each other. Because the players are both large and few, strategic gaming occurs between nations and the potential costs of conflict are large. Nevertheless, in the near future it is sensible to assume that governments of the major industrialized nations will play an active role in a wide range of industries through a myriad of industrial policies which seek to promote national interest.

Governments of NICs and LDCs can be expected to continue taking a fairly active role in the overall economic development process. There are two standard approaches: attempting by various means to control the level of foreign ownership in industry within the country; and aggressively selling primary commodities to acquire the foreign exchange necessary to finance economic development and social programs. Both of these are of particular importance for Canada.

With these observations in mind, it is possible to begin fleshing out a theory of world trade to explain trade in manufactures. There are a number of key factors — global enterprises, activist government industrial policies, technological innovation, and competition between low wage and high wage countries.

The sources of innovation, the starting point for the product cycle, will clearly no longer be concentrated in the United States alone. Major industrial innovations will be made by private and public research and development facilities in each of the major industrial trading blocs. In the 1930s, Schumpeter (1934) proposed a theory for closed economies in which he argued that competition between monopolists and oligopolists over innovation and the introduction of new products was a major engine of growth for capitalist economies. Some of Schumpeter's observations are pertinent to the present debate. There is nothing inherently virtuous about competitive markets with regard to the promotion of technological change. The race to be technologically in the lead will be played in equal parts by government and the multinationals. The players in this technology race will be large, and substantial resources will be devoted to it. However, a major factor tempering the enthusiasm of each firm and nation will be the extent to which it can retain the benefits of the R&D process. It is going to be particularly difficult for governments to hold on to the proprietary rights of any industrial research they fund. The multinational firms are efficient mechanisms for the transfer of technology for two reasons. First, while they have every incentive to retain for themselves the results and returns to the technology they develop, they have no incentive to retain them within any particular nation, regardless of where the research was conducted. Second, in some cases the knowledge embodied in new products can be acquired relatively easily by competitors.

The race for new technology will be hampered by the ability of any firm to retain the proprietary rights to the technology, and governments may be discouraged by the "leakage" through multinationals, exports of high technology products and other channels. Both firms and governments will attempt to slow the diffusion of new technology to other countries and competitors. This is an old policy. The British government, for example, tried unsuccessfully to prevent the spread of textile technology in the early nineteenth century, in order to retain their lead in textiles.[12] The innovating country benefits in the short and medium term if it can lengthen the imitation and diffusion lag to other countries, but slowing the diffusion of new technology is harmful from a world perspective. In a closed economy the patent system is one imperfect social device which attempts to overcome the discrepancy between private and social interests in the dissemination of new technology. Nothing comparable to the patent system exists in practice at the international level.

National governments clearly have an incentive, particularly on short-run employment grounds, to retain the technological lead within their own boundaries. Methods of achieving this are limited in democratic societies within a highly integrated international economic system. Attempts to limit the flow of ideas and new products in which technology is embodied are bound to prove self-defeating. Even the patent system has proved ineffective in closed societies for similar reasons. In the end, governments may come to accept the natural market mechanisms of technology transfer. Instead of devoting resources to retaining technology within national boundaries, they may decide to benefit when possible by international sales of technology and otherwise attempt to stay one step ahead in the technology race. The crucial questions are how this might be done and what the gains are.

The gains to participating in a technology race come from the potential rents to innovation. Innovation leads to significant quasi-rents when it makes possible the production of a new product, or a new means of producing an old product at lower cost, which either changes the condition of competition in an existing world industry or opens a completely new market. The new product or process confers a monopoly upon the innovating firm. Rents are earned if imitation by competitors is technically difficult or impeded by some means.

Dynamic firm-specific economies are often barriers to rent dissipation on new innovations. One such barrier is the familiar "learning curve" by which production cost falls as cumulative firm output grows. Another is the effect of being first to invest in production capacity. The first firm to invest, having sunk its costs, is irreversibly committed to the market over the short term, and thus is at a strategic advantage over its rivals. Being first may have a favourable effect on long-run costs, may discourage future competitors or capture brand loyalty, yielding significant monopoly gains or rents, although it may turn out to be a disadvantage in the longer term if a better product or process is developed shortly after. Thus, the innovation race leads to a subsequent production race, in which the market conditions may yield substantial advantage to the first firm introducing the product. If the entry barriers in the post-innovation phase are very substantial, then the returns from being the first can be great. The process is subject to great uncertainty. A firm's apparent lead may be wiped out by a technological development in some hitherto unrelated industry, e.g., the shift from mechanical to electronic watches. Nevertheless, even when the rewards are transitory they can be great.

Given the opportunities afforded by the current revolution in microelectronics, the big industrial powers can be expected to continue to engage in technology races. While the transfer of technology is relatively fast, particularly where aided by multinationals, the degree of scale economies or the dynamic aspects of competition in some industries will necessarily allow only a few firms to survive the competition.

If governments do not intervene to prevent technology transfer, there is certainly every possibility that production could end up in locations other than the country of the initial innovation. A useful working assumption is that for industries which receive substantial government support in the R&D process, it will be impossible to move abroad. Thus, for very large-scale industries, the major industrial country which innovates first will also be the site of production for that product. The aircraft industry is an excellent example. The two major firms in the production of commercial airlines are Boeing in the United States and Airbus in Europe. Both are government supported to a significant degree and scale economies are large relative to market demand. It is highly unlikely that the political process in their respective home countries would allow the production of either firm to move offshore.

The technology race between the major industrial nations will also take place in products in which the level of world industry concentration is unlikely to be as great as in some of the scale-intensive R&D industries. In these instances, normal market forces will have greater scope in determining the location of sales and production establishments. Governments will differ in their propensity to support the type of industrial research and development which fosters these industries. The smaller industrialized countries and NICs should be significant beneficiaries in this process as technology becomes available worldwide. There is no particular reason why innovation should not occur in countries other than the major industrial nations, although the sheer size of the larger countries means that the bulk of industrial R&D will be performed there.

The future impact of these technology races for trade in new or high technology products is uncertain. The large industrial nations are likely to be the major exporters of products in which there are significant scale economies in either R&D or production and marketing. Beyond this, it is doubtful whether much more can be said about the type of products which will be exported from a country. One pattern which has held up in the past is that innovation is related to relative factor costs in different countries. Thus, Japan and Europe can be expected to focus on innovation in the energy-saving area while the United States and Europe might continue to emphasize more labour-saving innovation than Japan, where wages are lower. Innovation can be expected to be focussed on meeting demands of the home market, since this is where consumer product testing is most naturally conducted. However, the global orientation of many firms doing research and development suggests that unless the government is directly involved, the location of R&D and the ultimate market for the product developed may be often unrelated.

In products for which scale economies of production are not important, the technology race is likely to occur in both oligopolistic and competitive industries. The transfer of technology should be fairly rapid and the ultimate location of production will probably be dictated in many cases on grounds of cost and labour market conditions. The famous Atari case in the United States is one example of a high tech firm that moved its entire production facilities to the Far East shortly after its inception. In other cases, production location will be dictated by the need to be near the customer. In some industries characterized by product differentiation, small-scale, flexible manufacturing systems are likely to prove best suited to local markets. In products such as these, technological innovation may actually reduce trade in final goods. Instead, production will be suited to local markets; the trade in goods will be replaced by trade in technology. Multinationals and other technology transfer devices should prove important in this overall process.

A different pattern can be expected for middle technology industrial products associated with the traditional "smokestack" industries. These industries are characterized by the sale of an established product, usually but not always with standardized methods of production subject to significant scale economies. These industries, which include steel, autos, heavy machinery and electrical equipment, are subject to two main trends. Technical changes may alter the scale required for efficient production, and automation may reduce the labour requirements of the production process. In addition, strong pressure exists to move production locations to low wage countries in order to increase cost competitiveness.

Pressure to move production is particularly acute for U.S. firms. High labour costs plague virtually all the traditional U.S. industries, with American workers earning two to five times what their counterparts earn in the NICs. Automation is one possible solution to the cost competition problem, but another solution is relocation. Many NICs have achieved the skill levels and overall infrastructure to offer very favourable terms to multinational firms. The U.S. steel industry is facing stiff competition from multinationals in Brazil. Ford announced in January 1984 that it was opening a major new auto assembly plant in Mexico. Where increased automation is feasible, it is just as viable in the low wage countries as in high wage countries.

There are two possible developments in these type of industries — either the massive protection we are currently witnessing in most of the industrialized countries or a fall in industry real wages which restores the competitiveness of the industries located in the major industrial countries. The probable outcome is a combination of both these developments, together with a rise in real wages and exports in the NICs and more progressive LDCs. If protection is the predominant outcome over the next decade, then we are likely to see a fragmentation of the world market. Each major industrial power will produce essentially for its own market. This option could have unintended internal consequences. Maintaining high real wages in these industries, by taxing the rest of the population through high prices, will set up powerful incentives for firms to hasten the automation process. In autos, for example, it would mean a much faster move to full-scale robotic plants. The negative employment consequences of protection, given the existence of labour-displacing technology, may be more adverse than an alternative adjustment which would keep wages down and employment up, at least over the medium term. Increased protection will have the side effect of generating considerable demand for industrial robots. Whether the country implementing the protection would gain from this or in fact end up importing the robots, would undoubtedly depend upon a complicated set of economic and political factors.

The scale bias of innovation in these industries could prove to be either the salvation or damnation of the industry as far as the major industrial nations are concerned. With the development of computer-aided design and computer-aided manufacturing (CAD/CAM) technology and flexible-based manufacturing processes, there is a tension between innovation which leads to increases in scale economies in production and innovation which reduces scale economies in both new and existing products. For example, technological innovations are changing the whole face of the steel industry by reducing the need for large-scale operations. In the technology race, large-scale enterprises have an incentive to innovate in large-scale production processes because they have the size to benefit, and these processes carry the additional advantage to existing firms of creating entry barriers. Consumers of the product and firms which cannot overcome the existing size barriers would tend to favour innovations that result in reductions in scale. There are obvious analogies on a national level. The big industrial nations will be interested in high technology innovations which are large in scale because these nations, with their large markets and resources, have an obvious advantage in capturing world market shares for products with large-scale economies of production.

In the traditional middle technology industries, the case is the opposite. If large-scale, standardized production remains significant in these industries, and labour continues to make up a significant share of total production costs, then strong forces dictate the movement of production to low wage locations. However, if labour costs and scale can be reduced simultaneously, there is a strong case for production to stay close to the market it serves. The flexibility to product differentiate and produce customized products without cost disadvantage will make location of production near to the buyer very important. Therefore, industries which experience innovation that lowers scale and permits product differentiation are likely to remain relatively immune from import competition. In the extreme case of complete custom production, one can think of the good as non-traded.

Reduction in scale, however, does not necessarily result only in customized product markets. If scale reductions and additional scope for product differentiation occur within an industry, the large country advantage will be dissipated. This type of technological change will give small countries greater export opportunities.

Aside from certain parts of the steel and machine tool industries, there are few examples of this type of reduction of scale in traditional industries. Standardized production and cost competition may continue to dominate many of these industries and where this is the case, there will be strong pressures to move production to low wage locations. However, the incentive for small and medium size firms to innovate along the lines suggested in the previous paragraph will be strong, and successful innovations may result in a reduction in the overall importance of trade in particular commodities.

With respect to primary products, factor abundance will naturally continue to be the primary determinant of trade. The most probable political development will be a greater trend toward government ownership and intervention in these markets in the NICs, LDCs and many developed countries. At the world level, the resources of the Communist countries will obviously play an increasingly important role in the world trade picture. In the near term, over the next three to five years, the pressure by NICs and LDCs to generate foreign exchange reserves will probably keep the level of competition high and the prices low in many of these markets. In the longer term, prices of raw materials may recover, resulting in both income transfers to the resource-abundant countries and strong incentives for material-saving innovations. Europe and Japan in particular have good reasons for being at the forefront of this innovation relative to the United States, which is relatively better endowed with some resources.

The overall pattern of trade in this scenario includes, first, a continuing major technology race by the major industrial blocs and considerable emphasis by governments on intervention in large-scale, high technology industry. Other innovation will be market directed but subsidized through tax, subsidy and non-tariff barriers. There will be strong political pressures for subsidized high technology industry to locate in the innovating country, but this will be tempered by the incentives of multinationals to locate production in the least-cost alternative. Overall, this will result in a tendency to equalize wages of workers of comparable skill levels across both the industrialized and newly industrialized countries. The United States, Europe and Japan should all continue to be strong exporters of high technology products. Whether any of these countries will be the overall winner will depend in good measure upon the extent to which they devote resources to R&D, the extent to which protection is adopted in each country, and the ability of each to retain the advantages of being the first innovator. The ability to devote resources to R&D will in turn depend upon the availability of skilled scientific and engineering personnel. In the short term this can probably be taken as given, but in the longer term it must be regarded as variable. All three industrial blocs have significant stocks of physical and human capital geared to R&D activities.

A trade surplus of high technology products for these countries should be matched by a growing deficit in middle technology standardized products and in the very labour-intensive, low-skill products of some old industries. At the same time, the average skill content of labour in the NICs should increase considerably.[13] NICs should increase in relative importance as exporters of high technology products, with the exception of very scale-intensive, high technology industry. Multinational or global enterprises will probably continue to be important as an institution of technology and capital transfer.

The absolute size of the NICs, however, will prove important as a limiting factor in attracting industry from the industrialized countries in many middle and low skill areas. Currently, the NICs account for a very small fraction of world trade, and while this share is likely to increase, constraints on the growth rate of NICs will prevent any significant change in the medium term. Some NICs are already experiencing labour shortages.[14] The key parameters are the rate at which these industries can be absorbed in the NICs and the pace of reduction in real wages in the industrialized countries. Furthermore, there is some significant wage equalization yet to occur between the industrialized countries themselves. Perhaps the greatest uncertainty is the extent to which technical change may reverse or exaggerate these trends. More certain, however, is that as imports from NICs increase, there will be strong pressures to provide protection for domestic industries in the industrialized countries. This has already taken place in a number of industries such as motorcycles, steel and autos, and could happen in others. Ultimately, the NICs will become fully industrialized, and the process of economic development will open a new chapter on world trade. There will be considerable competition among existing industrialized countries to gain access to these new markets.

In the postwar period, growth in the volume of world trade has been matched by a growth in the volume of capital flow, of both direct and portfolio investment. There is little reason for this trend to abate in general terms, although flows of foreign or direct investment may encounter increasing barriers to mobility for a number of reasons. First, governments will throw up barriers to prevent the departure of existing industry and perhaps to gain control of the outward flow of direct investment. Second, host governments in both industrialized countries and NICs may become increasingly hostile to foreign-based multinationals, unless the objectives of the government and the multinational coincide. The technology race among industrial countries will encourage governments to use the nationally based firm as the "chosen" instrument. Foreign firms may be viewed as direct competitors with national firms in the technology race, and this may raise barriers to inward flows of direct investment.

The U.S. government has been the most forceful proponent of reduced investment barriers, but this situation could easily change. In recent years, the United States has become host to an increasing number of non–U.S. based multinationals and has become a net importer of capital services. With low U.S. savings rates and substantial industrial innovation occurring in Japan and Europe, this trend can be expected to continue. A change in attitude toward foreign direct investment by the United States could mean a general increase in investment barriers worldwide. Protection of import-competing industries through tariff and non-tariff barriers could be replaced by an emphasis on export subsidies and controls on inward direct investment. For the time being, the direction in which things are moving is not clear.

Conclusion

In this chapter, we have discussed some basic trade theories, and traced actual patterns of world trade since World War II. The product cycle theory explained trade patterns well up to the 1970s. Subsequent changes in world trade were induced by the emergence of Japan and Europe as competitors to the United States, the rise in the relative price of energy, the industrial technology races induced by developments in microelectronics, and emerging competition from the newly industrialized countries. The last section provided a sketch of world trade in light of these developments. Awareness of the impact of these developments will be important in assessing the position of Canada in world trade and investment.

Chapter 3

The Classic Theory of Comparative Advantage and its Implications for Canada

Introduction

This chapter examines the application of the classic theory of comparative advantage to the Canadian economic structure, and explores its policy implications. This is the pre-eminent theory of trade within the conventional neoclassical economic paradigm and one of the cornerstones of conventional economics. The chapter begins with an examination of the logical underpinnings of the theory, in particular the factor proportions (FP) version of comparative advantage (CAV) developed by Heckscher and Ohlin, which is now the standard model of international trade. It then reviews studies on the pattern of comparative advantage in Canada. A review of the empirical tests of the theory and tests of the alternative "neo-technology" approach to trade are provided in order to place CAV in an appropriate perspective. These studies are largely non-Canadian but form an important background for this and following chapters. The rest of the chapter deals with the policy implications of the FP-CAV view of trade and economic structure, and certain difficulties that arise in applying the theory in the Canadian context.

The Factor Proportions Theory of Comparative Advantage

The factor proportions version of comparative advantage developed by Heckscher and Ohlin in the early part of this century is an extension of the analysis developed by Ricardo, which focussed on a single factor of production and relative costs in terms of that factor.[1] The FP version, as its name suggests, shifts the emphasis to relative quantities of productive factors which by assumption are not traded internationally. One of the most important assumptions in the FP model is that all countries have identical technologies. This is a natural extension of the assumption of identical costs in the classic theory of perfect competition. The model applies to a world in which information is freely available to all, at least in the long run, or in the case of a short-run analysis, to a world in which information as to technological advance is instantaneously available to firms no matter where they happen to produce.

Other crucial assumptions of the FP theory include identical tastes or demand conditions across all countries,[2] the absence of trade in factors of production, and constant returns to scale in the production of all goods. With these assumptions, it is possible to get some very strong predictions as to the pattern of trade between countries. In the simple two-factor version of the theory, with the two factors usually identified as labour and capital, the principal prediction is that a country will export that commodity which makes intensive use of its relatively abundant factor.[3] Thus, if the production of cloth is labour intensive and the production of automobiles is capital intensive, the theory would predict that a country endowed with relatively more labour and less capital than others would export cloth, as it would have a "comparative advantage" in cloth production.

Leontief's early tests of the theory on U.S. data (1954, 1956) were based on a two-factor (labour and capital) version of the FP model. The failure of the theory, or the "Leontief paradox," led to a search for a more general version of the FP model which explicitly handled many goods and many factors. This version, developed in the 1960s and 1970s, explicitly introduced the concept of a "chain of comparative advantage." The idea was that industries could be ranked in some order, with those higher on the chain afforded a more prominent position in export potential. There were some logical difficulties in determining where each industry belonged in the chain, and this led to the idea of the "factor content" of trade.[4] The basic idea underlying this concept is that by trading in goods, a nation is actually indirectly trading the services of its factors of production. Thus a capital-rich country exports its "capital services" by selling capital-intensive goods. Any pattern of trade in goods has an implied pattern of trade in factor services, even though the factors themselves, by assumption, stay fixed in the country of origin. With this extension the principal prediction of the theory is that a country will export those factor services in which it is relatively abundant and import those services in which it is poorly endowed. The chain of comparative advantage is expressed in terms of factors rather than goods; factors can be ranked in order, with those high on the chain in relative abundance to those lower on the chain. Goods trade is related to the factor content chain through identification of those goods and industries which use each of the factors relatively intensively.

Testing this theory empirically involves some serious problems which will not be discussed here, but one problem to be noted is that of measuring the quantity of factor services used in all industries in all countries. This must be done indirectly by examining the pattern of trade and production in one or, if possible, more than one country. Leontief's test was conducted on one country only — the United States.

Early studies in the FP tradition on Canadian comparative advantage include those by Wahl (1961) and Wilkinson (1968). More recent studies explicitly focus on the more rigorous concept of factor content and are better suited to the multidimensional nature of factor services.[5] The main interest is in what these studies reveal about the pattern of comparative advantage in Canada. Unfortunately, they are based on data from the 1960s, and it would certainly be desirable to update these. Another difficulty is that many of these studies use cross-section data, and thus explain only the short-run (annual) pattern of trade. The FP theory does not explain how factor abundance changes over time, so additional hypotheses are necessary for a proper test of a long-run theory. There are few time series studies of Canadian trade, even at a fairly aggregate level.[6]

In Table 3-1, the revealed chain for Canadian comparative advantage in terms of factor abundance, using the factor content methodology, is given for two studies — one by Postner (1975) and the other by Harkness (1983) — both using 1961 input-output data.[7] The disaggregation by factor type is different in the two studies, so the two are not strictly comparable. Examination of the chain reveals considerable similarity between the two, but also some significant differences. In the Postner chain, Canada's most abundant factor is non-renewable natural resources, while in the Harkness chain, it is base metal ores: capital appears about midway in the chain. In the Harkness study, the conclusions about skilled labour are mixed, with professionals, technicians and managers high on the chain and scientists and engineers low on the chain. In the Postner chain, university-trained labour as an aggregate is at the bottom of the chain. The methodologies employed in the two studies are different but both start with the same basic theoretical framework.

As this comparison clearly shows, investigators working on the same data set do not necessarily come to the same conclusion. Even in a more highly aggregated framework, investigators have come to different conclusions. Wahl (1961) found that Canadian exports were capital intensive, while Kohli (1975), working on a later data set and with a different methodology, found them to be labour intensive.

There appears to be considerable agreement, however, about two general facts. First, Canadian exports and the factor content of exports are certainly biased toward raw materials or resources. Second, imports of goods, and thus by implication factor content, are intensive in skilled

TABLE 3-1 Canadian Chain of Comparative Advantage Factors
Ranked by Relative Abundance

Harkness (1983)[1]	Postner (1975)[2]
Base metal ores	Nonrenewable natural resources
Forests	Renewable natural resources
Fish & game	Structures
Unskilled labour	Machinery
Iron ore	Labour (elementary)
Professional, technical & managerial labour	Labour (high school)
	Labour (university)
Capital farmers, farm managers & farm labour	
Pastureland	
Cropland	
Scientists & engineers	
Clerks & salesmen	
Non-metallic minerals	
Operatives	
Coal	
Petroleum & natural gas[3]	

Source: J. Harkness, "The Factor Proportions Model with Many Nations, Goods and Factors: Theory and Evidence," Review of Economics and Statistics 65 (1983): 784–800, Table A.1. Based on 1961 data set. Factor abundance on Canadian/Rest-of-World comparison. H.H. Postner, Factor Content of Canadian International Trade: An Input-Output Analysis. Study prepared for the Economic Council of Canada (Ottawa: Information Canada, 1975), Table II, p. 47. 1970 trade data. Factor ranking based on factor content of trade.

Note: While "Petroleum & natural gas" is the least abundant factor in Canada/Rest-of-World comparisons, it moves to fourth most abundant factor in Canada/U.S. comparisons. See Harkness (1983).

and professional labour of a technical and scientific nature. The conclusion, therefore, is that Canada has a comparative advantage in industries which are intensive in the use of raw materials and a comparative disadvantage in industries which use technical and scientific labour intensively. Little can be concluded about overall capital versus labour intensity.

The rest of this chapter deals with three questions. First, to what extent do tests support or deny the FP hypothesis against other alternatives? Second, accepting the theory, what are the policy implications of the revealed chain of comparative advantage? Third, what longer run considerations for trade and economic structure might be inferred from an FP framework, or what problems might arise from interpreting comparative advantage as revealed in a short-run analysis?

Challenges to the FP Theory

Two broad developments followed the failure of the early version of the FP theory of trade in Leontief's attempt on U.S. data. One, proceeding in the orthodox framework, attempted to resolve the paradox by including additional factors of production, in particular, skilled labour and human capital. The other was a more radical attempt to test a number of alternative paradigms, all of which attempted to explain trade patterns by hinging upon differences in technology among countries.

The inclusion of skilled labour and human capital in FP studies was generally regarded as successful by those who did it.[8] In particular, it resolved the Leontief paradox by explaining that U.S. exports were intensive in the use of skilled labour while U.S. imports were intensive in the use of unskilled labour. Thus the early studies, which aggregated labour types improperly, included substantial portions of the wage bill, which should have been viewed as the return on investment in human capital. In the human capital theory, developed in the 1960s, labour is viewed on a similar basis as physical capital. Through education and job training, the stock of skills of any given worker could be increased. As the United States had one of the most extensive public education systems in the world, it was argued they also probably had the largest relative abundance of human capital.

The human capital critique of the early studies is now generally accepted and many proponents of the FP theory would assert that, with the additional inclusion of natural resources, the FP model "worked" fairly well at explaining trade patterns.[9] A major revolt was brewing, however.

Empirical economists, and specialists in international business, found it increasingly difficult to accept a basic premise of the FP-CAV model; this was the assumption that all countries had access to identical technologies of production and a related assumption that the list of goods which were traded was somehow exogenously "given" and unaltered by economic activity. Economists such as Hufbauer, Keesing, Vernon and others proposed an alternative explanation of U.S. trade based on the notion that there were differences in technology between countries and that the United States was technologically more progressive than other countries in both process and product innovation.[10] There was consequently a "technology gap," with new products and processes flowing from the technologically progressive nations, in particular the United States, to the less progressive nations.

By the standards of contemporary economic theory, none of the technology-based trade concepts had developed a rigorous theoretical model of trade. Rather, investigators identified what was thought to be a list of important variables explaining trade. Measures of R&D input and output were constructed, such as the number of scientists and engineers employed in a given industry, expenditure on R&D as a percentage of sales, or the number of patents granted over a certain period. Other "dynamic" variables were included, such as the date of introduction of a product to international trade or a measure of product turnover in an industry. These variables were then included with more traditional factor endowment variables in an attempt to explain trade. The results were fairly dramatic when applied to trade in manufactures.[11] The technology variables were the predominant explanatory variables, and indeed the FP variables turned out to be insignificant in most cases. For 1960s data, the pattern of U.S. exports and imports could be explained almost entirely by the high innovation content of exports, versus the low technology nature of imports. The product cycle theory of trade was the most prominent and carefully constructed of the theories used to rationalize the results. Further corroboration was sought through a number of case studies on particular products and industries.[12] While admittedly the authors were looking for a confirmation, they certainly got it. It was clear that technology-based explanations of trade were very important.

The neo-technology hypothesis has received little emphasis in Canadian trade studies. This is evidence of the extent to which the comparative advantage approach to trade dominates the discussion of international trade in Canada. One study by Harry Baumann (1976) explicitly focusses on U.S.– Canada trade and tests the neo-technology versus factor proportions theories. For Canada–U.S. trade, a priori it might be thought that the FP theory would work relatively better than the neo-technology approach, since resources figure so prominently in Canadian trade. This turns out not to be the case in the Baumann study. The neo-technology variables dominate in explaining both imports and exports. This study also confirms a result which is consistent with the human-capital-augmented FP theory: imports to Canada tend to be technology intensive relative to exports.

Other approaches to Canadian trade focus on market structure variables. These theories are more recent and share certain features of the neo-technology approach. They are covered in Chapters Five and Six.

In my judgment, these studies destroy the viability of the FP theory of trade as a useful theory of trade in manufactured goods and probably, although this is more speculative, in services as well. Most economists, however, would still take the position that the FP view of trade in primary commodities is more or less accurate. Countries that have more oil than they can consume tend to export it — there is not much argument about this. Why the United States should export aircraft and Japan video recorders is more problematic. The difficulty with the technology-based studies is that they do not identify the causal patterns in any systematic way. In recent years, more effort has gone into looking at the underlying structure of innovation, production and marketing decisions from an international perspective. With more emphasis on market structure, it is possible to identify the nature of trade in manufactures. In any case, the FP model is deficient and some alternative is required.

Policy Implications of the FP-CAV Theory

While my interpretation of the empirical support for the factor proportions model of trade suggests that the theory is inadequate, it remains as the standard model of international trade used by economists. To the extent that trade is important to an economy, as in the case of Canada, it is also the theory most commonly used to explain the "economic structure," as reflected in inter-industry size, output and factor use. With this in mind, it is of considerable importance to appreciate exactly what the policy implications of that theory are.

Two general policy implications follow from the FP model, or from any model of international trade in which technology is taken as exogenous, all markets are competitive and resources are fully employed. These propositions form the cornerstone of the neoclassical theory of commercial policy. The first is the famous "gains from trade" theorem, which says that free trade is better than no trade. That is, it is nationally advantageous to engage in trade in the sense that the gainers from free trade could compensate the losers and leave all with higher real incomes than would be possible without free trade. The other proposition of interest is on the impact of tariffs. If all countries unilaterally impose tariffs against each other, all countries are worse off than with free trade. However, if one country insists on keeping its tariff barriers up, the best response by the other country is generally not to reduce its own tariffs completely. This is known as the optimal tariff argument.[13] The impact of these propositions has been profound. They are responsible for both free trade and protectionist stances taken by various countries at different points in time. Chapter Five looks at these points in greater detail. Both propositions are fairly non-interventionist with respect to internal markets. They indicate that competitive markets should be left alone and policy should be restricted to the imposition of tariffs.

The policy thrust of the FP model, though, is sometimes carried beyond these basic propositions. It is generally recognized that governments intervene in the economy in a variety of ways which affect the relative fortunes of industries, including tax and expenditure policies. The question arises as to whether or not certain industries should be encouraged. One position is to take the strictly neutral stand that no industry should be differentially treated. Whatever its merits in principle, this position can lead only to the admission of sin by those who profess to live by it. A less virtuous stance is to admit that government policy affects industries differently, but to take as a rule of thumb that industries in which a nation has a comparative advantage should, in some overall sense, be the favoured ones. It is difficult to find an intellectual defence of this position since it doesn't follow directly from the assumptions of the theory. Furthermore, it clearly has a mercantilist flavour to it, which rubs free trade economists the wrong way. However, this position is actively pursued in economic development policy in numerous countries. The usual justification is that it is better to promote export industries than import-competing industries, either because they bring in foreign exchange or because they use resources more efficiently than import-competing industries. Those of a more interventionist persuasion go even further and use the same arguments to justify a larger role for government. These arguments may sound reasonable and can be defended on a variety of "second-best" arguments.[14] Nevertheless, they do not follow directly from the purer versions of the FP-CAV theory.

Comparative advantage of one industry over another in this framework becomes an important signal of the appropriate direction for the planning process in government. Therefore, arguments about which sectors have a comparative advantage are likely to be quite vigorous, given that the interests on both sides have a great deal to lose or gain. In the Canadian context, using the data of the 1960s, the FP model clearly dictates that the sectors with comparative advantage are the resource sectors. This traditional conclusion has recently been called into question, but support of the resource sector has been a cornerpost of Canadian economic policy since Confederation.[15] The development of the transportation system, to give one example, was clearly intended to help the resource sector reach its export markets. If comparative advantage were to shift over time, the basic FP philosophy might be that economic development efforts by government should follow the shift, emphasizing development of those industries high in the chain of comparative advantage. The ability to favour the export industries, though, is always constrained by the political necessity of ensuring that the interests of the import-competing industries are not completely sacrificed. Protection becomes the major instrument by which incomes are protected in import-competing industries as the forces of comparative advantage shift. On balance, the export-oriented policy seems sensible enough if one accepts the basic underlying explanation of the determinants of comparative advantage.

The FP model can be used to derive some strong policy implications as to the longer term effects of government policy on trade and economic structure. A policy that changes the relative quantities of factor endowments over time will alter the nation's chain of comparative advantage. The non-interventionist position is that long-run changes in factor endowments, such as changes in the stock of capital through saving, are governed by the same market forces which dictate any decision to buy or sell, and that the best that can be done by governments is to leave well enough alone. A contrary position, which has many adherents, is that there is nothing sacred about the market-determined, long-run allocation of investment. In particular, there are imperfections in the markets for physical and human capital which make it desirable for government to intervene through policies to affect saving, education and job training. These policies should be chosen so that the long-run economic structure which emerges leads to the maximum social and economic benefit to both current and future generations.[16] For open economies this is essentially an argument for "engineering" long-run comparative advantage.

Suppose, for example, that an objective of government is to employ a substantial portion of the population in high wage/high technology industry. In the short run, there is no means by which this objective can be achieved. In the longer run, government can increase the stock of skilled technical labour by investing in education and skill-training programs. Under the FP model, ignoring the possibility of immigration, this means that the comparative advantage of the country in question should shift to those industries which use these factors intensively — i.e., high technology industries.

There are three potential difficulties with these long-run strategies, accepting the logical implications of the FP model as correct. First, the period of building up a stock of one factor, in this case human capital, involves an investment of current resources and hence postponement of consumption. This cost of creating comparative advantage by factor accumulation must be kept in mind when undertaking any policy to achieve potential long-term gains by expenditure on current resources. Second, the attempt to build up comparative advantage in a particular area will only be successful if the factor accumulation occurs relative to other countries. In a two-country world, if both countries attempted the same strategy within the FP framework, the initial structure of comparative advantage would not change and the main effect would be to lower the price of high tech goods and the wages of workers in those industries. The investment in human capital might be justified on some other criteria, but it would not necessarily lead to a change in the structure of comparative advantage between nations. Third, in any long-run perspective, tastes, technology and resource endowments are very likely to change, creating unanticipated changes in the structure of comparative advantage. Deliberate policy attempts to alter the structure of national comparative advantage must be prepared to deal with the risk that the policy will be ineffectual because the goal becomes infeasible or less valuable. An example would be failure of an attempt to develop a particular resource export market because of the sudden discovery of lower cost deposits of the resource in a foreign country.

There are clearly problems with attempting to engineer a long-run comparative advantage. Nevertheless, a number of policies implicitly or explicitly have such objectives. The following section further explores some additional problems with respect to the relevance of these arguments to the Canadian situation.

Problems and Prospects with an FP-CAV Perspective on Industrial Structure and Trade

Renewable and Non-Renewable Resources

This section discusses some of the basic issues involved in applying comparative advantage theory in its traditional form to the resource sectors of the economy. It looks at the trade implications of an apparent comparative advantage in resources, as revealed in the comparative advantage studies, or more directly through Canada's long history of trade surplus on exports of unprocessed and semi-processed materials.

Recent events may have reversed this long-standing trend in the Canadian economy. Many of the submissions to this Commission expressed doubts and concerns about the resource and primary sectors, including agriculture. Hard rock minerals may be the only sector in which Canada has a clear pre-eminence in terms of world supply. Conventional supplies of oil are running out and Canada has been a net oil importer since the mid-1970s.[17] I have neither reason nor expertise to question these assessments of future Canadian supply, but I would like to point out some problems with the traditional economic approach to the resource sector in trade studies.

The long-term supply of both renewable resources such as fish, forests and land, and non-renewable resources such as oil, gas and minerals is affected by the supply decisions taken in the short term. Careful management of a renewable resource is needed to avoid reducing the long-term sustainable harvest.[18] In non-renewable resources, every barrel of oil extracted today is one less barrel available for extraction tomorrow. Unfortunately, the trade studies completely by-pass this problem of trade-offs over time. Typically, these studies assume that the amount of current output in a resource sector is the relevant quantity of resource factor supply. This is a completely ad hoc assumption and renders the whole attempt to identify comparative advantage questionable. If an economy with a small stock of a resource chose to extract all of it in a single year and export some, a comparative advantage study using the above methodology would show a demonstrated comparative advantage in this resource. Obviously, the country would have no future comparative advantage in that industry. The extrapolation from a short term to a longer term comparative advantage in a non-renewable resource is only justified if the current flow supply of the resource is indicative of the longer term supply. If that is not the case, for example because the total stock of the resource is known and no further exploration will take place, then comparative advantage will shift over time as the industry depletes the existing stock.

Additional problems are caused by unanticipated shifts in the terms of trade which affect the economic viability of existing resource stocks. These shifts can occur because of discovery of reserves elsewhere, changes in technology which reduce the demand for the resource, or political events. Furthermore, primary commodity prices have historically been unstable, adding to the vulnerabilities of the resource sector. From a national perspective, comparative advantage in any particular resource sector is an uncertain thing in the medium and longer term. In terms of policy dictated by comparative advantage theory, the conventional static approach is not likely to provide any useful guidance. The theory, at a minimum, needs to be reinterpreted to deal with stocks of resource supplies rather than current flows of resource extraction or harvest.

The FP-CAV theory also fails to provide a convincing explanation of the lack of resource processing in Canada. Policies to increase resource processing, raising "value-added" in the resource sector, have been suggested by some commentators as a way to exploit our natural comparative advantage in resources. However, the "revealed comparative advantage" in the trade data seems to indicate otherwise, since historically so little resource processing has been undertaken in Canada. The explanation to this aspect of Canadian industrial structure lies in more careful examination of market structure, transport costs and locational perspectives in North American trade. These factors are not an important part of the FP-CAV theory.

Savings and Capital Accumulation

This section reviews the prospects for capital accumulation as a determinant of comparative advantage and industrial structure. There are two kinds of limiting factors: the extent to which physical capital is mobile in the short run, and the extent to which domestic savings determine investment in a small open economy.

In the classic Heckscher-Ohlin model of trade, all factors of production are treated as immobile between countries; that is, trade takes place in goods but not in factors. A theory of trade in goods which includes the assumption of capital mobility will yield fundamentally different predictions to one in which capital is assumed to be immobile. Mundell, in a classic contribution to the theory of international trade (1957), showed that, with all other assumptions remaining the same, allowing trade in a single factor of production such as capital has the effect of making trade in factors a substitute for trade in goods. Thus, capital movements replace movements in goods.

In the Canadian situation, the first issue to address is whether capital is mobile within a time period comparable to that in which goods are traded. Obviously, there are substantial differences across industries and across countries. In some industries, physical capital is literally on skates — oil rigs, for example, or heavy construction equipment. In other industries, capital is long lived and both location and industry specific; this has the effect of making capital immobile both across industries and across countries. This version of the Heckscher-Ohlin model is quite popular today. On the other hand, many types of capital (equipment and machinery, for example) are certainly mobile within a time period comparable to that over which contracts in international trade are binding.[19] The proximity of Canada to the United States makes the capital mobility argument quite compelling, perhaps more than in bilateral trade between any other two countries. In addition, the presence of multinationals, which of course are prevalent in Canada, has long been argued to facilitate the capital transfer process.

How does the capital mobility assumption affect comparative advantage arguments? In FP empirical studies for Canada, physical capital comes out in about the middle of the chain of comparative advantage. This means that within this framework, Canada has neither a comparative advantage nor a disadvantage in capital-intensive industries. Might this result be the outcome of artificial assumptions about capital immobility? On the other hand, there are industries which are capital intensive but are neither net exporters nor importers because the movement of capital into these industries has substituted for imports of goods which are capital intensive in production. Even ignoring aspects of market structure and tariff effects, this provides a partial explanation of the heavy foreign investment in some manufacturing sectors where setting up a branch plant to serve the domestic market substituted for export to that market.[20] If capital were immobile, as the FP-CAV theory assumes, the capital-intensive sectors would be net importers and would be even further down the chain of comparative advantage than existing studies show, possibly even at the bottom, displacing high skill industries.

If economic policy is based on some notion of the chain of comparative advantage, the policy significance of this last observation is quite important. Policy could be seriously misdirected if it is directed toward capital accumulation instead of other types of factor augmentation, based on a perception of the order of capital-intensive versus skill-intensive industries in the chain. The cost of inducing investment in a particular capital-intensive sector in order to shift CAV and turn a marginal net importing industry into a net exporter could involve more resources than it would take to turn a skill-intensive industry into a net exporter. At the same time, there is the more obvious problem of treating capital as internationally immobile, when it is in fact mobile. Adverse tax treatment of investment by either foreigners or domestics may cause an exodus of capital yielding lower returns to those factors of production, such as labour, which are immobile. When capital is mobile the incidence of any policy can be quite different to what a "factors immobile" perspective would suggest.

The more fundamental problem with engineering comparative advantage through capital accumulation, while not directly relevant to the FP studies of comparative advantage, is that over the long run the capital stock of any country is endogenous. In a closed economy, the savings by government, firms and consumers determine the amount of aggregate investment. Higher savings mean higher investment, and thus higher long-run capital stocks. In a world with trade in goods but no trade in financial assets, the equality of domestic savings and investment continues to hold. Foreigners are prohibited from purchasing domestic assets and domestic residents are unable to purchase assets outside their own country. Thus, differing rates of saving in different countries explain different rates of economic growth. In the longer run, differing rates of capital accumulation with closed world capital markets imply that countries with high savings relative to population growth achieve a comparative advantage in capital-intensive industries and higher per capita real incomes. This is a traditional explanation of the growth performance of Japan and Germany relative to the United States in the postwar period.

In Canada, the assumption of "no trade" in financial assets is clearly unrealistic. For much of Canada's history, financial capital was imported into the country. In more recent years, Canadians have become net exporters of financial capital. In addition, the integration of Canadian and U.S. capital markets is substantial. Canadian firms, governments and households, to a considerable degree, take the rate of return on financial investment and cost of capital as determined by world capital markets.[21]

Moreover, domestic savings need not equal domestic investment. Indeed, investment and savings can be viewed as independent processes. Savings are affected by domestic income and real interest rates set in the world market. Domestic investment is determined by the productivity of investments in the Canadian economy relative to those elsewhere in the world. The difference between domestic savings and investment in any given year is made up by a corresponding flow of foreign portfolio and equity capital into or out of the country.

In a small open economy which is an interest rate taker on the world capital market, the openness of the capital market means it is difficult, if not impossible, to engineer a long-run comparative advantage by attempting to change aggregate savings behaviour through tax policy or other means. At the microeconomic level, industrial structure can be affected by changing the profitability across industries of relative types of investment. Policy can attempt to focus on the investment side of the equation by changing the marginal private profitability of various investments, always keeping in mind that ultimately the private rate of return on investment must equal the after-tax rate of return on a world portfolio. The attempts to engineer a long-run comparative advantage by focussing on investment incentives can have unintended side effects. In particular, given that Canadian savers may be averse to financing the investment, a policy of subsidizing investment may actually result in a higher level of foreign ownership than is intended.

The fact that the capital market is open has never daunted governments from undertaking policies which affect the quantity and, in particular, the composition of savings. Many policies, such as favourable treatment of Canadian equities and restrictions on the composition of pension fund portfolios, are intended to effectively encourage a domestic bias in certain types of saving, thus lowering the cost of funds of certain domestic investments. As a means of encouraging long-run comparative advantage, though, this type of instrument seems unlikely to have any great impact. At the macro level, if savings by Canadian residents could be effectively contained within Canada, this would lead to an increase in domestic investment, an increase in Canadian capital stocks and a lowering of the marginal return of further investment. This in turn, however, would induce non-Canadians to reduce their investment in Canada, offsetting the additional savings by residents. Only if the entire domestic capital stock were held by Canadians could such a policy begin to have any effect. In terms of the composition of investment, sectorally targetted microeconomic policy can lead to permanent discrepancies between the domestic marginal productivity of capital in a certain sector and the rate of return established in world capital markets. This policy-created distortion could lead to capital accumulation in that sector and, in the longer term, could create the intended comparative advantage in that sector. But the cost of such a policy must be considered. In order to justify diverting resources to a particular sector, a good case must be made that social rates of return on that investment are substantially higher than private rates of return.

It is difficult to understand fully the potential long-run effect of investment tax-subsidy policies on long-run industrial structure. In theory, they should have a very powerful long-run effect on the set of industries which are established in any country, and their export versus home production potential. At the empirical level, we know little about the export effectiveness of tax-induced sectoral investment.[22]

Encouraging capital-intensive industries in an attempt to engineer comparative advantage seems a questionable policy for three reasons, ignoring for the moment the possibility of the social-private discrepancy in the return on investment. First, reinterpreting the results of the CAV studies seems to suggest Canada has a comparative disadvantage in these industries. Second, this policy may encourage additional foreign ownership — something viewed as politically and socially undesirable. Third, the attempt to raise domestic value-added by fostering these industries could be largely self-defeating. In a capital-intensive industry, the cost of each additional job is quite high in terms of added expenditure on capital. Unless there are some genuine external benefits in these industries, the additional wages paid to labour will be more than offset by the cost of the capital subsidy necessary to generate the additional jobs. From the perspective of neoclassical economics, this type of policy does not rank highly.

Human Capital and FP Theory

As pointed out in the previous sections, one of the major alterations to the basic FP model was to incorporate human capital explicitly in both the theory and empirical testing. From a longer run perspective in which the stock of human capital and mix in job skills of the labour force can be augmented through education and job training, the human capital approach offers a fairly straightforward means by which comparative advantage can be engineered. The basic idea is quite simple. By investing current resources in education, the stock of human capital in the economy can be raised. If this changes factor proportions between countries, so that the country's relative endowment of human capital rises, the country will shift its comparative advantage toward human capital/skill–intensive industries. This emphasis on human resources is one area of common agreement between economists who often differ on the role for government intervention. Why might this be the case?

The answer lies in a fairly broad acceptance of the notion of a "market failure" in the market for human capital and the scope for public provision of education.[23] Basically, the idea is quite simple. Each individual must bear the future risk of choosing a particular kind of work. In modern society, labour is so specialized that most people cannot train for more than one job or profession. Therefore, the individual who undertakes to acquire human capital is unable to diversify the risk he faces. The government, by undertaking to subsidize or publicly provide education at least partially, removes the reluctance of the individual to take the risk.

A different market failure which also operates in the human capital market is caused by what is known as the adverse selection problem.[24] Private capital markets are unwilling to provide an individual with loans anywhere close to the present value of an individual's post-training wage stream. The reason is that it is very difficult for a bank to assess the prospects of any given individual. Some students will not complete their education and it is often difficult for banks to recover bad loans granted to students. The net result is that the presence of "poor" students in the market for educational loans implies that "good" students must pay higher loan rates or be rationed in the amount they are loaned. Most economists would agree that market failures in the human capital market provide a firm case for public assistance to education.

The existence of the market failure means that public resources devoted to education are likely to have a far higher rate of return than other forms of investment by the public sector. Thus, support for education and job-training policy is more widespread amongst professional economists than in most other areas. In particular this support is offered by those who would seriously doubt the possibility of engineering a comparative advantage in anything.[25]

In the context of international trade, a long-run "engineered" comparative advantage based on human capital is probably the most meritorious of all policies based on factor accumulation. Since physical capital is mobile, there is good reason to believe that the FP approach tends to overstate the comparative advantage of capital-intensive industries. The ranking could possibly be reversed by properly treating capital as partially mobile. One policy choice is thus between accumulating physical, immobile capital or human capital.[26] Policies geared toward human capital are better on a number of criteria. The income distribution consequences are preferred, given that the beneficiaries are wage earners as opposed to capital owners. There are fewer leakages to the rest of the world, relative to physical capital accumulation policies, so that attempts to raise investment in human capital are likely to have a fairly immediate effect upon domestic residents. Attempts to raise physical capital accumulation domestically can give rise to transfers to foreigners and are subject to other problems discussed in the last section of this chapter.

The human capital approach to trade, however, is not without its problems. There is the question of whether universal or targetted programs should be adopted. Universal problems are more costly, and possibly less effective, in generating specific comparative advantage in some sectors. Targetting certain occupations and skills, an approach advocated through the concept of "manpower planning," involves the difficulty of picking tomorrow's winners. In summary, the approach has its problems but in a small open economy it is preferable to one based on supporting capital-intensive industry.

A final comment. Education and job-training policies have implications in numerous other areas of economic policy in addition to the trade concerns. These other implications may well dominate the trade and economic structure concerns.

Public Infrastructure and Regional Diversity

Public infrastructure and regional diversity are two topics which do not fit neatly within the traditional comparative advantage framework and have been given very little attention in the traditional theory. They are nevertheless of crucial importance in examining the basic issues of economic structure. The comments offered are in the spirit of amendments to the FP-CAV theory rather than a wholesale throwing out of the theory.

Historically, public capital goods, or social overhead capital, has played an important role in Canadian economic development. Transportation, communications, health care, education, and basic research and development are areas in which public sector capital plays an important role. The common element in the provision of public sector capital is the presence of either a pure public good problem, where individual free riding destroys the viability of the market system, or the presence of a significant indivisibility in production that makes large-scale coordinated investment important. In some cases, monopoly would be an alternative supply mechanism to deal with the large-scale investment problem, but generally the scale of enterprise is so large and the potential abuse of a monopoly so great that public sector involvement is called for. Different countries have different public capital intensities depending upon such factors as climate, geography, industry and resource base. In Canada, the large size of the country, together with a harsh climate and extensive but regionally diverse resource base, suggests the need for more per capita public sector capital stock than many other countries.

The doctrine of FP-CAV can be augmented to include the public sector capital as a factor of production. It seems patently obvious that this is indeed an important factor of production in many industries. Public sector investment policies must necessarily create a comparative advantage for some industries and a disadvantage for others.

There is little sense in arguing about whether the public sector should or should not supply public goods when it is clear that the provision of public sector capital is an important part of the overall economic development process. A more substantive argument hinges upon whether public sector capital formation should lead the economic development process or follow the lead taken up by the market sector. Economic theory has little to offer on this rather fundamental point.[27] The private profitability of any incremental private sector investment in a particular sector will depend upon the stock and composition of public capital. On the other hand, the social value of an additional dollar of public sector capital in a particular form will depend on the existing set of private sector activities. If, instead of leading, the public sector follows in the development process, it is not clear whether one ends up with the same allocation of economic activity.

My guess is that in the case of large-scale indivisible projects such as the building of airports or railroads, the initiative should clearly lie with the public sector. These arguments will be taken up further in Chapter Seven. For the purposes of the present chapter, this discussion has two implications. First, the FP-CAV view of industrial structure must, at a minimum, be modified to incorporate public sector capital as a productive input in existing methodology. If it then turns out that some industries in which Canada has a comparative advantage are intensive in the use of public capital, this provides an important argument for careful public sector investment with respect to its trade effects. Second, it must be realized in the planning process that public sector investment decisions, through their impact on infrastructure, can create a comparative disadvantage for some industries and a comparative advantage for others. This is obviously important for very large-scale projects.

The regional diversity of the Canadian economy is another topic which has not received a great deal of attention from trade economists, possibly due to a lack of data. Interprovincial trade statistics, however, point out the obvious.[28] The West and East are more dramatically specialized in resources than Central Canada and there is substantial interprovincial trade. In the standard version of the theory, each country is treated as a point in space — transport costs and geography play no essential role. In the case of Canada, this may seem a serious omission, and I believe that more detailed regional analysis would alter the view of comparative advantage given by the aggregate data. Canada can be thought of as either three or four economic regions, depending upon whether Ontario and Quebec are regarded as one or two regions. To be realistic, the theory must recognize the mobility of labour and capital between regions, with goods and factor trade as partial substitutes.

The most substantive change in explicit recognition of the resource base and location of the different provinces in the North American market would be the recognition that Ontario and Quebec do not have a comparative disadvantage in manufactures, particularly in skill-intensive goods. Certainly, Ontario exports a great deal of manufactures to other provinces, and some of these exports are skill intensive. Quebec, on the other hand, given the importance of labour-intensive industries in its economy, would probably have a comparative advantage as revealed by trade data in low-skill manufacturing industries. This is only a guess, not yet substantiated by careful empirical analysis. Any such study should attempt to control for both tariffs and transport costs.

The basic point is that using the FP-CAV theory for policy purposes can be misleading in a country such as Canada, which is so regionally diverse. To foster an industry simply because it is high on the national chain of comparative advantage without attention to its location, would be nonsensical for Canada but not necessarily for a smaller and more homogeneous country like Belgium. The concept of national, as opposed to regional, comparative advantage is dubious. The major practical problem for Canada is that the national approach emphasizes resources at the expense of manufacturing. The West has a comparative advantage in resources but Central Canada does not. Using national comparative factor abundance as a criterion for economic development seriously biases the outcome in inefficient ways. It encourages the fostering of resource-intensive industries at the expense of skill-intensive industries which, in an appropriate regionally disaggregated analysis, offer the greatest export potential at the margin. The tariff has exacerbated the problem to a considerable degree by fostering East-West as opposed to North-South trade. In the absence of tariffs, inter-provincial trade in manufactures would probably decline somewhat and there would be considerably larger exports of manufactured goods from the Central Canada Region. Thus, even with the FP-CAV framework, an explicit recognition of regions would force a more accurate view of comparative advantage in the country as a whole. It would also, perhaps unfortunately, intensify the whole problem of regional conflict by bringing greater attention to the fact that promoting the comparative advantage of one region could well mean creating comparative disadvantage for some industry in other regions.

Conclusion

This chapter has reviewed the arguments for and against the classic theory of comparative advantage for Canada, in the factor proportions version. The policy implications of comparative advantage theory have been discussed at length, in particular the possibility of changing the quantities of factors of production as a means of inducing a change in the chain of national comparative advantage. Some of the arguments, for example regarding the accumulation of human capital, were found to be reasonable and of wider applicability than envisioned in the basic FP model of trade. In general, though, the empirical support for the FP theory is weak. This, together with certain crucial omissions in theory, makes it an unreliable guide for policy making. The next chapter examines an alternative theoretical and empirical framework which focusses on issues more relevant to Canadian trade and economic structure.

Chapter 4

Economic Integration

Introduction

The deficiency of the factor proportions approach to trade and economic structure lead to the obvious question of available alternatives. In this and the next chapter, alternative approaches to explaining trade and investment are offered which may meet some of the criticisms levelled at the traditional theory. The emphasis is on two aspects of markets and economic exchange which have been studied most intensively in the field of industrial organization.

The first set of factors is broadly referred to as the "transactions cost" approach to the study of markets. This approach seeks to explain why certain types of contractual and exchange relations emerge. A central question in this theory is the reason for the margin between market and non-market activities. The names associated with this approach include Coase, Knight, Demsetz, Williamson and Arrow.[1] This chapter explains the implications of economic integration of spatially separated markets, the role of the firm in the process of economic integration and the possibility of "external" effects associated with economic integration. Considerable emphasis is placed on explaining why certain types of economic activity are located in certain places. The discussion also focusses on the role of market versus non-market transactions in the international trade context and the policy implication of this distinction.

The second set of factors in trade and economic structure is associated with the entry barriers approach to industrial organization pioneered by Bain (1956). This approach, treated in Chapter Five, emphasizes scale economies, product differentiation and oligopoly in explaining trade. Canadian economists have played a considerable role in developing this as the industrial organization approach to trade.

A fundamental question addressed here and in Chapter Five is why trade might take place in the absence of conventional forces of comparative advantage based on the different endowments of natural factors of production. This seemingly academic question is closely related to the question of how income and economic structure are determined within a nation. Other related issues are the meaning of economic integration, its likely impact on a collection of spatially connected regions and the role of policy instruments such as tariffs, taxes, subsidies and investment controls. A carefully articulated theoretical model is needed to examine these questions adequately. Unfortunately, such models are sadly lacking.

The ideas advanced in this chapter are based on what I and others regard as the logical implications of the transactions cost approach to international trade and investment. The literature on the multinational firm has used this approach more than other areas of international economics.[2]

The analysis here and in Chapter Five is based on economics; it also borders on some political and social questions. Economic integration of regions and countries invites a variety of political, cultural and historical perspectives which are beyond this study. They are important, both on normative grounds of making "real world" policy prescriptions regarding integration and also on positive grounds of explaining why integration might or might not occur in different ways.

Transactions Costs, Markets and Trade Between Spatially Separated Markets

The transactions cost approach to markets addresses some of the fundamental questions in economics — the nature and purpose of organized markets on which goods and services are traded and the reasons why some transactions occur within markets and other transactions on a non-market basis. The major explanation lies in the existence of transaction costs and the motives and opportunities which affect the economic behaviour of groups and individuals. These include the number of parties to a transaction, the extent of uncertainty in any given transaction and the role of social convention.

Williamson's *Markets and Hierarchies* (1975) is a classic statement of this theory. A standard axiom of this theory concerns the gains to be achieved through specialization of activities by labour. In Adam Smith's words: "The division of labour is limited by the extent of market." Another fundamental proposition is that information costs have an impact on the organization of production and exchange. Markets reduce the costs of acquiring the information needed to make economic decisions. Instead of dealing on a personal level with all possible sellers of a good, the buyer can deal with an impersonal market on an objective level. Of course, a degree of control and coordination is lost when transacting parties resort to market-conducted exchange. By internationalizing an ongoing and repetitive transaction into a non-market context, considerable coordination can be realized.

The firm is the institution in which non-market transactions of interest to economists routinely occur. By organizing labour within a single institution with established rules, the gains from the division of labour are realized. As information costs are reduced, including the cost of monitoring and enforcement of contracts (either implicit or explicit), there is a greater tendency to non-market exchange. In general terms, the theory emphasizes that the efficiency of resource allocation depends in important ways on the organization of production and exchange. Market and non-market contractual and exchange relations are varied and determined endogenously by a number of forces. Government policy and changes in the external environment have a considerable impact on these arrangements and thus on the efficiency of resource utilization in the economy.

The greatest weakness of the transactions cost approach is that it comes very close to being tautological. It does, however, lead to a theory of trade in the absence of comparative advantage. In the simplest terms, it sees the starting point of trade as the division of labour or the gains to specialization, independent of possible skill or endowment differences of the individuals. Economic development has been associated with an increasing division of labour. This division of labour necessarily creates trade either in a "market" in which several individuals participate and formal rules are established, or on the level of barter between individuals. Imagine a number of spatially separated economic centres or regions which are identical in terms of population, labour skills and resource base. In the complete absence of transportation costs or communication costs between regions, the "division of labour" hypothesis and the existence of transaction costs would dictate that trade take place as a natural consequence of the efficiency gains from specialization. Goods are produced within firms, and markets are established for the firms' primary output.

What distinguishes the different regions in the first place may be natural transportation networks, local resources, culture and historical accident. Distance is of course one of the main factors causing economic separation of regions. "Agglomeration economies" is the term regional economists use to explain the spatial concentration of economic activity.[3] These cover a host of economies both internal and external to firms, some based specifically on proximity in location, which arise as economic activity expands within a region. The increasing division of labour within and between firms is one of the most important economies.

The same type of economies which explain why firms emerge as the means of organizing production also explain trade between regions, even if factor endowments of the regions are similar.[4] Organized interregional markets emerge and the nebulous process of economic integration of regions begins. The extent and pace of economic integration depends in subtle ways upon proximity, the volume of trade, and the nature of goods which are traded. The sources of agglomeration economies within regions extend to interregional economic transactions. The process is closely related to economic growth, transportation and communication and, of course, politically created barriers to interregional economic transactions.

In understanding Canadian trade, it is useful to think of the North American continent as a large number of closely integrated but spatially separated markets. Each market is characterized by a set of factors of production — the area's labour force — which, in the medium run, is specific to that location. There is a set of commodities which are traded within but not between regions. These include such non-tradables as fresh-baked bread, haircuts and garbage collection. It is clear that the definition of a non-traded good depends upon the relative transportation costs. For example, daily newspapers, once available only in major cities, are now available nationwide.

All other goods are traded, either through market or non-market arrangements. These traded goods include some services. An important part of the trade in services is the labour services provided by one part of a corporation to another part of the corporation. Intrafirm trade of both goods and services is an important part of the total economic interaction between regions and does not occur through formal market arrangements. All regions are connected by a transportation and communication system which facilitates the flow of goods, services and people, together with the flow of information, which is important in the conduct and organization of production and exchange. In the absence of comparative advantage effects, these transportation and communication costs are one of the most important determinants of the extent of specialization between regions and hence of the overall pattern of trade.[5]

Historically, Canadian economic integration within North America was fundamentally altered, at least for much of the period before World War II, by the existence of tariff barriers which fostered an East-West orientation to trade in manufactured goods. The question of economic integration with the United States poses some fundamental questions for Canadian trade patterns. A principal issue today is whether the locational basis for manufacturing in Central Canada is likely to change as integration proceeds. The resource-based nature of trade in eastern and western Canada is unlikely to change. The Wonnacotts argued, in their study of Canada–U.S. trade in the immediate postwar period (1967), that the proximity of Central Canada to the large midwest U.S.

market meant that complete integration of the two economies would be unlikely to cause production to shift from Central Canada to some other region within North America. The shift in economic activity within North America to the southern and southwestern United States in the last decade has raised some questions as to the relevance of this argument for the remainder of this century.[6]

My view is that the old perspective of looking at transport costs and distance to market as a significant determinant of location of new industry or relocation of old industry is for the most part irrelevant, given that transport costs represent a low share of total cost of most goods. Transport costs are rarely the most significant determinant of location.[7] The existence of an economic infrastructure and skilled labour force in Central Canada, together with agglomeration economies will result in a strong persistence for economic activity to locate within Central Canada, quite independently of intervention by governments. The existing level of economic integration of Canada within the U.S. market is the most important determinant of this persistence. The links between the two economies, in terms of ongoing contractual and informational relations between firms, customers, distribution networks and financial markets, constitute an enormous sunk investment between the two economies. New industries locating in Canada benefit from these links. Empirical and theoretical models of trade and location which ignore the existing economic links between the two countries can easily come to different and incorrect conclusions about industrial location.

The locational choice of industry, however, may be altered when external shocks occur, such as technological change and the emergence of low-cost foreign competition. A fall in transport and communication costs may cause some industries to move production sites if other factors are conducive to relocation. As markets become integrated, the analysis of location choices requires much closer attention to product market structure and the nature of factor price determination in regional markets. If factor prices are perfectly flexible, a high degree of firm mobility may have a greater impact on equalizing factor returns across regions than a shift in the location of production. This crucial point is taken up later, in the discussion of industrial policy.

External Scale Economies: Firms and Markets

This section explores in further detail the nature of contractual relations between regions, with emphasis on the possibility that changes in these arrangements may lead to external economies. The analysis focusses on changes in the organizational structure of firms, and market relationships between firms, their suppliers and customers.

Companies may be classified as having a regional, national, multinational or global perspective.[8] An interesting feature of the modern capitalist firm is that most are not limited to a specific region. Through experience and active search for profitable opportunities, many firms acquire a market horizon which extends far beyond their initial home base. This extension of the firm's horizon or market span is a major impetus for economic integration and a determinant of trade.

The modern industrial firm in a traded goods niche inevitably participates in more than one regional market. Indeed, the concept of a regional market holds little interest as a unit of study. Trade in any particular commodity occurs in a large number of interconnected regions and individual participants include firms which are involved in many of the markets. The degree of overlap determines the extent of market integration. "Perfect integration" could be defined as a state of market awareness such that any profitable opportunity, no matter where its location, is recognized by all participants in all regions. This condition probably comes closest to the concept of the perfect information conditions postulated in the abstract ideal of pure competition. Transactions in traded goods become more regionally integrated as the market span of firms increases and as transportation and communication costs are reduced.

Greater regional integration contributes to the extent of the markets and therefore to greater division of labour and more efficient arrangements of exchange, both within firms and within markets. A number of examples of this process come to mind.

When the downstream market becomes large enough to justify the overhead costs of a larger organization, vertical integration may displace less efficient spot market contracting for material from upstream industries.[9] The optimal organizational structure of a firm appears to depend upon the type of market in which it participates. There is considerable evidence that the modern innovation of a multidivision corporate structure is dependent on the existence of larger markets. Vertical integration and multidivision corporations are organizational responses which lead to greater efficiency in the internal allocation of resources as the market size expands.[10]

Another example of organizational change is horizontal merger and diversification. In this case, the effect of economic integration on the firm's efficiency is achieved primarily through increased economic interaction with other firms in export, R&D, financing, distribution and marketing. Economic integration permits horizontal mergers which exploit the public input aspects of a firm's overhead activities by consolidating financial and managerial transactions from separate lines of business within one organization. Without integration, these mergers are not profitable because there is not sufficient interaction with other firms.

Economic integration also permits improved matches between buyers and sellers in factor and product markets. A reduction in trade and investment barriers permits buyers and sellers to expand their horizons in searching for partners in mutually advantageous transactions and this expansion leads to a rise in the average quality of the match, in terms of net benefit received by both parties. This, in fact, is a simple prediction of the modern search theory of markets. Since a great deal of trade is in intermediate goods, where matching buyers and sellers is important, the potential benefits can be quite important. This type of interaction exhibits strong scale economies, as has long been suggested in the literature on spatial agglomeration. As integration proceeds, the benefits of expansion increase more rapidly than the increase in the size of the population from which buyers and sellers mutually search in order to make exchanges.

In analyzing the effects of economic integration of a small and a large country, it is clear that the benefits of improved matching of buyers and sellers accrue largely to the small country. As a simple example, consider a market with 100 buyers and sellers in Country L, and 10 buyers and sellers in Country S. With complete integration, the total market increases to a size of 110. This represents an elevenfold increase in the market size for the small country, versus a 10 percent increase for the large country. The effect is even more dramatic in terms of the total number of potential matches of buyers and sellers. Before integration, there are 10^2 matches in Country S and 100^2 matches in Country L, for a total of 10,100 matches. After integration, there are 110^2 matches, or 12,100 matches. Of these, residents of Country S account for 2,200 potential matches. Thus, the small country experiences a twenty-two-fold increase in the number of potential matches.

In the literature of urban and regional economics, there are numerous examples of external economies of city size. Some of these economies are industry-specific while others are more general. Many external economies are related to transactions and communications, and would be relevant also to economic integration between countries.

Larger markets don't necessarily lead to larger firms. As the size of the market expands, some activities that have been carried on within the firm may be handled more efficiently by a separate enterprise outside the firm. The larger market makes this activity viable on a stand-alone basis and contributes to both productivity and profitability. This is an example of the division of labour hypothesis that is limited by the extent of the market. A prominent example is the emergence of specialist firms in the financial services industry and in the production of particular types of telephone switching equipment, the latter activity being previously carried on by the large, integrated electronic manufacturers.

The effects of market size on firm and market organization structure and specialization promote increased economic efficiency through improved allocation of transactions between market and non-market mechanisms. Naturally, changes in structure and specialization occur with economic growth in general, but economic integration encourages these processes by increasing market size. These organizational changes can be regarded as external economies in that individual firms do not include in their own "internal" calculations the effect on overall market integration of their own output decisions or decisions to change organizational structure.

It is extremely difficult to provide reliable estimates of the contribution of external economies to economic growth and productivity. These economies do not lend themselves to objective identification and statistical measurement, partly because they are amorphous in nature and partly because of the problem of distinguishing between the effects of economic integration, technological change and other factors of economic growth when all are taking place at the same time. However, studies of the economic integration of nations such as those by Balassa (1975) on the European Common Market have placed great emphasis on the effects of external economies stemming from integration.

The available evidence on external scale economies is highly aggregative and compounds internal and external scale economies. Walters, in her study of Canadian economic growth (1970), attributed more than 80 percent of the residual growth rate, after accounting for factor inputs, to scale economies. Balassa, in his study of European economic integration (1975, p.113), assumed that the aggregate increase in trade between member countries led to total scale economy gains, including both internal and external economies, of about 30 cents on every dollar of additional trade. Richardson (1978, chap.3) reports a number of studies in the context of urban growth supportive of the existence of agglomeration economies, but the evidence seems highly variable.

Other indirect evidence on the existence of external economics directly relevant to the question of economic integration exists in the literature on the multinational firm. Globerman (1979) is one of a number of studies showing that multinationals promote greater efficiency through faster technology adoption, improved management techniques and upgraded labour force skills. These benefits subsequently spill over to other domestic firms through labour mobility, creating external economies. Since the emergence of multinationals can be viewed as part of the process of economic integration, this lends support to the hypothesis that external economies of scale accompany the process of economic integration. Although the quantitative estimates of external economics are few and generally unreliable, it seems fair to conclude that they are important.

Firms: Location and Market Strategy

An essential prerequisite to understanding the pattern of trade and investment in manufactured products between regions is an understanding of the motives which determine the location of various activities of the firm. These motives relate to the general concept of market strategy of the firm articulated by business policy economists and spelled out clearly by Porter (1980). The basic point is that as the firm extends its span beyond a single region, its marketing, management, R&D, and production activities no longer must all be located in the same region. The study of multinational enterprises (MNEs) has attempted to explain what determines the location of various activities of the large-scale corporation across various countries.[11] In examining some basic hypotheses advanced about location decisions, most attention has been focussed on how the firm decides whether to export from the home region or to open up a branch plant (foreign direct investment).

Porter (1980) distinguishes three basic types of MNEs and analyses for each type on the relation between location, firm strategy and market structure. The exposition which follows is based on his analysis.

One type of firm strategy concentrates on achieving scale in the production and competes primarily on cost. This strategy is successful only where there is a degree of product standardization and the market is reasonably large. Clearly, the span of firms of this type extends beyond the local market, and often embraces national or world markets. A low-cost distribution system and substantial investment in capital are necessary.

The second type of firm strategy is based on product differentiation. The firm may concentrate on certain local segments of an industry, but the emphasis is generally in terms of meeting a product spectrum, rather than a regional orientation. Firms of this type have a strong R&D base and emphasize innovation in product and process technology. Skilled labour is the most important labour input on the supply side. Equally important is a strong marketing base, with close coordination between marketing and R&D in order to keep pace with market demands.

The third type of firm strategy is described by Porter as a "focus" strategy. Firms of this type concentrate on either product differentiation or cost competition to serve a few customers, as opposed to the entire market. Considerable emphasis is placed by the firm on serving the needs of these few customers. Production, R&D, marketing and other activities focus on this end.

Clearly, certain types of industries attract one of these types of firms more than others, so that an industry can be characterized to some extent by one of these strategies. Over time, firms within an industry may shift emphasis from product differentiation to cost, as the product cycle hypothesis suggests. In the context of international trade, it should be recognized that systematic forces are important in determining which types of firms and which activities of each type of firm will locate within a region.

The activities of the modern industrial firm can be classified into three categories: (a) head office activities, which include central management, R&D, product development and finance; (b) production; and (c) marketing and distribution, including all aspects of customer relations. This division is somewhat arbitrary and any multidivisional organization conducts some of these activities within each division and some at the overall central management level. The basic issue, however, is where such activities are generally located. The forces which determine the location of head office activities are not necessarily those which determine the location of production. There are eight basic determinants of location.

- The extent of scale and scope economies in production, marketing, R&D and management. Scale economies may induce centralization of any one of these activities. They tend to coincide with the production of standardized commodities requiring low-skill labour. Scope economies, defined as the cost advantages of combining activities under a single location or organizational umbrella, induce a centralization of all activities at a single location.
- Cost differences due to factor price differences, transport costs, tariffs or other government policies.
- The extent and mode of anticipated competition in any market. High versus low entry barrier locations will result in a firm choosing the low entry barrier location as an entry point, other things being equal.
- Barriers to exit, or sunk costs which induce a firm to stick with its present locational pattern, even though new entrants face a different set of incentives.
- Cultural and regional preferences of management. Management generally has a bias for location close to its "roots," but the bias becomes weaker as the firm grows larger and gains experience in global or multiregional markets.
- Political and economic stability and the assurance of a stable supply of crucial inputs in various regions.
- The tax treatment of corporate and salary income by regional tax authorities. The ability to minimize the "tax cost" of doing business by shifting locations can be a powerful determinant of the location of various corporate activities.
- The comparative advantage effects of a location in terms of the relative abundance of various raw materials.

A great deal has been written about the firm's decisions to locate its various activities in response to these eight factors. A rough connection can be made between the type of strategy in which a firm competes (product differentiation, scale or focus) and the general locational pattern for firm activity across regions. Table 4-1 examines location decisions in regions which are not integrated. Regions are distinguished on two criteria, absolute size and per capita income. Comparative advantage effects are ignored. In practical terms, a region may be a country, a large region within a country, or many small countries which are closely linked. The emphasis is on economic as opposed to political boundaries. Assignment of entries within the table is fairly straightforward and follows from the definition of firm strategies and the determinants of location decisions. The assignment should depend on the specifics of each industry and is, of course, only crude. Substantive theoretical and empirical argument supporting this assignment are presented in Chapter Five.

The table indicates that small regions with high wages have trouble attracting the production activities of firms with scale strategies. They are more successful at attracting marketing and production activities of product-differentiated firms, and the head office, production and local marketing activities of firms with focus strategies. Finally, if raw material and transport costs are significant, comparative advantage effects remain important in determining the production activities for all three types of firms.

The separation of firm activities means that countries may well attract one type of firm activity but not another. Large countries have obvious advantages in being able to hold a diversified mix of firm types and firm activities. The general implications for a small country such as Canada are as follows:

- Large-scale production activities are at a competitive disadvantage in Canada unless the availability of special raw materials outweighs the wage cost disadvantage.

TABLE 4-1 Firm Strategy/Activity Location Matrix by Country Type

Industry/Firm Strategy

	Product Differentiation	Scale	Focus
Large, high income countries	HO S & P activities if skill requirements high enough	S & HO	S, P, & HO
Small, high income countries	Some S for local market. Some P activities. Some HO activities.	Odd S & HO activities.	P & HO S only for local market.
Low income countries	Some P activities in lower skill production (component assembly, etc.).	P activities.	None.

Notes: HO denotes head office, including R&D, finance & management.
S denotes marketing and distribution.
P denotes production.

- Firms with a focus strategy might well locate all firm activities within Canada, particularly if their customer is based in the United States.
- Head office and production activities of some product-differentiated industries are not at a competitive disadvantage within Canada. The marketing of these firms will, in some cases, have to be located close to the market and hence not within Canada.
- If there are scale economies in head office activities or strong complementarities between head office and production activities, then product-differentiated industries will be at a competitive disadvantage in small countries.[13]

The conclusion seems quite grim. Without comparative advantage effects or protection, manufacturing industry activity of all types seems generally disadvantaged in the small country. However, it must be recognized that Canada is integrated to a great extent within the North American market and, in some cases, within the global market. This means that the second, third and fourth points are irrelevant within a free trade arrangement which assures the full benefits of a large integrated region. Because complete free trade does not exist, these constraints play some part in the development of Canadian industry and the location of economic activity within Canada.

Trade and Income Determination

How can the pattern of locational bias among firms and industries be translated into a pattern of trade? In the short to medium run, meaning a period of up to ten or fifteen years, there is considerable rigidity in the location decision of firms because of the presence of sunk costs in both human and non-human resources, and the absence of effective competition forcing least-cost solutions. In particular, these rigidities create quasi-rents to location-specific factors of production, as well as to the owners of the proprietary resources which distinguish a firm from its competition. Not the least of these are the results of product development within the firm through research and development. These quasi-rents in the form of profits and wages are an important part of regional income. Other more conventional rents accrue through the effect of entry barriers such as brand loyalty, scale economies and rents to specific natural resources. Within an integrated economic region, incomes tend to be equalized across labour of similar types, while between non-integrated regions the process of income equalization is much slower.

The pattern of trade between regions is dependent upon the pattern of location of economic activity. The analysis here focusses on trade in manufactures, ignoring trade in primary commodities. The three activities of firms induce an implicit pattern of market and non-market trade in goods and services both within the firm, and between the firm, its input suppliers and final customers. Total trade between regions depends upon the number and size of firms engaged in the production of any commodity and the distribution of the various activities of these firms across regions.

The firm has no role in the classic theory of international trade. All trade is market-conducted and hence the location decision of any given firm is regarded as insignificant and overridden by aggregate considerations. More realistically, the typical firm in many industries is distinguished by such assets as its management, product lines, distribution networks, customer loyalty and supply networks, all of which impart uniqueness to the firm. This uniqueness implies that the location decisions of individual firms have a significant impact on economic activity within a given region. A decision by one firm to shut down a plant within a region does not automatically imply that another firm will open a similar plant. This may seem obvious but is not usually recognized in neoclassical trade theory.

The location decision which has greatest impact on trade in goods is the decision regarding location of production plants. The concept of "footloose" production is a dramatic example of a sensitive locational decision. If there are no sunk costs in a particular production location and production is completely independent of other activities of the firm, the production activities are literally "on wheels." The impact of a shift in the location of production means that the region from which the plant departs experiences a reduction in exports and an increase in imports of the commodity which the plant produced. In a plant which produces for a large market, the export effect is dominant. In a global industry in which the plants produce for the world market and there are relatively few plants worldwide, the regional gains and losses stemming from a shift in production can be dramatic. In the long run, the factors which become unemployed will eventually be employed in some other activity, but the adjustment period can be long and workers whose skills are specific to the firm and industry will suffer irretrievable losses. It is not surprising therefore that the relocation decisions of multinationals attract considerable political concern.

The non-market aspect of trade generated by firms with regionally diversified activities is less dramatic but equally important. In Canada intrafirm or "tied" trade has received considerable attention.[13] A vertically integrated firm with many plants may produce components in one location and ship them to another location for assembly. Here they may be sold in the local market or exported. The important determinants of this trade include transport costs, scale economies of specialized versus diversified plant production, skill levels of work forces in alternative locations, and customs procedures and practices among countries. One implication of this type of trade is that it tends to make foreign direct investment a complement of trade. The decision to locate a plant abroad is accompanied by a decision to export certain components to that plant. If the firm was initially exporting a product in finished form, the decision to invest abroad instead of exporting may reduce the trade in commodities and increase the trade in factor services. As mentioned before, the tariff can influence this decision.[14] The nature of the industry is an equally powerful influence. If customized production is important, product-differentiated industries will tend to locate production next to the customer, inducing direct investment by the firm. On the other hand, if there are important complementarities between production, R&D and marketing, then scale economies in the production process will tend to induce concentration of production and head office activities in one region, and export of the final commodity.

It should be noted that the question of ownership becomes somewhat irrelevant in a global market context. One reason is that capital markets become more integrated, and individuals hold internationally diversified portfolios, so that a firm may have an internationally mixed set of owners. Another reason is that, to the extent that firms do have a national identity, the fraction of foreign ownership in any given country in the traded goods sector would, on purely random grounds, tend to be proportional to the share of all other regions in total world trade. Thus, in the absence of comparative advantage, and assuming that the ultimate location of firm production is independent of the firm's national origin, in a country which accounts for 5 percent of world trade, foreign firms should account for about 95 percent of domestic trade. Of course, location decisions are not random, and governments in particular worry about the ownership of those firms doing business within their boundaries.

A final aspect of intrafirm trade is the implicit or explicit trade in technology and management services which is generated by a regional diversification of production, sales and head office activities. It is extremely difficult to come to any quantitative assessment of this trade because of lack of objective ways of measuring it.[15] Nevertheless, it is important because of the income it generates for the exporting region and the external benefits it provides to the importing region. As in the case of physical investment, trade in these services becomes a substitute for the trade in the goods these services produce. The decision by a firm to move a head office or R&D facility has important income consequences for the region from which the move is made and the receiving region. A region which can capture these activities in the medium run can sustain a higher level of regional income. It is worth noting that importing the services of the technology and then exporting is not the same thing as having the firm locate R&D within the region and then exporting. The region in which the innovation is performed captures a share of the quasi-rents from this activity to the extent that it accrues to regional labour and capital. Firms will locate head office and R&D

facilities where they are most cost effective and the infrastructure and skill level of labour force is appropriate. This will necessarily impart a bias toward large regions with highly skilled labour forces or toward regions with amenities which attract skilled labour.

The implicit trade in technology and management services will continue to be an important and possibly increasing part of total trade as the share of world income going to innovation and monopoly rents increases. The pattern of this trade across countries, given the inherent indivisibility in firms' various activities, will depend importantly upon the location decisions of firms with respect to their management and R&D activities.

The process of economic integration has a profound impact on the location decisions of firms. As economic integration of regions proceeds, the economic horizon of local entrepreneurs expands. This expanding horizon in turn accelerates the speed of integration; both effects work in the same direction and lead to the type of efficiency gains referred to in the previous section. When regions are balkanized or non-integrated, the decision of a local firm to change the location of production generally has a major impact. When the regions are national states, the decision has the connotation for the firm of "going international." The firm perceives this as taking a significant risk and often requires additional backing in terms of financial resources. This perceived risk of going over a regional and political boundary can often discourage a firm from setting up a new plant abroad, when economic efficiency dictates such a production decision. Instead the firm may resort to export, or fail to enter the new market altogether. Economic integration removes this impediment, as participants within the larger market attach less risk to location changes in economic activity. For many local firms, the simple act of exporting becomes routine, and goods which previously were not traded now cross the old regional borders routinely.

Policy Implications

Various policy implications of economic integration have been discussed throughout this chapter. This section expands on some of the major policy implications of certain aspects of integration. These include: (a) the mobility of firms across national and regional boundaries; (b) the existence of external economics associated with the economic integration process; and (c) the particular problems posed by non-market transactions.

A government which has jurisdiction over many regions can be a positive force in the process of integrating those regions. A wide variety of public projects, including education, culture and defence, can hasten or hinder the process of integration. However, governments have less power, and typically fewer incentives, with respect to integration with regions outside their political domain. The integration process necessarily reduces the ability of the government to affect economic outcomes within their own jurisdiction. For example, a small economy with a large fraction of its factors of production devoted to trade will bear the full brunt of the international business cycle, and there is little its government can do about it.

The same can be said, though, with respect to policies aimed at influencing economic structure of the region or sets of regions within a country. As the process of integration occurs across political boundaries, the firms of any one political jurisdiction become less sensitive or vulnerable to the policies of all jurisdictions. The opportunity of carrying on the same line of business from a number of political jurisdictions gives the firm a great deal of freedom, while hampering the ability of politicians and bureaucrats to affect internal outcomes.

The only completely effective way for governments to surmount this problem is to widen the scope of political integration at the same time that economic integration takes place. This has occurred to some extent with the European Common Market. The process of integration within a country may result in increased mobility not only of firms but also of labour. The problem of governing regions then becomes even more difficult because their political constituency can change with population migration.

Mobility, however, is a relative concept with an important temporal dimension. Investments have varying degrees of location specificity and longevity. Generally, produced goods are more mobile than factors, and some capital goods are more mobile than people. Nevertheless, there will be some industries in which production is genuinely footloose and the policy response to footloose industry is an important aspect of a nation's trade/industrial policy.

Crudely speaking, there are two alternatives in "tying down" an industry in the absence of strong comparative advantage effects. One approach is to raise trade barriers so that production is geared to the domestic market. The other approach is to keep trade barriers down but create barriers to factor movement. The most common way of doing this is to subsidize a firm's expenditure on location-specific investments, creating a sunk cost which makes it unprofitable in the short run for the firm to move in response to external shocks. With the reduction in trade barriers under the Kennedy and Tokyo rounds, this latter form of industrial policy has become common. Another way to create barriers to factor movement is by direct government ownership of footloose industry. This too has been used, to some extent, in Canada and the European countries.[16]

Both types of policies amount to protection and both have negative consequences for aggregate world economic efficiency. The competition among nations to retain or attract multinational production through competitive subsidization could have larger negative consequences for domestic real income than tariff protection has had in the past. The problem arises because multinational enterprises are active participants in the game being played between nations to attract industry. By playing one government off against another, the MNE can extract a great deal of surplus from the successful bidder. There is no guarantee, for example, that labour employed by the MNE in the winning country will benefit, as would be the case under tariff protection. The transfer will be primarily from the taxpayers of the winning country to the shareholder of the multinational. If these shareholders are foreigners, the domestic real income cost of winning could be very large and must be balanced carefully against the employment gains.

In short, the protection, one way or another, of footloose industries presents a genuine dilemma for policy makers. For small open economies, playing either game can be very costly. Sensible trade/industrial policy should avoid either form of protection. For industries which are not footloose, at least in the medium run, exit and entry barriers figure prominently in the location decision. The discussion in this case shifts naturally to market structure and will be deferred to the next chapter.

The sources of certain types of external economies have already been discussed. Some of these economies are industry specific and others are more general and related to the process of economic expansion. The main policy implication is that trade and investment barriers inhibit both market and non-market transactions between economic regions and thus prevent the full realization of these external economies. This is particularly true for a small economy integrating with a large economy. A further question is whether the existence of these economies calls for additional policies beyond the reduction of trade barriers. For example, to achieve maximum efficiency, external economies in an industry require an additional subsidy on output if the industry is competitive. The logic of this argument is correct, but to implement it in practical terms is extremely difficult. The problem is even more complex for general or environmental external economies, because quantitative knowledge of these economies is so imprecise. In the absence of this knowledge, extreme caution in intervention is a sensible course of action. The great advantage of free trade is that it permits a small open economy to realize the greater portion of these external economies without engaging in fine tuning at the microeconomic level.

One view of industrial policy is that it is concerned with "positive" adjustment to external shocks. In the discussion of economic integration and external economies, it was noted that as integration occurs, firm and market organization tends to evolve in fairly natural ways. As the economy adjusts to external shocks, including foreign competition and technological change, similar adjustments are likely to take place. Vertical and horizontal merger, divestiture of existing firms, the creation of new firms and internationalization or externalization of economic transactions are responses which can be expected. A policy of positive adjustment must be carefully designed not to hinder these forms of adjustments. On the other hand, it is difficult to identify those cases where the adjustment should be assisted. Specific issues are discussed in Chapter Seven. In general, the complexity of economic organization suggests that a pragmatic, piecemeal approach to industrial policy may be the only practical alternative.

The final policy question I should like to focus on here is the special problems created for policy by non-market transactions. Intrafirm or tied trade and technology transfers by MNEs are perhaps the most obvious examples in the trade literature. Non-market transactions create particular problems for government policy since they can seldom be monitored as easily as market-based transactions. A notable case in point is the growth of the underground economy in response to the personal income tax system. This type of response by the private sector makes government management of economic activity even more difficult and results in less efficient exchange arrangements. This in turn may lead to frustration on the part of government and bureaucrats, with further intervention and costly monitoring of the internal activities of firms. If substitution between market and non-market transactional arrangements is relatively easy, then traditional tax and subsidy instruments may be quite ineffective or have uncertain unintended side effects. In such cases closer collaboration between government and the private sector may be an appropriate institutional response, particularly if the number of firms involved is small.

The conventional theory of economic policy approach, in which the public sector mechanically manipulates private sector agents by changing taxes and subsidies, may not be an appropriate analytical framework in these circumstances. Given a large degree of uncertainty as to firm response and lack of information as to relevant market parameters, a cooperative bargaining approach between public and private sector may be considerably more practical and less wasteful of public resources. Since a significant portion of total international transactions are non-market based, industrial policy will have to be realistic in the way it intends to affect economic outcomes.

Chapter 5

Entry Barriers and Competition in the Small Open Economy

Introduction

This chapter shifts focus from that of the previous chapter in several substantive ways. First, the discussion is concerned generally with an economic environment in which the level of economic integration is taken as given, with emphasis on the effects of trade and investment on a small open economy. Second, the background analytics for the material in this chapter come largely from the treatment of entry barriers in the study of industrial organization. The "industrial organization" approach to questions of trade and investment has a long history in Canada and offers a perspective quite different from that given by the factor proportions model. Another change in emphasis is the implicit acceptance of the concepts of a "domestic firm" and domestic versus foreign markets. As the previous chapter emphasizes, the distinction between foreign and domestic firms can be misleading as it de-emphasizes such things as location decisions by firms, but it remains a useful distinction for many purposes. What must be kept in mind is that unless the domestic firm is owned by residents of the country, the question of ownership is irrelevant. It will also be irrelevant if the return to capital is determined entirely by conditions in the world capital market and all rents show up as returns to labour or other factors of production specific to the home country. Some of the general implications of relaxing these assumptions are straightforward and will be covered in Chapters Six and Seven.

This chapter deals first with static entry barrier theory and its implications, and then with dynamic theories of competition. Some of the material on static entry barriers is not new, and is covered by Wonnacott (1983) and my own monograph (Harris, 1984b), but the basic arguments are worth repeating because they are still novel for many economists used to working in the Heckscher-Ohlin tradition. Finally, this chapter is predominantly concerned with the manufacturing sector, where comparative advantage explanations of trade are particularly lacking. Dynamic entry barriers created through industrial innovation are covered in Chapter Six.

Static Entry Barriers

This section details the effects of the static entry barriers approach to trade. This approach to industrial organization has a long history in economics, beginning with the important work of Joe Bain (1956). Only in recent years has explicit theoretical work been done which incorporates entry barriers into an international trade framework. In this section attention is focussed on three traditional entry barriers: scale economies internal to the firm; product differentiation; and absolute capital requirements.

Scale Economies

Scale economies have received a great deal of attention in Canada.[1] One of the standard arguments against protection in the Canadian economy is that it inhibits the achievement of scale economies by Canadian firms. It should be stated at the outset of this discussion that economies of scale are an important reason for trade between countries that are otherwise identical. The reason is that gains from specialization can be achieved by having countries specialize completely in the production of separate sets of commodities.

The crucial observation is that conditions of perfect competition are not compatible with significant firm-level scale economies. Monopoly, or some other form of imperfectly competitive market structure, is the "natural" outcome of free market forces. Some critics of the neoclassical perfect competition model take this observation as sufficient to justify intervention in the market. These critics support their view with the following observation: depending upon the nature of the market structure, trade is not necessarily mutually beneficial with significant scale economies in production, assuming that all firms and countries have access to the same "best practice" technology. Unfortunately, this tells us little about which country is likely to gain and which will likely lose. The basic idea is that if the world market will support only one firm, the country which ends up with the monopolist may benefit at the expense of the other.

These are just some of the many possible effects of scale economies on trade and imperfect competition. Existing theory tends to present a list of possible cases rather than provide any definitive answer.[2] It is necessary therefore to resort to identification of the important forces at work.

The emphasis on scale economies in the Canadian trade policy context has focussed on two things. First is the observation by Eastman and Stykolt (1967) that the domestic tariff, by protecting firms from foreign competition, may encourage domestic oligopolistic pricing practices, which in turn induce operation at inefficient plant scales. Related is the tendency for protected domestic and foreign firms to produce an overly diversified product mix within the plant, with short production runs and high unit cost. Wonnacott and Wonnacott, in their study on free trade between Canada and the United States (1967), placed considerable emphasis on the U.S. tariff, which denies Canadian producers access to the large U.S. market and hence restricts them to output levels too low to reap full economies of scale in production. The inability of firms to rationalize is responsible for the relatively inefficient Canadian manufacturing sector. Productivity differences observed between the United States and Canada during the 1960s were as high as 33 percent.[3] The significance of scale economies goes even further. The revealed comparative advantage of Canada in resources, and the net deficit on manufactured products during the 1970s, was due in large part to the tariff-induced inefficiency of the manufacturing sector (Harris, 1984b). At the same time, it is widely agreed that the Canadian tariff historically induced a significant degree of foreign ownership in manufacturing.[4]

There are three substantive empirical issues in the contemporary Canadian debate on the role of scale economies. First, what is the empirical magnitude of scale economies at the firm level, and will they diminish or increase in the future? Second, what has been the effect of tariffs on Canadian manufacturing in the past? Three, what is the implication of all these results with respect to free trade and protection?

The empirical significance of scale economies remains problematic, with statements supporting almost any possible position.[5] Industrial organization economists, using a variety of methodologies, have attributed great significance to these scale economies as a determinant of industrial structure, and observed that larger scale economies relative to the market size indicate a more concentrated industry structure. Engineering studies largely support this view. On the other hand, statistical studies based on observed samples of plants have, with few exceptions, revealed only modest scale economies. This issue has never been adequately resolved. Detractors of the statistical approach argue that the samples have never had enough variability to determine the full extent of the true scale economies. Studies of revealed market structure, however, are in uniform agreement that for many industries firms show no sign of getting smaller, whether absolutely or relative to market size.[6] The fact that firm size is keeping pace with market size is particularly telling. If technology does not change as the economy grows, scale economies should prove less significant and concentration levels in industry should decline. There are many supporters of the view that technical change over the past few decades has been significantly biased toward larger scale operations. The innovation process has been geared toward reducing labour costs and increasing the efficiency of mass production. In the postwar period, most manufacturing industries moved to assembly-line production methods.[7]

What of future scale economies? Some have argued that scale economies are now declining in a large number of industries. The development of CAD/CAM technology and flexible manufacturing processes will mean the scaling down of a large number of processes.[8] This has already happened in the steel industry and parts of the retail industry. Unfortunately, there is no way to resolve this issue through statistical study, at least yet. Recent technological change has been so rapid that the general scale bias of innovation is impossible to pin down. It is likely to be highly uneven across commodities.

It is important to recognize that scale economies can affect all aspects of the firms activities — product development, production, distribution, marketing and management. It is possible for scale economies to diminish in one area and increase in others. Most economists have focussed on scale economies in production, but the information revolution created by technological innovations has considerably reduced the cost of non-market coordination. Firms can now coordinate activities internally which were previously conducted through market transactions. This may lead to increased vertical and horizontal integration and consequently an increase in the firm size needed for maximum efficiency. Work by Rumelt (1974) and others on corporate organization clearly point in that direction. While this evidence is not conclusive, it suggests the possibility that scale economies in a number of areas may actually rise.

Statistical work on the effect of the Canadian tariff on industrial structure in Canada is less controversial. A string of studies, beginning with the work of Eastman and Stykolt, has documented the bias toward small scale and industry concentration induced by heavy domestic protection in the postwar period.[9] More recent studies (e.g., Baldwin and Gorecki, 1983) have also shown that with the reduction in tariffs following the Kennedy and Tokyo rounds of the GATT, Canadian industry has moved toward a more rationalized industry structure, as predicted by the theory. Much of the adjustment toward free trade may already have taken place, given that tariffs by the mid-1980s will be down to an average of 5 to 6 percent across all manufacturing industries. The Wonnacotts (1982) and Cox and Harris (1985) agree that gains to Canada from a reduction of foreign and domestic tariffs from their pre-Tokyo

Round levels to zero would result in income gains to Canadians of about 8 to 10 percent of GNP. In both cases the arguments hinge on the presence of scale economies. These are extremely significant gains, and strong evidence in favour of the free trade position.

The scale economies argument, though, can be pushed in other directions. Particularly troublesome for Canada is the possibility that scale economies may create entry barriers in export markets. This is just one example of the two-sided role of the entry barrier methodology. If scale economies in an industry are quite significant, then even after tariff barriers decline a domestic firm from a small economy base may find entry into a foreign market very difficult, at least in the short run.

Evidence for the 1970s suggests that with tariff reduction over the last 15 years, this has not been a problem, at least for many industries. Canadian firms have made inroads in industries which are fairly scale intensive industries, reversing the pattern of trade noted in the 1950s and 1960s.[10] While scale economies may create significant short-run barriers to entry to Canadian export firms, in the longer term, entry opportunities appear to be equalized in most industries.

Entry is more problematic, though, in industries for which scale economies are so significant that the world industry is highly concentrated. Some of these industries are closely related to the U.S. defence sector. These industries with scale economies at the world level could probably not exist at all within a small open economy in the absence of government intervention, unless there were significant comparative advantages favouring this location. If such an industry is already established, however, it would probably survive even in the absence of domestic protection. This argument might have to be modified if the domestic market accounted for a large fraction of the world market. The removal of protection, both domestic and foreign, could allow a firm from a small open economy to gain a share of the world market, particularly if it had formerly relied on high-priced tariff-protected intermediate inputs. There are, naturally, few such firms in a small open economy. Certain defence industries and commercial aircraft are examples. In most cases, technological change is so important in these industries that it is difficult to assess the impact of long-run scale economies.

The automobile industry has generally been regarded as having world-level scale economies, but this view is now questionable, given the large number of entrants in the past two decades. The industry is of special significance to Canada because of its large employment base, and the special nature of trade in automobiles and parts between the United States and Canada under the Auto Pact. Specific issues of this sector are discussed in later chapters, after issues of innovation and dynamic competition are covered.

Product Differentiation

In industries where the product is not standardized and where product differentiation is the key to competition, there is yet another reason to trade. Different countries can specialize in particular lines of products, realizing intra-industry gains from specialization. The model of monopolistic competition provides a theory which focusses not on the entry barriers but on the welfare implications of changes in product variety. There is general agreement that trade between countries is beneficial because it increases the product variety available to consumers.[11] It has, however, been suggested that tariffs may be welfare-improving in industries characterized by genuine product differentiation because of an under-supply in product-differentiated industries relative to non-differentiated industries in a free trade equilibrium. This argument is, at least for the moment, generally regarded as an intellectual curiosity. On the export side, product differentiation opens up the prospect of entering foreign markets through a strategy of non-price competition and meeting selected market niches. Scale economies are less of a barrier and competing on product is an important channel by which a small country may export successfully.

The industrial organization literature has focussed not on the positive welfare aspects of product differentiation, but on the observed positive correlation across industries of high product differentiation with high concentration.[12] Many such industries, particularly in consumer goods, consist of a number of product oligopolies competing with one another through brand competition. In some cases, the result may be wasteful brand proliferation and image creation. Closely related is the role of advertising in creating entry barriers by creating differentiation in the eyes of the consumer. There is an active debate between those who regard advertising as primarily a device for conveying useful information to consumers and those who regard it primarily as a serious entry barrier.

If one views product differentiation and advertising as entry barriers which lead to concentration and high profits rather than ways to satisfy varying consumer needs, the policy perspective changes slightly. First, the domestic tariff may be viewed as encouraging wasteful product differentiation by inducing collusion on prices and non-price competition among domestic oligopolists. A reduction in protection could lead to an increase in cost efficiency of production and a fall in consumer prices. On the export side, the problem is quite different. A significant barrier to a domestic firm entering a foreign market could be the product differentiation of foreign competitors. In particular, brand loyalty created by large-scale advertising or large fixed costs associated with providing a full line of competing products may impede entry into a concentrated foreign industry. The ability to product differentiate may facilitate entry, either through price competition, given a reduction in foreign tariffs, or through finding a product niche. Multinationals may play a significant role in such industries. If they are part of the industry to begin with, the tariff reduction merely gives them an opportunity to shift the location of alternative product line production. For reasons alluded to in Chapter Four, they may choose to produce one of their products in the small country for export to the foreign market.

The possibility of world market concentration through defensive product differentiation and advertising by incumbent firms means that, to export successfully, a firm must overcome these barriers. As in the case of scale economies, this may create problems in the adjustment to free trade. On the other hand, the possibility for non-price competition through product differentiation may actually reduce the problems in exporting successfully.

Historically, Canada has exported little in the way of consumer goods. Some might interpret this as evidence of a revealed comparative disadvantage for a small open economy in producing consumer goods tailored for the large U.S. market. This seems unlikely, given the cultural similarity between Canada and the United States. A more adequate explanation lies in the existence of high entry barriers in a number of the consumer goods industries, together with the U.S. tariff. These factors have been prohibitive enough to discourage Canadian imports in the traditional industries. The bias against product-differentiated exports could disappear with free access to the U.S. market if the entry barriers can be overcome. A final word of caution is that the emphasis on the static theory may be unduly biasing the case. In many industries, product differentiation means product development and dynamic innovation, and matters are somewhat different from that perspective.

Absolute Capital Requirements

A major entry barrier referred to in many studies of market structure is the absolute size of capital requirements for an efficient size firm in many industries. This barrier is distinct from scale economies and is motivated by the observation that capital markets for industrial firms are imperfect in that existing firms have a lower cost of capital on external borrowing and recourse to greater internal financial resources than a new entrant, who would typically have to raise most of the necessary financial capital through external borrowing. The theoretical rationales for these imperfections are not well understood. Undoubtedly, the risk element of entry into a concentrated industry plays an important role. There is substantial evidence of the risk to entry and how this affects the cost of capital to new firms.[13]

The implications of this capital market imperfection in an open economy context are not yet fully understood, but some important observations can be made. Capital market imperfections are one explanation for the presence of multinationals in concentrated industries, since multinationals have recourse to corporate financial resources and are not dependent upon the capital market of any one country. The cost of capital to firms in Canada is slightly above that of similar firms in the United States (Daly, 1979, p.19). One plausible explanation is that Canadian firms are smaller on average than U.S. firms in similar industries and thus face greater risk, raising their cost of external finance.

Observation of these barriers does not carry with it any immediate implication of "market failure"; there may be good reasons why the capital market charges these firms a higher rate on their borrowing. Nevertheless, the existence of capital market imperfection is used as a rationale for defending the many provincial and federal programs to aid small business and some programs to aid medium size business. It is in fact the only substantive argument for these subsidies other than Keynesian-type arguments on the employment benefits of supporting smaller firms relative to large firms. One thing that can be said for this type of policy is that it is superior to restricting foreign investment. A general principle of optimal economic policy is to locate the corrective device closest to the source of the problem. If there is a capital market failure, subsidizing capital is the right thing to do.

Barriers to Export from the Small Open Economy

In the discussion of the three barriers to entry, it was noted that each may constitute an entry barrier to export for a domestic firm from a small open economy. Thus, as trade barriers are reduced, some firms may have an opportunity to export but that opportunity may be significantly hampered. There is a parallel argument on the import side; large firms from large countries may find it relatively easy to penetrate the domestic market of a small economy. The evidence which exists on this question is sparse. What does exist is based mostly on European data.[14] The conclusion of these studies, though, is more or less in conformity with the view just expressed. Firms from small countries have difficulty establishing an export market in industries which are relatively concentrated, due to either scale economy or product-differentiation barriers. Perhaps more telling are the studies reported in the export marketing literature. There are many tales of small firms who attempted to establish an export market but simply gave up.

Another form of supporting evidence is provided by the studies on trade patterns and market structure variables (Hufbauer, 1970, and Gruber et al., 1967). In these studies there is often an attempt to control for static entry barriers, such as scale economies and product differentiation. There are numerous studies on 1960s data which show that small countries have a comparative disadvantage in scale economy industries. This is consistent with the hypothesis that entry barriers to export are present in scale economy industries which prohibit entry by small domestic firms. It is also consistent with the hypothesis that these industries are precisely those facing the largest tariff and non-tariff barriers to trade. Large countries can overcome these barriers by relying on their domestic market alone to realize scale economies and, thus, capture the export market. Unfortunately, the studies do not adequately discriminate between the two hypotheses. In Baumann's study on Canada–U.S. trade (1976) he finds, for example, that Canada tends to import in those industries in which there are firm-level scale economies, thus exhibiting a revealed comparative disadvantage in these industries.

A major problem with the trade studies using market structure variables is that many of them fail to account for the possibility of intra-industry trade. It is possible that market structure may be less than perfectly competitive, but substantial two-way trade occurs within a particular commodity because the industry is based on both sides of a border. Balassa has repeatedly emphasized the importance of intra-industry trade and intra-industry rationalization in response to reductions in trade barriers and external shocks.[15] The revealed comparative advantage approach completely breaks down when intra-industry specialization is accounted for. A country could be a small net importer of a given commodity in a scale-intensive industry, yet be a substantial gross exporter of the same commodity. Does this indicate a comparative advantage or disadvantage? In my study of Canadian trade (Harris, 1984b), I found that, within a fully static approach, incorporating intra-industry trade and scale economies led to a dramatically different picture of industry trade barriers, rather than a focus on net trade balances across industries. An industry which was a net importer before a reduction in trade barriers could, depending upon conditions in foreign and domestic markets, become a substantial net exporter after a reduction in trade barriers.

Summarizing the evidence, a good case can be made for the existence of barriers to export at the level of the individual firm. However, attempts to identify those industries which may suffer potential problems due to these barriers should not be based only on the export potential revealed in trade data. A more careful market structure analysis is required which focusses on the individual firm's entry prospects in each foreign market.

Getting at a consistent theoretical story behind the existence of export barriers is a task which remains to be undertaken. The argument thus far been based upon the idea that concentrated foreign markets are characterized by entry barriers which make entry difficult for any firm, including a possibly more efficient home firm. Small countries are thought to be particularly disadvantaged because they tend to foster a higher percentage of small firms.

A different argument might well hinge on the presence of barriers to export in particular, as opposed to barriers to entry in general. There is certainly some evidence of economies of scale in exporting, because of the fixed costs of acquiring the necessary information to market abroad and setting up necessary foreign distribution networks.[16] Both of these problems could, in principle, be circumvented by resorting to specialized export marketing firms which spread these costs over a large number of exporters, and this is in fact the case in a number of industries. In foreign industries which are concentrated, however, this type of strategy is unlikely to work, because the number of firms that could potentially enter the industry is very small and the information and distribution networks are likely to be highly specialized to the particular industry. If the information in an industry is product and competitor specific, the scale economies to exporting cannot be overcome by export marketing firms. These arguments suggest that scale economies in exporting are most likely to constitute an effective barrier in those industries which are characterized by a small number of sellers. The positive association between foreign concentration, entry barriers and economies to scale in exporting all tend to reinforce each other. The story needs to be extended to a dynamic setting. Export barriers have a strong temporal dimension. If a firm can overcome them once and enter the export market, the costs to exporting will become sunk costs and should prove no further hindrance to the firm. Empirical work emphasizing the dynamic aspect of export barriers remains to be done.

What type of policy response does the presence of export barriers call for? Banks and other financial institutions may be worried about the potential success of a Canadian firm entering the U.S. market. This would lead them to charge a higher interest rate to the firm than would be charged a new entrant entering the same market from a U.S. base. The fundamental question is whether this discrimination is based upon the origin of the firm or its status as an entrant per se. It may simply be that the expected failure rate on entry to foreign markets is higher than on domestic entry. A number of reasons alluded to earlier could explain this, including implicit cultural and informational barriers to the exporting firm, difficulties managing distribution and sales from a distance, etc. Does the presence of such risk provide an argument for subsidizing new firms trying to enter an export market? I think a good case can be made here, although the emphasis should be on subsidizing entry into the market rather than sales after entry has been successfully completed.

One argument is that the government has greater ability to pool risk than private capital markets, and should therefore subsidize risky activities to take advantage of investment opportunities. This is a standard argument in support of the proposition that public investment should be discounted at risk-free interest rates. However, some doubt has been cast upon the supposed superior ability of the government to pool risk relative to private financial capital markets.[17]

A more substantive argument hinges upon the dynamics of firm growth and entry. Consider a small country with a number of small to medium size firms previously oriented to the domestic market, attempting for the first time to enter a foreign market in which the incumbent firms are significantly larger. The presence of barriers to entry makes it difficult for the small country to establish a presence in the industry. Private financial markets looking at the prospect of successful entry by these small firms judge it to be sufficiently risky to charge rates of interest on loans that are prohibitive for most of the potential entrants. If by some means, a large potential entrant could be created, this single large firm would have a greater chance of succeeding than the collective chances of many small firms. The question of size is crucial in many industries; without a sufficiently large firm, the chances of successful entry are nil. The best course of action would be for the small firms to merge. However, the dynamics of merger are notoriously capricious and the importance of grasping the export market early is great. There are two courses of government action: direct intervention to encourage the merger of a number of small firms, or subsidization of some of the smaller firms. While the former course of action may be preferable, it may in many cases be impractical because individual entrepreneurs are reluctant to give up their companies. The "market failure" that government intervention must try to correct is the failure to foster the creation of large firms. The market for corporate control is not sufficiently perfect to produce a domestic firm which is the optimal size for entry. The general subsidy is the next best alternative. This will raise the chance that some fraction of the entering firms will succeed. A firm which successfully establishes a presence in the industry will face reduced capital costs in the private market. Market forces should ultimately dictate the most profitable strategy for the successful firm. Once the export market is established, the subsidy can be removed. In industries with significant entry barriers in the foreign market, failure to undertake such a policy would mean the long-run loss of a significant market.

It is important to recognize those cases in which the above argument is not relevant. It is not relevant when domestic firms are the correct size for entry to a concentrated foreign market, or in those cases in which size is a matter of indifference. Small firms can achieve successful entry in competitive markets and in some markets where innovative product differentiation is the major form of competition. The general question of size of firms and the dynamics of entry take us naturally to the next topic.

Dynamic Theories of Competition

The static entry barriers approach to market structure has long been recognized as inadequate. Most of the time, the theory ends up trying to deal explictly with a dynamic factor in a relatively ad hoc way. Empirical investigation of hypotheses suggested by the theory of entry barriers has tended to concentrate on the static approach because of a lack of adequate time series data. In recent years, however, advances in the field of industrial organization have led to development of a more complete dynamic theory and serious attempts to test the hypotheses suggested. This section explores some of the implications of this dynamic industrial organization approach to trade.

The dynamic entry barrier approach attempts to explain the evolution of firm and market structure over time. It helps to explain why some firms stay large even when all firms in the industry face the same objective static entry barriers. The theory generally emphasizes the importance of being first. In the trade area, it has tended to be applied to potential export-oriented growth industries — of course, one country's exports are another's imports, and hence, natural questions regarding protection occur. From the small open economy perspective, this theory recognizes the role of the firm, as opposed to the industry, in the economic process. Large successful firms in particular are more important than small, unsuccessful ones. In a small open economy, an industry can often consist largely of one or two firms. Tailoring trade and industrial policy to deal with this fact generally means a shift of focus from the industry level to the firm level.

Pre-emptive Large-Scale Investment

Awareness of the advantages conferred upon the firm which is large relative to its competitors led to the theory of strategic dynamic pre-emptive investment.[18] The basic idea is that the firm which is first to expand by investing in fixed and irreversible firm-specific capital puts its competitors at a disadvantage. These firms observe the large competitor and refrain from taking an action — such as expanding productive capacity — they would have taken had the other firm not forestalled them. The strategic threat posed by the first firm to expand is only credible to the extent that its investment involved costs which are genuinely "sunk" or irrecoverable. This theory recognizes the strategic importance of "burning one's bridges." A basic precondition for this type of strategy to work is some type of indivisibility, such as scale economies in production or R&D, which keeps the competition limited to a few firms; thus the market structure, at best, is competitively oligopolistic.

The theory may explain why incumbent firms in concentrated industries appear to undertake unprofitable investment with the sole intent of keeping out entrants. The U.S. antitrust case involving Alcoa is a major example of such behaviour. In practical terms, the theory predicts that the basic competition is over timing of investments to expand productive capacity to serve a future market. While there are great benefits to being first, there are also great risks. If market conditions and technology change rapidly, the initial investment may soon become obsolete and a second firm can profit from the first firm's mistakes. Nevertheless, an aggressive pre-emptive strategy by incumbents is often thought to dominate the more conservative "second mover" strategy; consequently, pre-emption is an important factor in explaining firm behaviour and industry structure.

This theory of market structure has a number of implications in the context of international trade. First, consider the problem of firms attempting to enter the export market as foreign trade barriers are reduced. Local foreign incumbents in those industries, faced with removal of protection, may engage in defensive pre-emptive investment against foreign entrants. There is every reason to believe the incumbents have the incentive to pre-empt, and will be reasonably successful in those industries where costs can be sunk for relatively long periods by investment in real capital. Heavily mechanized industries with strong scale economies and low resale value of equipment would be natural candidates.

This theory has implications not only for Canadian exporters but also for import-competing firms in Canada, which could attempt to use this strategy in response to reduced levels of protection. This would be unfortunate because the strategy perpetuates an inefficient industrial structure and causes inefficient and excessive investment within the industry. Fortunately, most of our import-competing industries are not heavily capital intensive, so the problem is not likely to be serious. On the export side, though, the reduction in foreign tariffs in some industries could increase entry barriers against Canadian firms, lengthening the adjustment to a free trade industrial structure and, in some cases, perhaps eliminating the prospect of establishing an export market at all.

A more popular application of the pre-emption theory concerns competitive national industrial policies.[19] The basic idea is that governments try to use their subsidy policies in highly concentrated industries strategically, pre-empting other nations' firms by subsidizing their own first. If they succeed, the winning country shares in the monopoly rents and the cost of the subsidy is more than justified. A more likely outcome is that every country attempts the same strategy and all lose, with substantial overinvestment in the world industry as a whole. Under certain circumstances, however, the result may be similar to an optimal tariff, that is, for one country to subsidize exports even if all competing countries do so. For this to hold true, no country can have a clear head start, and all participating countries must have sufficient market power such that their subsidy policy has an important effect on their firms' sales. This is clearly an argument which can be used to justify protectionism. There are a number of problems with the practical relevance of the argument which will be discussed below in connection with dynamic protectionism.

Competition on the Learning Curve

Another aspect of pre-emptive competition is grounded in the concept of dynamic scale economies which arise through the presence of learning-by-doing effects in the production process. The learning curve is an empirical summary of these effects, which postulates that unit costs of production decline with cumulative output. The learning curve was popularized by the Boston Consulting Group, an influential corporate consulting firm, as a way of aggressively pre-empting competitors. A substantial body of empirical evidence documents the existence of a learning curve effect in many industries.[20] The basic idea is that, as production of a new product begins in the plant, labour and management need time to discover the most efficient production methods; there is also a learning-by-doing effect on any given task on the production line. Some observers find that Japanese industrial policy has attributed great importance to the learning curve effect as a means of cost-reduction.[21]

In order for the learning curve to be an important competitive mechanism, the learning effects must remain with the firm; i.e., they must not be easily portable to other competing firms. It is believed that in many cases portability of learning between firms is low or at least subject to long lags.

The basic application of the learning curve to pre-emptive competition is that the firm which is first to start down the learning curve gets ahead in the race to achieve lowest cost. By keeping prices close to cost, the leader in the race will deter the competition from continuing. This is an ideal form of pre-emptive investment because there is no doubt that the winner is at an advantage. The learning curve strategy tends to emphasize price competition relatively soon after the introduction of the product, rather than competition through product differentiation. Lower prices mean higher sales; higher sales mean faster learning and lower future costs. It can even be rational to price well below cost in the early phases of production. The payoff, of course, is monopoly rents in the future.

We now turn to a further examination of the trade policy implications of pre-emptive strategies.

Dynamic Protection Arguments

As suggested in the previous section, the arguments of dynamic pre-emptive strategies in non-competitive industries provide a rationale for subsidy or protection which is similar to the dynamic external economy argument used in the standard infant industry argument. The important difference between the "old" and the "new" infant-industry argument is that economies are held to be internal to the firm and the product market is non-competitive in the new version. The idea is to use a subsidy to foster a winning firm which has a significant world market share in an internationally oligopolistic industry. In many ways, the emphasis is quite different to the usual market failure arguments for government intervention, which presuppose the benefits of competitive market structures. In this case, the basis for intervention is to get a piece of the world monopoly. It should be recognized that these monopoly rents may be the return to technological innovation — a subject that is dealt with in the next chapter.

The other important difference between this new infant-industry argument and the old one is the "hysterisis" of the market dynamics; that is, the long-run outcome is not independent of short-run actions. A firm which successfully pre-empts a competitor in the short run may retain the lead forever, given the dynamic irreversibility of investment. In the international context, a country which allows itself to be pre-empted may permanently lose an export market. The stark contrast between winning and being pre-empted means that all countries have a strong incentive to engage in protectionist-type policies in these industries. The standard argument on externalities associated with an infant industry suggests a subsidy, as opposed to tariff, as a first-best instrument. The presence of hysterisis in the market dynamics may well reverse this ranking. A tariff, by guaranteeing the domestic firm a market, assures the long-run survival of the firm. A subsidy may enhance the prospects for survival but cannot guarantee it. If other countries are subsidizing, retaliation by tariff protection may be a better way of ensuring survival of the domestic industry.

If all countries resort to protection, though, the whole idea of getting access to the world market falls apart, as also does the case for subsidy. The risk of this type of pre-emptive strategy — in which investment in productive capacity is the vehicle for pre-emption — is great. It could easily result in excess capacity in the world industry, which in turn could lead to aggressive price cutting and the type of destructive competition observed in the 1930s in some industries. For a small country the downside risk of such a strategy is extremely high. Failure to get access to the foreign markets spells disaster. If domestic firms undertake such a strategy on their own, that is one thing. But government participation or encouragement through subsidy is an unwise course of action.

If the vehicle for pre-emption is the learning curve, the arguments for protection and subsidy are subject to the same general risks but the logic is closer to the genuine infant-industry argument. If the domestic market is large, protection in the early phases of the industry can directly contribute to increased sales and can speed progress down the learning curve. In very small economies the domestic market may not be large enough and a subsidy on output would be the more effective instrument.

It is clear that large countries, because of the size of their domestic markets, have an advantage in this type of competition if protection is allowed. In the absence of protection by all concerned, the competition is not so heavily stacked against the small country. In this case, if a number of countries provide subsidies to start their domestic firms down the learning curve about the same time, and all are equally successful in sales, none should be at a cost advantage relative to the others because of the learning effect. Ultimately, they will all share in the world oligopoly. The policy could have a good side effect to the extent that the learning effects are transferable to other products and the industries in question are genuine infants. It should not result in massive excess capacity, as in the previous case.

The real risk in this type of pre-emptive strategy is the "leap frogging" effect — the risk that the first firm down the curve may be cut out of the market by some new product development. On the other hand, the existence of the learning curve effect in an established product is a significant entry barrier for a new competing product. Video disc players are an example of a product which was effectively leap frogged by the introduction of low-cost video-cassette recorders. Learning economies were claimed to be substantial in both cases. On the other hand, there have been numerous personal computers technologically superior to the IBM-PC, but the general consensus is that the IBM has them beat, at least for the time being. The other risk in this type of competition is that the learning economies may not materialize or may be less significant than was anticipated. This may not be such a bad outcome, especially for the small open economy. It offers improved access to the industry and avoidance of yet another oligopoly in the world industrial structure. The down-side risk in this case is not so great.

The real problem with focussing a policy on dynamic scale economies is the transient nature of the object being pursued. The policy must focus on the firm during a particular stage of its development. For industries in which they are very important, targetting at the level of the firm may be necessary. In industries in which the small economy has a good reason to compete — i.e., a factor cost advantage or expertise and technology in a particular area — policies which foster development of such industries may be justified.

In arguing the merits of protection versus free trade in industries which are characterized by dynamic entry barriers, it must be admitted that economists know precious little about the determinants of industrial evolution. The empirical evidence suggests that large firms have a tendency to stay large, but that over a long period there can be substantial turnover among firms. While the theory discussed in this section offers some hope of constructing a more coherent view of industrial dynamics, the empirical work supporting this theory is in its early stages.

Nevertheless, the question of trade and industrial policy will not wait for academics to sort these issues out. As in the discussion of export barriers, the theory suggests that the process of adjusting to either external shocks or a reduction in trade barriers may be more difficult than the traditional analysis would indicate. A recognition of dynamic entry barriers offers countries strong incentives to intervene in the process of firm formation and growth. The "winner take all" nature of the competition may mean that export losses on investment could be large. Where individual firms are large relative to the size of the economy, this could have significant negative consequences for real income in small countries. The best that a small country could hope for would be free trade; the "deep pocket" of the treasury of large governments would thus not constitute a threat to the export industries of the small open economy. Open access to the world's markets is the most important condition for small country participation in these industries.

At present, the chance for complete free trade seems slight. Industrial subsidies and contingent protection are increasingly prevalent throughout the world. What is the optimal policy of a small open economy in these circumstances? Certainly in the case of Canada, trade and industrial policies should be formulated with a view to keeping the U.S. market as open as possible. These policies should not be based on those industries which involve large down-side risk, that is, industries characterized by large-scale fixed investment. Instead positive industrial policies should be used whenever possible to foster those industries with the potential of providing genuine dynamic economies embodied in labour. This type of investment has the least risk and the highest potential pay-off. It will be important to develop those policies which focus clearly on the basic objective — accumulation of experience in the early phases of product development.

Summary

In this chapter, the implications of static and dynamic entry barriers for trade and investment have been examined. A number of observations emerge.

- Entry barriers, conventionally thought of as determinants of market structure, can explain the existence of trade in manufacturing goods in the absence of comparative advantage effects.
- The long-run implication of the existence of static entry barriers is that the gains to free trade in a small open economy can be substantial.
- In the short run, static and dynamic entry barriers may prove an impediment for domestic firms from a small open economy in entering

the export market. Positive adjustment policies to assist entry into the export market may be called for, particularly as trade barriers are reduced.

- The dynamic irreversibilities of pre-emptive firm investment mean that the adjustment process poses particular risks for the small open economy. Competitive subsidization of large-scale productive capacity should be avoided. Positive industrial policy should focus on industries with potential for learning-by-doing economies.
- The small open economy with some industries that have potential for dynamic scale economies has a strong incentive to foster free trade and to refrain from inducing retaliatory protection. Positive industrial policy should focus on those industries and products where the dynamic economies are based on the acquisition of skills by labour and management, rather than investment in physical capital.

Chapter 6

Schumpeterian Competition and the Small Open Economy

Introduction

One of the most widely agreed upon propositions in economics has been the importance of technological progress in explaining the growth of real income in the industrialized countries since the beginning of the industrial revolution. Indeed, there are numerous studies establishing that technological progress is the single most important explanatory factor in explaining real income growth. Schumpeter (1934) put forward the proposition that monopoly power is not necessarily bad, as demonstrated by static economic theory, because monopolists are the major technological innovators in a capitalist economy. Schumpeter's notion was that the presence of monopoly power allows a firm to capture some of the rents from innovation, relative to a competitive industry where the rents quickly dissipate through imitation. At the same time, monopoly power gives a firm the financial resources to undertake the expensive industrial development process. His reasoning was that as a consequence of entry barriers, monopolistic industries tend to be more technologically progressive. A related proposition of Galbraith (1952) is that large, as opposed to small, firms ought to be either more able or more prone to undertake R&D. Both propositions have been widely debated and subjected to empirical testing. Some of the evidence will be reviewed in the following section. In recent years, with the high degree of technological competition in numerous industries, there has been a renewed interest in the Schumpeterian vision. This chapter explores the Schumpeterian perspective in some detail with respect to its implications for trade and investment policy.

It is clear that a conceptual framework which involves imperfect competition and entry barriers is essential to understanding the process of technological innovation. Many studies have shown that economic factors play an enormously important, if not an overwhelming, role in the determination of the rate of technological progress.[1] Competitive theories in which rents to innovation do not exist are woefully inadequate. As remarked in previous chapters, an important role has been attributed to technological innovation as one of the empirical determinants of trade in manufactured goods. The task that remains is to construct an adequate theory with which to organize these observations. The Schumpeterian perspective offers at least the beginnings of such a theory. The policy implications which emanate from such a view may be quite different from the traditional "public good" view of technological innovation in which most of the existing technology policy is framed.

The public good approach to technological progress focusses on the idea that once an invention is discovered it has the properties of a public good, in that it can be made available to all potential users at zero marginal social cost.[2] On the other hand, because private individuals cannot appropriate all the potential returns from use of a new product or process, the private incentives lead to an under-investment in R&D. The patent system is one imperfect means of attempting to move private incentives in the direction of the social incentives.

The Schumpeterian hypotheses have received increasing attention because a number of scholars have come to believe that the public good view of technological progress is too narrow and one-sided. It ignores the fact that the process of technology transfer is subject to considerable private cost, making technology more like a private good with appropriable benefits. The existence of exogenous and endogenous entry barriers in many industries provides the means by which firms can capture the quasi-rents from R&D. At the same time, technological progress affects the nature of entry barriers, and thus market structure in the long run is endogenous. The public good approach to innovation has focussed on the use of the patent system and government subsidy of industrial R&D as policy tools. The Schumpeterian perspective shifts emphasis to entry barriers, the technology transfer process and policies which impinge on market structure, such as combines policy. The debate at present is in a state of flux, although there remains considerable agreement that the social rate of return on R&D is higher than on many other forms of investment.[3]

It is fairly obvious that social incentives regarding industrial R&D are significantly different in the small open economy than in a closed economy. First, there is the conventional problem of leakages both into and out of the economy from the R&D process. Hence, the emphasis on the technology transfer process in the international trade context and, in particular, the role of the multinational as a vehicle for the transfer of technology. The public policy debate, though, does not seem to have come to any definite conclusions about the proper role of the government toward R&D in the open economy. In Canada, the Science Council has been an active proponent of activist government support of high technology industry and indigenous Canadian R&D.[4] The Economic Council of Canada, in its 1983 annual review, stresses the importance of the technology transfer process, and the role of international trade and investment in facilitating this transfer. In my own view, both are correct, at least in part. This chapter offers another perspective of industrial R&D and the technology transfer process.

The main issue discussed in this chapter is the role of industrial R&D in the open economy. The importance of basic, non-commercial R&D is an important part of the whole story which will be covered in Chapter Eight. All that need be said at this point is that technological opportunity is determined to a great extent by investment in basic R&D worldwide which is almost entirely government supported; and further, that technological opportunity, in turn, is one factor in the industrial R&D process which tends to emphasize the economic factors.

The basic perspective on market structure and trade remains as in the last chapter. Thus, economic integration is assumed to be less than complete and the distinction between national and global firms is maintained.

The Schumpeterian Hypotheses: The Evidence

There is substantial literature on testing the basic Schumpeterian hypotheses, together with numerous additional hypotheses as to causality. On one of these hypotheses there is some basic agreement, but on others the evidence is much less conclusive. In broad terms, there is agreement that a positive correlation exists between concentration and technological innovation, which is strongest at moderate levels of concentration. The direction of causation, though, is not one-way. In general, numerous other factors affect the relationship and the pattern seems highly variable across industries. The hypothesis that large firms are more efficient and effective at doing R&D has received considerably less empirical support, and investigators have come to quite different conclusions, often on the same data base. It is worth restating that most of the studies give no particular emphasis to international trade and investment. The literature on diffusion and technology transfer is far less extensive.[5]

The following is a list of widely accepted conclusions regarding the connection between R&D, firms and market structure.[6]

- There is no substantial support for the hypothesis that in most industries there are significant scale economies in the R&D process itself.

There are a few notable exceptions, such as the aircraft and other defence-related industries.

- In considering the relationship between firm size and R&D, there is no significant evidence in terms of either inputs to, or outputs of R&D, that large firms are more R&D intensive, or provide greater R&D output than smaller firms. The evidence suggests that medium size firms are prone to spend the most on R&D and to operate the most productive R&D establishments. A major qualification to these studies is that they do not control for the R&D participation rate. Large firms, on average, are more likely to have an R&D establishment than small and medium size firms.
- There is a positive correlation between concentration and R&D, indicating that R&D increases more than proportionately up to moderate levels of concentration and diminishes rapidly thereafter. The relationship is weakest when technological opportunity is high.
- Both technological opportunity and demand-pull explanations of innovation receive substantial support and seem to be complementary. Demand-pull, or economic opportunity, seems to be by far the dominant short-run influence on industrial innovation.
- Interfirm rivalry is an important determinant of industry expenditure on R&D seems to be most significant when rivals are of approximately equal size, rather than in circumstances when the industry size distribution of firms is highly skewed.
- Entry barriers in the form of scale economies (both static and dynamic), product differentiation, and absolute capital requirements appear to be important determinants of R&D, although the evidence is weak. It appears easier for smaller firms to enter and be successful during entry phases of the product cycle. In later phases, post-invention competition explains why moderate to large size firms have an advantage in the technological competition. Traditional entry barriers have an important role in determining the nature of this competition.

These six observations summarize the extent of current knowledge in the field. Each hypothesis has its critics and there is some disagreement as to the suitability of the methodology used in some of these studies.[7]

The issue of foreign ownership and R&D continues to attract a lot of attention in Canada, but far less research has been done on this matter than on the issues listed above. Early studies in Canada tended to support the view that there was no difference between foreign-controlled and domestic firms or that foreign firms actually did more R&D, contradicting the view that branch plants of foreign enterprises tend not to undertake R&D.[8] More recent studies take a more diverse view of the relationship between R&D and foreign ownership.[9] The real problem is that the question is not founded on any specific hypothesis about market structure, corporate control and innovative performance. To make a claim that foreign-controlled subsidiaries are engaging in practices which are either inefficient or detrimental to national interests requires a more complete understanding of the technology development and transfer process than simple correlation between expenditure on R&D and foreign ownership.

It is widely recognized that from a world perspective, R&D activity is a good predictor for the presence of multinational enterprise within any world industry. From the Schumpeterian perspective, for example, multinational enterprises (MNEs) appear in either technologically progressive industries or those which are moderately concentrated. On the other hand, at least for U.S. multinationals, there is also agreement that about 90 percent of R&D has in the past been done within the United States, confirming the importance of scale economies in centralizing the location of R&D activities. In recent years, though, there has been an increasing tendency among MNEs to decentralize the R&D function. It is too early to tell whether this trend to "world product mandating" will continue (Caves, 1982, chaps.1 and 7).

The technology diffusion and transfer literature offers some general conclusions about the speed of the imitation and the extent to which new technology is appropriable by the innovating firm. Generally, the conclusion is that the diffusion process is far from being a public good. Imitation can be quite slow, and the "first in" on a particular class of innovations in either product or process invention can capture a large amount of the benefits. Within national markets, the diffusion process has both public good and private good aspects. There is some evidence that industrial innovation is biased toward those innovations which cannot be easily imitated, as one would expect, and also some evidence that speed of diffusion is positively related to the competitiveness of the industry.[10]

There is clearly a host of environmental factors which affect the diffusion process. The most significant of these is the manner in which the market for information works. There seems little doubt that the extent of economic integration of regions is an important determinant of diffusion rates. There have been some international comparisons of diffusion of new technology. One study (Globerman, 1974) showed that Canada has had a particularly slow internal diffusion rate. The Economic Council (1983, p. 55) takes the view that the small scale of Canadian industry explains this at least partly. Their argument is that diffusion involves the adoption of technology which is scale intensive; in the postwar period, Canadian industry was not at a scale suited to this type of technology. An implication of the general hypothesis is that if the scale bias in new technology has been reduced, the rate of diffusion should increase within small open economies.

Diffusion, of course, is a general description of the advance and spread of the use of new technology. Some of this occurs through specific market and non-market transactions in which the externality effect is minimal.[11] All costs and benefits are appropriately internalized in the transaction. In studying these transactions, at least part of the diffusion process is understood. The other part of the diffusion process occurs through the general spread of information, and non-appropriable imitation of new technology. The public good view of technology has emphasized this feature of the process, and economists have yet to quantify it in any reasonable way (Scherer, 1980, chap. 18). Trade in goods and intangibles such as scientific and managerial services, though, plays an important role. Recent efforts by the U.S. government to restrict the export of certain types of computers is reminiscent of the attempts by the British in the ninteenth century to halt the export of textile machinery so as to maintain their lead in the textile industry (Cooper, 1975). Migration of skilled labour is another important part of the diffusion process. The rate of non-appropriable technology transfer is an important indicator of the degree of market failure in the R&D/technology transfer process from the world perspective. It should be remembered that from the perspective of the small open economy, world market failure works clearly in favour of the smaller economies. By relying on technology spillovers from other countries, small countries can "free-ride" on the technology developed elsewhere.

The technology transfers which do not suffer from market failure are, at least to some extent, those involving intrafirm transfers of technology, licensing of technology, joint ventures and mergers which are motivated by the desire to internalize the benefits of a new technology. The multinational enterprise as a purveyor of technology transfer has been studied fairly intensively. A number of studies have shown that information, once developed, still has substantial cost associated with transfer. Thus, a basic precondition for the functioning of an exchange of property rights is present. There are a number of problems with the "arm's-length" market approach to technology transfer through licensing. A number of factors are at work here: the complex nature of the technology product, the uncertainty and scope for opportunism on the part of one or both parties, and finally, the small numbers involved in any technology transfer. These factors suggest that a non-arm's-length approach, in particular the setting up of a foreign subsidiary, may be an efficient way to handle the transfer. Licensing tends to be resorted to in those circumstances where the seller faces a substantial capital market imperfection or other entry barrier in the foreign market which prohibits capturing the benefits associated with an internalized transfer (Teece, 1977). It is difficult to draw definite conclusions as to the efficiency of the international exchange of technology. The literature and evidence, on balance, suggest that the process is reasonably efficient. There is no evidence to suggest that, from the perspective of a small open economy purchasing technology, the exchange is biased against the buyer in any fundamental way.

Schumpeterian Competition and Market Failure in R&D

In recent years, empirical observations on market structure and innovation have led to some theoretical models in the economy of Schumpeterian competition over product and process innovation among oligopolist firms. The developments are quite recent, but they have given a much clearer picture of the forces at work.[12] This body of theory, in general terms, has predictions which are generally consistent with the empirical observations made above. They start with the assumption that the race to innovate is a genuine competition and that at least over the short term the benefits to the technology are proprietary. In the longer term, monopoly rents from being the sole provider of the product or process will be eroded by the introduction of new products and processes, including successful imitations.

An important part of the theory is the presence of either static or dynamic entry barriers in the post-innovation phase of the competition. These barriers allow the winners of the technology race to protect their market over the medium to short run and to collect revenues which not only cover product development costs but also provide above-normal rates of return on total investment. An important and related observation is that the technological competition tends to be pre-emptive and contain elements of irreversibility. Thus, if one firm gets ahead, there is a strong likelihood it will retain that lead for a considerable period through its ability to pre-empt subsequent competitors. Investment in R&D thus creates entry barriers and leads to concentration. The evidence supports the hypothesis that success in innovation is inter-temporally correlated — "success breeds success."[13] Thus, being successful today raises the probability of success in the future. The presence of entry barriers creates substantial lags in the process of competing down quasi-rents to successful initial innovators. The existence of the lags means that new entrants in a Schumpeterian race are most likely to succeed by getting into an area where established firms do not have significant advantages.

The theory, in addition to providing a rationale for the empirical predictions noted above, has also produced one additional, consistent result. In the absence of spillovers between independent, industrial R&D labs (i.e., if there are no public goods effects), there is a general presumption that from the perspective of an industry in a *closed economy, the technological competition produces too much investment in* R&D by the industry as a whole. This is a fairly striking conclusion and is at odds with popular interpretation of the Schumpeterian benefit of technology races among oligopolists as conducive to economic welfare. Balancing out against this tendency, however, is the possibility of the spillover effects which, as in the conventional story, tend to lead to under-investment in R&D.

The Open Economy

How can these theories be applied to the *open economy*? First, it should be noted that if all sales are in the export market, the primary national social benefit of the Schumpeterian competition is not an advance in the pace of introduction of new products or processes, but rather a share in the quasi-rents which are earned by participating in the race. A small open economy can, of course, enjoy some of the benefits of the advance in the pace of innovation by importing, without participating in the Schumpeterian competition. The existence of entry barriers and the dynamic nature of the competition means that import prices include quasi-rents which persist even in the long run. A small country with a firm that participates in such a race will share in these rents if it achieves a degree of success which is in accordance with the industry average. Losing in any particular race means a transfer of wealth to the winners through high product prices — an unavoidable but necessary transfer. Finally, the pre-emptive nature of the competition has the consequence that a country which refrains from competing early has substantially reduced chances of competing later on. This induces a technology gap which has been emphasized in the neo-technology literature.[14] A con-centration of successful innovators within one nation leads to higher national income and a trade surplus in high technology products for a considerable period.

Literature on the technology gap, including the product cycle hypoth-esis, maintains that innovations in one country which move with a lag to other countries, create higher wages in the innovating country. This proposition finds support in some theoretical work although the empirical evidence supporting it is only indirect. The main form of evidence is that used in support of the product cycle, which established that the United States exported technology-intensive goods in the 1950s and 1960s, and at the same time U.S. industrial labour received higher wages than comparable skilled labour elsewhere.[15]

There has never been an explicit connection made between the trade literature and the industrial organization literature on R&D. In the latter, partial equilibrium estimates of the social return to industrial R&D based on a closed economy assumption are quite high — often in the 30 to 50 percent range.[16] Yet these estimates do not include any of the returns to domestic labour which would be earned if R&D was the means by which a technology gap is maintained. In an open economy context, if the basic idea of the technology gap theories is correct, the national social returns to R&D which allow the maintenance of a gap may be far in excess of the conventional estimates.

In a Schumpeterian competition, the technology gap is endogenously determined by the relative success of firms in different countries. To the extent that the gap is narrowed, wages should tend to be more equal across countries. This does not, however, reduce the significance of industrial R&D for national income levels, given the existence of world Schumpeterian competition. Any country which fails to participate by investing in R&D will necessarily produce the low technology goods; these, in turn, will pay lower wages and, hence, lead to lower national incomes in the long run. In an open economy framework, the main social return to R&D is in the form of super-normal profits on equity, but a great deal of it may be in the form of higher wages to domestic labour. How can this be?

There are really two questions to be answered. First, how do rents persist in a Schumpeterian competition for any length of time? Second, do these rents include a return to labour in the innovating country? These two questions are closely connected. The answer to the first question, at least with respect to rents earned by owners of the firm, is given in the R&D literature. As noted already, the key answer lies in the existence of entry barriers in the post-innovation phase. Evidence on private rates of return to industrial R&D clearly support this proposition. The "success breeds success" hypothesis means that successful innovation implies a higher probability of future successful innovation, which reinforces the persistence of rents in the Schumpeterian competition. Since the calculations of private rates of return on industrial R&D do not include a correction for this persistence-of-success effect, they are biased downward. On the first question, therefore, there is strong evidence supporting the existence of barriers which prohibit imitators from achieving the same degree of success as the initial innovators.

The second question is much more difficult. How can labour capture some of these quasi-rents? As noted, if labour does, then the rate of return to a nation on industrial R&D may be much higher than suggested in the literature. Quasi-rents to a nation must be redefined by using some opportunity cost of labour. One extreme suggestion would be to use the wage rate of the lowest wage country in which the product could be produced. Labour might capture some of these rents in two possible ways. If the labour market is competitive, with an inelastic supply curve of labour to the successfully innovating firm, then as the firm's demand curve shifts outward the equilibrium wage will be driven up. Suppose, for example, that the supply curve of labour is completely inelastic, labour is used in fixed proportions with other inputs, and these inputs are in elastic supply to the firm. A shift in a monopolist's demand curve to the right will cause a large fraction of the increase in revenue to accrue in the form of higher wages to labour. A number of factors contribute to an inelasticity of supply of labour in the short run, including immobility of firms and workers and lags in the supply response of skilled workers to changes in industry demand. The competitive labour market assumption, though, is a far from accurate view of the situation. In most Schumpeterian industries, workers acquire on-the-job skills and experience which make them more productive within the firm than in alternative employment. At the same time, this makes them more productive than a new worker to the firm's work force. Labour becomes a quasi-fixed factor and the relationship between the firm and its workers can be described as a situation of bilateral monopoly. Both groups have considerable bargaining power, as the monopoly power of the firm is transferred to some extent to its workers. This, in turn, means that labour captures a significant fraction of the firm's revenues over non-labour costs.

There is some corroboration for this in U.S. studies on the relation between industrial concentration and wages. The evidence indicates a positive correlation between quality of workers and industry concentration, although the direction of causation remains uncertain.[17]

A successful Schumpeterian firm can attempt to avoid paying labour any "rents" by shifting the location of production. This type of policy is at best a short-run solution. Unless there are no worker-specific learning effects, so that inexperienced workers with comparable initial skills can carry out the production activities in any alternative location, the firm's production workers will have acquired some of the firm's rents. Of course, to the extent that the firm is reluctant to shift production to other countries, the workers in the innovating country will capture a larger share of the monopoly revenue.

The distribution of world labour income depends not only upon the distribution of factor endowments, including the endowments of human capital, but also on the distribution of successful Schumpeterian firms across countries who produce for the world market. All major industrial countries will undoubtedly have some of these firms. Factors explaining relative success are suggested by the trade and technology literature. These include investment in industrial R&D and the level of human capital in the labour force. The current microelectronics revolution suggests that the share of world income accruing to Schumpeterian industries is likely to rise. Therefore, those countries which are relatively more successful in these industries will be characterized by higher incomes to both capital and labour.

Governments clearly have incentives to create barriers to firm mobility in these industries. If the successful firm can move its production facilities abroad, the country will lose a source of income and employment. At the same time, all governments have incentives to foster the development of potential domestic Schumpeterian monopolists by a variety of policies, including the subsidization of industrial R&D. These incentives differ in fundamental ways between small and large countries.

Is there a small open economy market bias in industrial R&D against Schumpeterian industries? If so, does it constitute a genuine market failure? The term "market failure" is perhaps inappropriate; from the perspective of indigenous firms from a small open economy attempting to penetrate the export market, the failure may be not in the R&D process itself, but in the existence of the entry barriers which accompany the post-innovation phase of the competition. On average, these entry barriers affect smaller firms more adversely than large firms. To the extent that small countries foster smaller indigenous firms, this places the country as a whole at a disadvantage. An optimal industrial structure may be more concentrated; if it were more concentrated, the firms would, on average, undertake more industrial R&D because of the increased chances of success in the post-innovation phase of the competition. Thus, in terms of the overall competition from innovation through selling the final product, the Schumpeterian industries in small economies suffer from relative disadvantage in industrial structure. There is considerable evidence suggesting that small countries export a disproportionately low volume of intensive goods.[18] The evidence, though, is primarily from the 1960s and early 1970s, and there are some industries in some countries which are notable exceptions.[19] The approach of looking at historical trade patterns as evidence of natural market tendencies suffers from the usual problem that the existence of protection seriously biases the results against small countries exporting in concentrated industries. There may well be a market failure of sorts; if the share of world income going to technology-progressive industries increases, the revealed bias against small countries could become more important than it has been in the past. More recent studies for Canada tend to present a more diversified view on the relation between exports and R&D.[20] A number of studies point to a positive connection between exports and R&D intensity, although the causality and implications of this are not clear. One telling statistic is that the Canadian share of exports in fully finished manufacturers increased from 8 percent in the 1960s to 30 percent by the end of the 1970s, although much of this rise was in automobile trade.

The Open Economy Policy Perspective

In a small open economy which accounts for a fraction of the world's basic and industrial R&D, it is natural for most of the technology which is used domestically to be developed elsewhere. I also take it as given that the development of technology around the globe explains in important ways the patterns of trade among countries in manufactured products, as noted in the technology studies of trade covered in Chapters Two and Three. The Schumpeterian and public goods aspects of R&D create conflicting and opposing policy incentives in large and small countries.

Even within a country the incentives are different in the export, import and non-traded goods sectors.

The Large Country Perspective

Within the export sector, the large country would like to hold or at least slow down the transfer of technology abroad, to the extent that the rents accruing nationally from the technology are dissipated by the transfer. In the import sector and in the transfer of input-relevant technology, however,any country would like to see the rate of international diffusion increase, particularly if it occurs at a zero cost. From the Schumpeterian perspective, in the export market a large country would like to see its domestic firms win in any technological competition and collect the winner's rents. The large country would favour a large expenditure on innovation in these industries, and would benefit through world industry concentration to the extent that it ends up receiving a larger absolute monopoly rent.

As large economies generally have a smaller traded goods sector, the Schumpeterian and the public good arguments yield opposing policy implications toward R&D directions on internal market criteria. From the public good perspective regarding technology diffusion, the large country should encourage the speed-up of diffusion internally although not internationally. From the Schumpeterian perspective, it would wish to moderate any excess tendency of industry to spend on R&D and at the same time avoid other harmful effects of excessive industrial concentration.

Choosing a balance between these opposing incentives is obviously difficult. The discussion on the role of technology transfer in the United States reflects an uneasy tension between these approaches.

Large countries have incentives to discriminate in protection policy between large and small country competitors. Protection aimed against small countries can effectively exclude most of the small country's potential export market and weaken the viability of the small countries' Schumpeterian firms. Hence, through protection the large country can eliminate a significant fraction of the competitors of its own domestic firms. It cannot practise the same type of policy toward other large countries without risking retaliation. This retaliation could cost them a large part of the world market and reduce the potential returns from their own Schumpeterian industries.

One means of implicit protection by large countries against small countries is to bias technology policy toward innovations which are designed for large-scale production. While there is no direct evidence that policy has consciously been directed this way, there is evidence that innovation can be directed toward or away from scale-intensive production methods (Blair, 1972). The two types of protection policies interact effectively. Protection against the small countries in scale-intensive industries is more effective at deterring small country entry to the world industry than protection against non-scale based industries.

Both types of incentives to protect are tempered by the concern of the large country for free trade and trade policies which are non-discriminatory across countries. But in the absence of global free trade, small countries have obvious incentives to seek insurance against these large country protection policies by seeking trade alliances which assure them access to large markets.

The Small Country Perspective

Within the small country, the logic of the public good and the Schumpeterian arguments as to social incentives is the same as for the large country, but the importance to the international aspects is much greater. This leads to some fairly natural implications for technology policy.

A large number of traded commodities are natural candidates for a Schumpeterian competition. This is because the imitation process is slow, either because of effective entry barriers or because the cost and benefits of technology transfer are effectively internalized in exchange through market or non-market contractual arrangement.

The key point pertaining to the small open economy's participation in Schumpeterian industries is the following:

> The social incentive to subsidize Schumpeterian industries is greater in a small open economy than in the large closed economy.

There is nothing perverse in the logic of this argument. First, it follows simply from noting the relative importance of the negative aspects of Schumpeterian competition in closed economies and the relative unimportance of these effects on national welfare in the small open economy. The small country is unconcerned about its impact on world industry concentration and is more concerned with receiving the benefits of technology spillovers than with halting them. Second, the small firm size in small countries, leading to a non-optimal industrial structure for participation in a Schumpeterian competition, implies that the amount of resource provided to those industries is less than would be socially optimal in a free trade situation.

It is difficult to determine the appropriate instrument that would allow an optimal industrial structure to develop. Subsidy of the R&D process, while correcting the propensity of small firms to engage in less R&D than larger firms, does not automatically ensure that the firm will reach the appropriate size to overcome the entry barriers in the world market, including trade barriers. Subsidy of R&D may go only part way to correcting the problem, but changing the R&D base is at least a necessary precondition for successful firm entry and subsequent growth. It is inherently difficult to attack the issue of firm size more directly. Additional policies which encourage appropriate firm size in the post-innovation phase need further consideration.

Schumpeterian industries are typically concentrated and subject to moderate entry barriers, in the form of either scale economies or product differentiation. From the small open economy perspective, the risk of unsuccessful entry attempts may be reduced somewhat by focussing on product differentiation industries, relative to scale economy industries. The observed technological progressiveness of medium size firms suggests that policies should give substantial encouragement to these firms as well. It is not clear that future technological competition will be most intense amongst industries with scale economy barriers. If it is, it may be those in which post-innovation competition is affected by the presence of dynamic scale economies within the firm. There may be significant learning curve effects on producing and distributing a new product or using a new process innovation. While noting the relative incentive between small and large countries to engage in Schumpeterian competition, there is a significantly greater risk of failure for firms from a small country participating in such a race. This risk can be a serious social and private deterrent.[21]

Given the prevalence of MNEs in R&D intensive, concentrated industries, they have been active participants in these Schumpeterian races and no doubt will remain so. There is no reason for the small country not to encourage these firms to locate production facilities within their borders. If R&D facilities also come with the firm, so much the better. It would not pay to subsidize the MNEs to the same extent as a domestically owned firm if the Schumpeterian rents accrue largely to foreign equity holders. However, as noted earlier, there is a good case that specialized R&D labour inputs capture a significant portion of the R&D rents. Accepting this, it would be both economically sensible and politically prudent to design government policy toward industrial R&D to be non-discriminatory between foreign and domestic firms.

The small open economy faces the difficult choice of backing either many firms or a few firms within Schumpeterian industry. As noted previously, there is substantial evidence that success in the post-innovation phase increases with firm size. Thus, to back many firms through universal policies may be nationally detrimental, given limited resources. On the other hand, subsidy at the R&D level should be guided partially by the observation that diversification, through support of more than one industrial R&D laboratory, increases the overall chance of success. Designing a policy which balances out the pre- and post-innovation phase of the competition is difficult.

A final and important observation on the relationship between Schumpeterian competition and trade policy: free trade, by expanding the size of the world market in Schumpeterian commodities, means larger rents to success and a faster pace of innovation. All countries, but in particular small countries, have an incentive to reduce trade barriers. Protection, by reducing the access of small countries to the large country markets, reduces both the probability of successfully capturing a market and the absolute size of foreign-generated Schumpeterian rents from a successful innovation. This argument is quite independent of the question of scale economies in production.

In non-Schumpeterian commodities and industries, the emphasis of industrial technology policy will focus, naturally, on the economy as a buyer of technology. It is in the small open economy's interest to free-ride when possible and to speed up the transfer of technology across international borders. When technology is purchased, the objective is to pay the lowest price. Of course, the line between Schumpeterian and non-Schumpeterian industries will not be clear in some cases, but some general principles seem evident.

First, free trade should be an obvious positive force in the process of technology transfer. A small country benefits significantly by importing technology through the importation of foreign-produced capital goods. Free trade, by assuring market access, reduces the incentive of large countries to develop technology which is biased toward large-scale production.

Second, multinational enterprises should not be discouraged. They are a well recognized instrument of technology transfer. Discriminatory policies toward MNEs would lead to a reduced flow of international technology.

Third, economic integration in general should be encouraged. To the extent that integration reduces the transfer cost or increases the speed of transfer through better informational channels, the relative benefit to the small country will be much greater than to the large country, because of the greater stock of technological opportunity existing in the large country. To the extent that the large country fosters both basic and industrial R&D on grounds of the public good aspect of information, the small country will benefit from this subsidy in proportion to its degree of integration with the large country market.

Technology Transfer versus R&D

In the technology policy arena, inevitably, some decision must be made about the allocation of scarce public dollars. In the small open economy context, this conflict is nowhere more apparent than in choosing to emphasize technology transfer versus indigenous industrial R&D. From an economic perspective, this brings to the fore the nature of the interaction between buying and selling technology. To "package" technology transfer and indigenous industrial R&D within the same policy "bundle," while perhaps natural, can be seriously misleading since it gives the impression that one is a substitute for another. It would be more enlightening to treat them from independent perspectives. Thus, technology transfer policy should compete with transportation policy as much as with R&D policy.

A technology policy which takes R&D and technology transfer as independent is unlikely to emerge. To many, the obvious question is: "Should we import technology or produce our own at home?" This approach ignores the fact that the small open economy is primarily a receiver, as opposed to a transmitter, of technology and that its interest in industrial R&D is concerned mainly with potential export sales. The presumed substitutability of the two activities is a misperception rather than a fact. It is obvious that Canada must import a great deal of technology. In terms of the preferred general bias in technology policy, the relevant question should be: "Where is the greatest market failure likely — in the technology transfer process or the R&D process?" There are a number of arguments involved in addressing this question.

First of all, are technology transfer and R&D substitutes or complements in achieving the delivery of a continuing stream of new products or processes within the firm? In many cases, the two methods are complements, since a new product builds upon existing technology. Efforts to develop a new product in a Canadian industrial R&D lab would inevitably involve the use of up-to-date technology as an intermediate input into innovation production function. This recognition of technology as an intermediate input would, on balance, favour a complementary relationship at the aggregate level between technology transfer and indigenous R&D.

In a longer term, inter-temporal context there are significant external effects between the two. A Canadian firm which employs an indigenous R&D work force will contribute to the appreciation, recognition and transfer of technology from abroad. These effects on "technological awareness," of course, go beyond the firm to the general industrial marketplace. The transfer of technology may directly cause indigenous R&D as the individuals involved in the transfer realize that significant modifications are needed for the Canadian market.

The substitutability issue is sometimes posed with regard to the delivery of a specific product or process. If an equal amount of known expenditure on either indigenous R&D or technology transfer will produce exactly the same final product, should technology policy emphasize the R&D or technology transfer route? The assumption of equal and certain cost is highly fictitious. In general, the cost and outcome of the R&D process is highly uncertain. Furthermore, the static nature of the comparison is dubious. R&D investment focusses on future potential products and processes, while investment in technology transfer focusses on known technology produced as the result of past R&D in foreign countries. Again, these highlight the fictitious nature of the substitutability assumption. However, even accepting the comparison as described, the externalities associated with the R&D process would seem to be greater than with the technology transfer process; in particular, the value of the experience and know-how gained by the technical people involved in an indigenous R&D effort should be recognized. Because these external benefits are much greater, given the equal current cost assumption, policy should favour the R&D as opposed to the technology transfer route.

The approach toward technology transfer versus R&D should not be phrased in either/or terms, but to the extent that it is necessary to take such a view, the existing evidence and economic theory suggest a more substantial market failure in the development of Schumpeterian industries within the small open economy than in the technology transfer process.

Thus, technology policy in choosing one versus the other should emphasize the indigenous development of industrial R&D. Trade liberalization policies and those assisting economic integration are more effective instruments to deal with technology transfer than any imaginable form of targetted or broad-based subsidization of the technology transfer process. In my view, this is the bottom line. While I have no objection to general environmental policies to correct perceived failures in informational markets across international borders, I am extremely doubtful about their general significance in the Canadian case. Canada's proximity to the United States, and substantial trade and investment flows assure a degree of integration in which the public good aspect of information transfer works in Canada's favour. Nevertheless the market failure in the industrial R&D process within Schumpeterian industries works against the small open economy. Technology policy should clearly be designed with these factors in mind.

Conclusion

In this chapter, an industrial organization approach toward trade in high technology manufactures in the small open economy was presented. The implications of dynamic theories of non-competitive Schumpeterian industrial markets were developed. There are significant gains to be had in the small open economy by participating in the Schumpeterian competition in product differentiated industries. Technology policy should emphasize correction or market failures in the indigenous R&D process, rather than interference in the technology transfer process. The market failures in that process, to the extent they exist, clearly work in favour of the small open economies rather than against them. Free trade enhances the benefits of both the technology transfer process and Schumpeterian competition. The most difficult question which remains is to choose the policy instruments for encouraging Schumpeterian industries and firms.

Chapter 7

Industrial Policy in the Small Open Economy

Introduction

This chapter examines the question of industrial policy or strategy. The potential usefulness of an industrial policy as an addition to the menu of traditional policy instruments has been vigorously debated in the last few years. The chapter does not review all facets of that debate in any exhaustive fashion.[1] Much of the existing literature is too inconclusive, argues from vague philosophical positions and often uses incorrect economic argument. Some of my impatience with this literature stems, no doubt, from my view of these matters as an economist.

However, much of what has been said certainly strikes me as reasonable. In the discussion of current economic policy, it is sometimes necessary to resort to argument not founded on a comprehensive set of statistical studies. In the case of the current shifting patterns of the international division of labour, compounded by the rapid extent of technological change which microtechnology is inducing, a more visionary and eclectic view of some of these matters is required. Traditional economists arguing from the neoclassical perspective have been notably hostile to the idea of industrial policy.[2] Basically, an industrial policy proposes some type of intervention in the market system which is not based on any of the standard arguments of market failure or public goods that economists like to resort to. An astounding variety of industrial strategies are being pushed these days. It is difficult even to classify them. Most attempt to incorporate some perceived desirable feature of the "Japanese model." They all involve exhortation to business, labour and government to get on with "adjustment," whatever that might entail.

It is important to recognize the general effects of the overall package of industrial policies on the economy. Furthermore, in a period of significant structural change within the economy, government must decide what types of structural change to encourage and what types to discourage. Some types of policies are better than others, and doing nothing is not a politically viable option. Failure to propose positive adjustment policies will only result in defensive protectionist policies which are the worst form of response.

Among the possible classes of industrial policies, there are important differences hinging on the extent of government directed central planning. I am a priori opposed to strong central planning solutions, on the usual grounds that the market system is good at resource allocation and bureaucrats are not. I also regard central planning as politically unacceptable to the Canadian population. Given these basic constraints, there remain some very important issues as to the particular directions industrial policy should take.

Most of the industrial policy literature has been written in the context of the large economy, particularly the United States. The literature on industrial strategy in the small open economy is notably thin by comparison.[3] This chapter reviews some recommendations which emerge from the industrial policy perspective. Every country has an extensive array of tax, trade, regulation and public expenditure policies which are industrial policies in that they affect microeconomic resource allocation in a variety of ways. What is at issue is whether these instruments should be pushing in new directions.[4] A general theme is the case for policy activism in nurturing new industries and tearing down old ones. Underlying this theme is the implicit or explicit belief that comparative advantage can be engineered. The perspective offered by the theories expounded in Chapters Three through Six are relevant to these arguments.

In the small open economy, industrial policy and trade policy are almost synonymous. However, in the tradition of the existing literature, industrial policy refers here to a collection of policies which affect industrial economic structure.

This chapter is concerned primarily with the small open economy as a single national state. The issues of regionalism and federal-provincial conflict are covered elsewhere and in other studies for this Commission.[5] Needless to say, these are of the utmost importance in the Canadian context. Therefore, policy in this chapter refers to policy by all levels of government.

The chapter first considers some basic conceptual issues in the examination of industrial policy in the small open economy. Some of these observations are general but many are specific to the Canadian case. Policy considerations are then examined with respect to public infrastructure, education, basic R&D, losing industries, the dilemma in the basic industries, and finally, high technology industries. The analytical and empirical framework for the discussion has been laid out in the previous chapters.

Economists and the Theory of Policy

A good starting point is the theory of economic policy, which suggests that policy makers must first delineate the goals, and then get on to process, agenda and instruments. The four basic economic goals of benevolent-minded policy makers may be summarized as follows:
1. a high aggregate rate of growth in average real income;
2. stability in real income, across both time and regions;
3. opportunity for stable and meaningful employment by all citizens; and
4. a degree of equality in the income distribution consistent with a social consensus about economic justice.

Other goals could be added, but these are sufficiently general and exhaustive for my purposes.

The process and conduct of economic policy is greatly affected by intellectual positions or schools of thought. Classic economic theory tends to be concerned exclusively with the first goal. The emphasis on free and competitive markets stems from the association between the maximum efficiency of resource allocation, without regard to distributive consequences, and the vision of ideal competitive capitalism. Most mainstream economists temper this position with some version of Keynesian macroeconomics, or one of its intellectual offspring, which deals expressly with goals 2 and 3. It is worth noting that the ability to hold on to both theories simultaneously has resulted in considerable schizophrenia in economists. The difficulty is that neither theory includes the other in any consistent way.

This intellectual division has been promoted, quite pragmatically, by dividing economics into macroeconomics and microeconomics. In macroeconomics, either a Keynesian or Monetarist aggregate model is used and emphasis is placed on fiscal and monetary policy. For microeconomics, the competitive neoclassical equilibrium model is the pre-eminent paradigm. This separation of problems and theory was reasonably comfortable until the 1970s, when the productivity slowdown, intense foreign competition in many sectors, and the general failure of macroeconomic policy to deliver on the goals of employment and inflation put the entire economics profession on the defensive. This state of affairs remains largely unresolved. It explains in part why the economics profession has not been as vigorous as it might be in criticizing industrial policy.

There are two factors explaining the recent popularity of industrial policy. First, it became clear to many that the competitive neoclassical model of resource allocation was inadequate, because the assumptions of perfect competition and flexible wages and prices were grossly inaccurate. The inflexibility of wages and prices meant, for example, that the primary response to a negative shock in the demand for labour was a fall in employment and not a cut in wages.

This observation, of course, is the crux of the argument used in Keynesian economics as a case for aggregate demand management. But it also has a profound impact on the view of resource allocation at the microeconomic level. For example, it means that adjustment may be a slow and lengthy process. Economic efficiency in such a world becomes secondary to the short-run costs of displaced and unemployed resources. Further, the pattern of adjustment across sectors is heavily dependent upon the relative Keynesian effects across sectors. Industrial policy can thus be rationalized as an extension of the Keynesian macro approach at the microeconomic level. At the moment, no consistent theory exists which encompasses all these factors, but the outline of such a theory seems clear.

Second, at the macro level, the policy failure of both Keynesian and Monetarist models has produced considerable skepticism about economic theory. Part of this skepticism has focussed on the basic microeconomic theory of markets and another part on the policy process itself. The failure of macroeconomic policy has pushed some to search for alternatives in the belief that the so-called macro-failures might not be the problem after all. Rising unemployment after each business cycle, which showed increasing resistance to aggregate demand pressures, was one indication that something might be wrong. This general dissatisfaction with macroeconomic policy led some to look for solutions in the microeconomic policy area. Their hopes found expression in the concept of industrial policy.

The case is probably not as stark or schizophrenic as this. Many economists still believe that their basic theories are more or less correct. Others believe more appropriate theories already exist, but have not yet been absorbed by the bulk of the profession. Some simply admit to one intellectual schizophrenia.

It is essential to appreciate the current state-of-the-paradigm situation because of the influence it has on economic policy in Ottawa, Washington and other centres where economists from within the bureaucracy and from outside participate in the policy process. The apparent failure of the orthodox approaches has created an intellectual vacuum which will be filled one way or another, and the policy agenda can vary widely, depending on whether non-interventionist or interventionist views predominate. At the moment, the politics of the situation seems to be the dominant force in the resolution of any given economic problem, because no economic theory of sufficient credibility exists as a legitimate base from which expert or technical argument can act as a constraint on admissible arguments. While evident in the macro area — where supply-siders face off against monetarists, against Keynesians, and on the deficit issue — the same is true in the industrial policy area. While agreement can be had on goals, there is little agreement about process.

My own view is that the description offered in previous chapters is the appropriate paradigm on which to conduct microeconomic policy. This means, in particular, careful attention to the scope for changing the margin between market and non-market transactions and an appreciation of imperfect competition and industry dynamics. However, it is also necessary to recognize that the Keynesian "failures" due to rigid labour markets are an important feature of the Canadian economy. No other OECD country has a worse record on strikes, and we still have a higher rate of inflation than most. While there is no comprehensive theory explaining these rigidities, their existence must be recognized. As a practical matter, this means recognizing that a fall in demand in any industry is likely to have large negative effects on employment in the short to medium term, and relatively smaller effects on the real and nominal wage in the industry.

This eclectic position on the appropriate theoretical framework means that difficult choices must be made in balancing the goal of real income growth and the goal of stability in income and employment. For the most part, these are conflicting goals. In the small open economy, the problem of social risk is often put forward as the basic case against opening up domestic markets to trade.

For the small country, external shocks are often more powerful than internal domestic shocks, causing instability in the domestic economy. The most important external shocks are changes in the terms of trade, the level of world demand for the small country's exports, technological developments, resource discoveries and political disruption that has economic consequences. An integral part of economic policy is to manage the risk imposed on the economy by these shocks.[6] This argument is simplistic in that it ignores the economy's access to world capital markets, which offer important channels for risk reduction, particularly to owners of physical capital. On the other hand, some specific and immobile factors of production have no market through which to diversify the risk in their income streams. Resource owners, and in particular labour, must bear the risk imposed by external shocks. Because some shocks are large and are imposed on the economy as a whole, the government, and the specific factors in the country, have no way to diversify this risk. The classic example was the OPEC shocks in the 1970s. Policy can attempt to even out the incidence of the shock through taxation, expenditure and transfer policies.

In the areas of industrial policy, the problem of social avoidance of risk comes up squarely in the issue of free trade versus protection. It can be argued that free trade increases the social risk exposure of the economy, and that protection can mitigate it. Free trade, by increasing the share of GNP devoted to trade, magnifies the effect of external shocks. The international business cycle is probably what worries people most. Increasing Canada's share of economic activity devoted to trade necessarily ties Canada to the world business cycle. The basic issue, however, is whether the domestic business cycle is moderated or exaggerated by the international business cycle. A highly unstable domestic economy could actually be stabilized by participating in world markets. As economic integration occurs, the large market size allows diversification of economic activity, which results in stabilization of average levels of demand. To the extent that scale economies are important in the small economy, this stabilization effect can be quite important in maintaining productivity. Therefore, the trade-off between growth and stability in real income may not be as severe as is commonly thought.

Public-Private Sector Interaction: Planning and Targetting

Much of the debate about industrial policy revolves around the question of possible public sector intervention in traditional private sector decisions, such as plant closures and the allocation of investment funds by financial institutions. The reputation and legends of the Japanese Ministry of International Trade and Industry are often the driving force in those who propose such intervention (Johnston, 1982). The logic of the argument hinges on the assumption that private capital markets are not functioning correctly in making crucial allocation decisions. A centralized approach offers the benefits of a more direct coordination of resources without reliance on an imperfect, and perhaps poorly functioning, system of uncoordinated corporate and financial market decision making.

The issue of whether decentralized markets, in a fundamental area such as the allocation of investment, are or are not superior to an administrative system of allocation goes straight to the heart of ideological and philosophical difference among individuals of varying political persuasion. There is no objective way to resolve this debate. In the United States, the majority view is probably that market mechanisms are vastly superior to administrative procedures. Part of this argument is based on belief in the virtues of non-political decision making. The free market view is still dominant in Canada as well, although there are probably a greater proportion of opponents of this view. In Europe and Japan, the neoclassical free market school of economics is not nearly as strong. This in part reflects the greater tradition of intervention in those countries than in Canada and the United States, where extensive centralized economic control existed only during World War II. Business, labour and politicians have views on this matter quite independent of what economists think, which are strongly held and conditioned by many years of tradition. This study deals only with the type of intervention which has been traditional. In Canada any form of extensive direct intervention, either in the allocation of industrial capital by the banks and financial institutions or formalized intervention in decisions within corporate boardrooms of the private sector, is unlikely and infeasible and is therefore not discussed here. Even without such direct intervention, however, it is obvious that governments have a substantial impact on the allocation of investment and the decisions of firms. Government policies with respect to competition, tax, subsidy, procurement and trade all affect private sector activity. Collectively, these policies constitute industrial policy.

To what extent should these policies be targetted to goals in specific sectors or firms? Many would argue that targetting is an impractical and harmful policy and that industrial policy should be broad-based and neutral in its coverage if not its impact. Thus, it is all right to have investment incentives but not incentives which encourage investment in the widget sector, or in any particular firm within the widget sector.

The opponents of targetting have a number of arguments which seem quite sensible.[7] First, identifying the winning and losing sectors and firms in a sensible way would require an elaborate cost-benefit framework and a set of appropriate criteria as input to the cost-benefit calculations, and it is doubtful that either could be done.[8] Second, the political ramifications of picking winners and losers are significant and largely negative. Politicians would be seen as favouring certain groups, compromising the integrity of the whole public sector intervention process and inducing wasteful rent-seeking by firms and industry groups hoping to be among the chosen few. Third, circumvention of the market framework would weaken the risk-reward incentive structure for entrepreneurs, reducing efficiency in management and the overall market allocation process.

While there is some truth to these observations, the whole question of targetting seems to have gotten a lot more attention than it deserves. As a matter of fact, targetting occurs all the time in industrial policy. Any casual reading of the history of Canadian industrial policy gives the overwhelming impression that both sectors and firms are routinely targetted for specific policy intervention.[9] Crown corporations are one very prominent form of highly targetted industrial policy.

There are some good reasons for targetting. First, as to the general sectoral breakdown of winners and losers, I think the potential winners and losers can be identified with reasonable probability. Most economists would agree that Canada's losing industries are the labour-intensive footwear, clothing, knitting and parts of the textile industries. This is borne out by the trade statistics. The potential winners are more difficult to identify. There is general agreement about the winning industries on a world scale, but the question is whether Canada can get a piece of these industries.

For a small open economy, many objectives of industrial policy, such as regional employment or capturing a share of a specific market, require the targetting of policies to specific firms. This has long been accepted as normal practice in the case of municipal and provincial industry policy, because some firms are so large relative to the local or provincial economy, that intervention must, of necessity, deal with specific firms. The same is true on the national level in a number of industries in which scale economies dictate that single firms be dealt with in order to make efficient use of scarce government financial resources. This means close government collaboration with both domestic and multinational firms on an individual basis. Targetting policies to specific firms does lead inevitably to politicization of the whole industrial policy process. Furthermore, the one or few firms that are targetted may not always be the most efficient, although this problem can be mitigated by sound intelligence.

In an economy the size of Canada's, and one which is so regionally diverse and large in area, industrial policy necessarily involves a considerable degree of targetting. This is inevitable, given the size of modern corporations relative to the Canadian market. In many cases, a broad-based industrial policy would be financially unsound and give rise to inefficient bureaucratic structures. Imagine trying to encourage a Canadian aerospace industry by offering across-the-board subsidies to all comers. Given the scale economies in the industry, the subsidy would have to be above some critical minimum level per firm. If more than one firm took up the offer, the financial cost could be enormous. It may not be necessary to target industrial policy to specific firms in an economy the size of the United States. In Canada, the size of the economy and the nature of the market structure leave little choice.

This does not mean broad-based policies are not preferred in some cases. For example, a universal tax-incentive or subsidy program would probably be the most effective way to encourage a substitution away from certain types of energy use in all industries. In neoclassical economics, there is a strong bias toward these types of policies because they fit naturally into the competitive neoclassical framework, where the firm is indistinguishable from the industry. In competitive industries, broad-based policies can almost always be used to achieve the objectives. As argued in Chapters Six and Seven, though, competitive industry structures are not likely to prevail in a number of the traded goods industries.

Free Trade versus Protection

Free trade versus protection, or "continentalism" versus "nationalism," is undoubtedly the key issue in terms of an overall guiding principle in the design of industrial policy. The successive rounds of the GATT have resulted in much more "free" trade than immediately after World War II. Canada in particular, with its historically high tariff structure on manufacturers, has opened its market substantially and gone a long way toward getting access to world markets. In recent years, concern has been generated about the rise of new protectionism. This involves both the use of selective import substitution policies such as quotas, dumping duties and other forms of contingent protection, and also the expanded use of subsidies to exports.[10] In Canada, the multilateral approach to reducing trade barriers is being replaced by a bilateral approach directed toward the United States. Most Canadians now recognize the importance to Canadian industry of gaining access to the large U.S. market, but many would stop short of bilateral free trade because they believe that the manufacturing sector would suffer under such an arrangement.[11]

Discussion about trade policy is sometimes hindered because the term "free trade" as used in classical economics is a misnomer. Within the classical literature, free trade was viewed in relation to trade between countries in which the natural market structure was perfect competition in all industries and the only role for government in the economy was to erect tariff barriers on imports. This conception of trade and trade policy is hardly relevant to today's situation, although some of the logic of the classical free trade argument remains intact, as discussed in Chapter Five. Perhaps it would be helpful to replace the term "free trade" with "fair trade." In any case, the perfect competition defence of free trade is irrelevant.

A substantial body of research shows that trade barriers are extremely costly to the Canadian economy. The chief cost is the promotion of an inefficient manufacturing structure. This is true no matter what other policies the government might follow or whether or not perfect competition exists. As made clear in Chapters Six and Seven, the presence of oligopolistic world industries makes open markets all the more important to a small open economy such as Canada's.

The commitment to freer trade should be a pre-eminent feature of Canadian industry policy, and it should include a commitment to the free flow of investment. Reduction in trade barriers should remove most of the inherently negative aspects of foreign investment. Since foreign direct investment is an important part of the export activity of Canadian firms, Canada must be extremely wary of engaging in discriminatory policies toward foreign investment which might encourage retaliation. Given that the move toward world free trade seems to have slowed, the shift to an emphasis on bilateral free trade with the United States seems to be the natural next best alternative. A free trade area with the United States, covering at least most industrial and resource commodities, should be a desirable longer term objective. At the same time, we should not lose sight of the growing importance of trade with countries in the Far East, including Japan, China and the newly industrializing countries. There is a potentially large market for Canadian resources and manufactured goods in these countries which has only begun to open up. The continued high rates of protection by Canada against these countries' imports is not likely to serve our long-term interests. Trade policy should take immediate steps to encourage a more even-handed treatment with these countries.

Emphasis upon Pacific Rim trade, as opposed to European trade, is where economic forces are clearly leading. It is time this was recognized. Bilateral economic and diplomatic efforts to expanding trade between Canada and these countries should be pursued.

Another aspect of Canadian trade policy which deserves comment is the call for implementation of contingent protection devices in Canada similar to those which exist elsewhere which provide a legitimate means of protection against "unfair" competing imports (Lazar, 1981). One thing is certain. There is a strong Canadian interest in avoiding contingent protection by the United States. Two potential countervail cases in 1983, a lumber case in the Pacific Northwest and a case of subway cars sold to New York City, both emphasize the extreme exposure of Canadian exporters to U.S. countervail legislation. Fortunately, neither attempt at countervail by U.S. producers was successful. However, recent events in steel, for example, suggest that a Canadian industry can be threatened even though it is not the primary target of U.S. protection.

While Canada has a great deal to lose from this type of protection, it is doubtful that it will gain much from a symmetrical policy. Any gains it might have would be very short term in nature. The main value of contingent protection is not in the redress of so-called unfair competition, but in the implied threat value of the protection. The threat impinges upon all exporters and governments, and thus modifies their behaviour accordingly. The threat to Canadian exporters of U.S. countervail is very great indeed. Yet the threat of a Canadian countervail to many companies exporting to Canada would be very small, given that Canada accounts for only a small portion of their total market. There is no sense in imagining that contingent protection legislation in Canada will yield a comparable degree of protection to that given to U.S. producers by U.S. countervail. In search for a workable Canadian–U.S. free trade arrangement, it is imperative that these potentially dangerous effects of contingent protection be understood.[12]

A healthy concern for retaliation by other countries must be always kept in mind in the conduct of export-oriented industrial policy. Subsidy of exports through a variety of means, including favourable export financing, is bound to attract attention. Other methods of encouraging exports should be pursued. It must be recognized that the technological competition being waged among the industrial nations means that subsidy is going to be prevalent in many industries. Furthermore, subsidy, like other non-tariff barriers, may be hard to detect. Government and corporate procurement policies can explicitly or implicitly subsidize a domestic industry in ways which are particularly hard to measure. The general support of R&D policies through government contracting policy and interaction between public and private research organizations are almost impossible to pin down as objective subsidies in any sense. Therefore, a fact of future trade is that the Schumpeterian competition in high technology industries will be heavily influenced by the participation of individual government. As subsidy is likely to be so prevalent, Canada should push within the GATT framework for clearer determination and definition of the rules governing subsidy and for some agreement as to the overall limits on subsidy. A real danger is that unconstrained world-wide subsidy competition could ultimately trigger widespread conventional tariff and quota protection, with harmful effects on all countries. Unfortunately, this seems to be the direction events are currently taking.[13]

In summary, an overall guiding principle of Canadian industrial policy should be continued emphasis on the free flow of goods and services across borders. This includes, incidentally, the flow across interprovincial borders. It is essential for Canadian industry to have access to a large market if it is to remain competitive. This means either the U.S. or world market. In the present environment of rising protectionism, the most reasonable course of action is to get assurance on access to the North American market.

Strategic Posture of Industrial Policy

Beyond the principle of access to world markets, at least three possible approaches to industrial policy can be identified which are available to the small open economy. These are referred to here as the defensive approach, the parallel approach and the differentiated approach. Each is set in the context of a particular strategic posture toward the major trading partners. Each trading partner is assumed to have a collection of policies which significantly influence domestic industrial structure. It is recognized that the small country is unlikely to affect the general policies of the large countries. The three approaches essentially cover the possibilities that might be taken in the design of industrial policy.

The *defensive* approach to industrial policy starts from the position that the main purpose of industrial policy in the small open economy is to react to the industrial policies of the large countries, so as to neutralize their harmful effects and at the same time exploit any advantages the small country might have.[14] In the language of modern game theory, this is a non-cooperative approach, with the small country taking reactive defensive measures as opposed to strategic offensive measures. The non-cooperative aspect of the policy basically reflects pessimism as to the prospect of affecting the outcome of industrial policies of the larger countries at all. In particular, the possibility of special bilateral arrangements is regarded as infeasible; the Most Favoured Nation principle of the GATT, for example, is designed to foster this attitude. The reactive approach reflects the desire to avoid the risks of taking offensive strategic actions, which could result in very damaging retaliation by one or more of the larger countries.

The defensive approach, while fairly conservative, can serve as the basis for a great deal of industrial policy of the tit-for-tat sort. If all countries engage in active subsidization of exports and protection of certain key industries, the small country can do likewise on grounds that this is the best it can do within a reactive, internationally non-cooperative policy framework.

The *parallel* approach toward industrial policy is motivated by the particular importance of a large country to the small country's economic well-being. In Canada, the importance of the United States is without question. Parallelism implies adopting a set of policies which coordinates as closely as possible in style and content with the large trading partner. This is a cooperative but reactive approach to policy, in that the large country's approach to industrial policy dictates the small country's approach. The emphasis is clearly on achieving the maximum benefit by explicit economic cooperation. It would mean, for example, that if the United States were to choose an activist industrial policy route, Canada would do likewise but would be certain to coordinate with the United States on those aspects of the policy where competition was a danger or where mutual gains were clearly identified. Thus, if the United States were to intervene explicitly in some industries, the Canadian government would have to intervene as well, to ensure mutual consistency in the overall policy. Similarly, if the United States were to pursue a free market industrial policy, the Canadian government would have to do likewise. The small country benefits from such a policy in two ways. First, it uses industrial policy as a bargaining device in maintaining access to the large country's market. Industrial policy becomes a tool of trade policy. Second, there is an "umbrella" effect of the large country's policy on the small which is particularly valuable in situations of economic conflict with third countries. For example, if the United States were to lobby Japan on access to certain high technology markets, it might be willing to bring Canadian firms under its lobbying umbrella if it saw Canada as a natural ally in its overall economic fight. In order to create that perception, Canadian industrial policy is designed to reduce political conflict and to maximize Canada–U.S. economic integration.

There are a number of problems with such a policy. Not the least is that it greatly constrains the political independence of the small country. On the economic side, it emphasizes the gains from explicit and coordinated cooperation but de-emphasizes the economic costs such a policy can impose. The cost can show up if the large country pursues a policy course which is going to impose potential or actual costs on the small country. In the Canada–U.S. context, this type of conflict could arise if the type of unilateral U.S. industrial policies deliberately prevented Canadian firms from gaining access to the U.S. market or resulted in Canada–U.S. competition in third country markets. This could seriously compromise the benefits underlying the whole framework. Furthermore, the form of U.S. industrial policy may not be suited to the particular structural problems of the Canadian economy. The single-minded pursuit of harmony could result in policies which at times were inappropriate. A good example might be deregulation in some sectors. Deregulation might work in the large U.S. domestic market because the preconditions for competition exist, while the Canadian domestic market might not be large enough to support a competitive market structure. If Canada were to deregulate in an effort to coordinate with U.S. policy, this could pose problems within the Canadian market. The reality of the parallel approach to industrial policy is that it must be tempered by a degree of caution as to unanticipated harmful consequences of large country policy. However, the risks may well be offset by the benefits of explicit cooperation. [15]

The *differentiated* approach to industrial policy is quite different from the other two. It emphasizes an explicit and strategic emphasis on differentiating the policy approach toward industry from that offered by the large country neighbour. [16] It also emphasizes unilateral and independent policy initiative rather than a cooperative decision-making framework. The idea is that the small country can benefit from strategic specialization which offers an alternative to that which exists in the large country. This is achieved by emphasizing development of a different economic structure and differences in the overall policy approach. In Canada, such an approach would mean explicit emphasis on the resource sector, as opposed to the manufacturing sector where U.S. interests largely lie. If the United States were to pursue a relatively non-interventionist approach to markets, the Canadian government would do the opposite. For example, it could set prices and wages, providing greater price stability than the United States and attracting certain types of economic activity which needed such stability. The Canadian government could also actively pursue negotiations on plant locations by multinationals from those European countries where government/business interaction is more accepted than in the United States. The Canadian government could emphasize the use of government-run cartels as a means of exporting. It could offer an extensive social system of health, education and public good provision to attract certain types of labour. Many other examples could be provided.

The usefulness of this approach hinges on the possibility that the industrial policy might create sufficient differences in the two countries to allow the small country to gain from specialization in all aspects of economic activity without attracting retaliatory action by the large country. The most striking implication of this approach is the possibility that comparative advantage could be engineered in those industries where the United States does not have a comparative advantage. If one accepts the legitimacy of engineered comparative advantage, and if the United States continues to pursue a non-interventionist strategy, then Canada could pursue a strong interventionist approach to industrial policy following a differentiated strategy. Policy would be geared toward building those industries in which the United States was losing comparative advantage or never had a comparative advantage. The major drawbacks are a reliance on the non-interventionist nature of U.S. industrial policy, faith in the ability to intervene effectively, and belief that retaliation against strategically aggressive Canadian industrial policy would not occur.

Any actual industrial policy will reflect some mixture of these three "pure" forms. In practice, Canadian industrial policy should emphasize a balance between the parallel and differentiated approaches. The relative emphasis between the two depends upon the course of action taken in the United States and structural differences between the two economies. The parallel approach offers great advantages but must take into consideration certain structural differences between the Canadian and U.S. economies. Parallelism should be pursued, for example, in the design of broad-based tax policy, the treatment of foreign investment and trade policy. All broad-based policies should be designed to encourage the flow of goods, services and enterprises across the U.S.–Canada border and to maximize the benefits from economic integration. To the extent that the United States pursues a more activist industrial policy, Canada should respond in like manner to avoid losing the U.S. market.

The differentiated policy approach should be practised in those areas where structural differences between the two economies are greatest and industrial policies which are not broad-based are called for. There are a number of areas where Canadian industrial policy is explicitly targetted. These included regional policy, high tech R&D policy, and policy toward public infrastructure in certain sectors. When targetting is involved, policies should not be constructed to parallel the U.S. approach. They should be geared to the specific concerns at hand and should avoid impacts elsewhere in the economy.

Adopting a parallel approach does not mean deliberate acceptance of the U.S. policy route, nor does it deny the possibility of unilateral action when there are clear benefits to doing so. Rather, it recognizes the benefits to coordination. Environmental policy is an example. It is clear that Canada has strong interests in pursuing a more rigid enforcement of environmental standards on acid rain. These interests should be pushed vigorously in Washington, but nothing is lost by pursuing our own environmental policies at the same time, even if the United States is reluctant to do so. The differentiated aspect of industrial policy must be tempered by recognizing where we risk competition with U.S. interests. Indeed, this may be the overriding concern in choosing a balance between the two policy postures.

The defensive approach to industrial policy could be justified in a worst-case scenario in which the United States closes off its markets to Canada. In this case, we would have no other alternative. At the present time, it provides a framework which forgoes too many benefits and is too conservative in its goals to be recommended as a central principle of policy design.

In concluding this section, I admit to being skeptical about any general scheme for policy analysis other than a fairly pragmatic one. To incorporate all aspects of political and economic reality in a few general principles seems dubious. Nevertheless, the search for order in an untidy world is a compelling one for the social scientist. Some specifics of industrial policy are taken up in the following sections.

Mega-Projects and the Resource Sector

Part of any industrial policy is the role afforded to public sector infrastructure. These include activities which are generally thought of as public capital goods, such as roads and communication networks, and other activities in which minimum efficient scale is so large that public sector monopoly is preferred to private sector provision. In the case of very large and risky projects, the risk aspect can be used to justify the public provision of the project; the argument is simply that private capital markets find the joint combination of the scale and risk associated with the project too great to undertake financing. The public sector, through its superior risk-bearing abilities, is able to finance the activity or at least provide loan guarantees to reduce the risk of private sector financing.

Another compelling argument for public sector provision is the presence of pecuniary externalities induced by the complementarity of economic activity. Thus, some private sector activity might be unprofitable without the joint provision of a road network in an undeveloped area of the country. However, if both are provided jointly, they are socially worthwhile. Existing market signals do not provide adequate information for the private sector participants to realize the potential economic value of the activity, but the public sector may not provide the road network because no current demand for the road services is perceived. Intervention on economic development grounds is justified in this case by the public sector. It must not only provide the road network but also induce the private sector to undertake the complementary activities.

Both these arguments form the basis for the provision of a great deal of public sector infrastructure. The arguments are as compelling today as they ever were. In the populated regions, though, they tend to play less of a role, because public infrastructure tends to be largely in place and additional large-scale projects are not necessary. Mega-projects will continue to be an important part of the total industrial policy package in Canada because of the importance of resource sectors in the hinterland. These include transportation projects, hydro-electric projects, and exploitation of oil and gas reserves.

The recent failure of the mega-projects strategy in the energy sector owing to the fall in world energy prices has led to some questioning of this type of strategy. This failure should not be taken as general condemnation of large-scale public sector investment. Needless to say, all such investment is risky and careful cost-benefit analysis is needed in each case. But the public sector must take the role of actively scanning the economy to determine the possible need for such projects.

Beyond recognizing the importance of mega-projects, there remain two basic policy issues for the resource sector. First, there is the difficulty of planning, given the uncertainty in resource prices. As remarked in previous chapters, there is no reason to expect these prices to exhibit more stability in the future than in the past. The lesson of the National Energy Program is that one must not place too much faith in any one set of price forecasts. The second problem is that the entire issue of trade in resource products, particularly energy, needs to be examined in the light of Canadian–U.S. trade policy.

The following are suggested as possible resolutions, at least in part, of some of these problems. First, the goal of self-sufficiency in energy should be abandoned as a planning tool. The idea that a small open economy like Canada's, in which there is no argument based on "strategic supply" considerations, should be self-sufficient in anything in today's integrated world economy, finds no basis in any sensible economic calculation. The primary consideration in resource policy should be the net economic benefits contributed by this sector in terms of income and employment. Second, Canada should seriously consider the concept of free trade with the United States in energy, minerals and forest products.[17] There are two reasons for this. First, the U.S. market is the only natural one to guarantee an export market for those energy products, such as gas and hydro-electricity. Second, a guarantee of U.S. long-term supply in energy would give Canada significant bargaining power in seeking access to the U.S. industrial market. As repeatedly emphasized in Chapters Four through Six, guaranteed market access is crucial for the development of new high technology industries in Canada and for the maintenance of some existing basic industries. (This is discussed in greater detail later in the chapter.)

There is little a small country can do about uncertainty in resource prices, with the possible exception of engaging in long-term contracts. Even these are notoriously difficult to enforce, as Canadian gas producers are discovering. Fortunately, the employment consequences of this uncertainty are not significant, because of the capital intensity of the resource sectors. The only practical policy with respect to the development of resources is a wait-and-see attitude. When development investment seems called for, it obviously pays to get the best advice you can. Public sector stabilization of resource prices, analogous to what occurs in some agricultural products and current energy policy, is something that many regard as highly dubious. It smacks of the kind of intervention which can quickly lead to excessive drains on public sector resources and inefficient resource use. The problem of unstable prices for resource allocation, however, is real enough. Corporate and industrial planning can be seriously hampered by price instability, and fluctuation in exchange rates has caused similar problems for firms involved in international trade. Given the importance of the resource sector to Canada, the size of investment required for development and the risks involved, the whole question of resource price stabilization needs further consideration. The recent experience should not be given too much importance. From the viewpoint of the industrial export sectors, price stability in energy inputs could prove to be an important advantage in the fight for world market share. This is perhaps one area where Canadian comparative advantage could be used in a strategically important way. In negotiating a free trade arrangement with the United States, an important part of that arrangement might be a policy on price stabilization in resource commodities.

Education and Job Retraining Policy

One thing everyone agrees on in the trade and industrial policy area, no matter what their political or economic persuasion, is that policy regarding human resources is of the utmost importance in terms of long-run productivity and income growth. In the U.S. industrial policy debate, every commentator has agreed on the importance of human resources to the long-run vitality of the economy. Even the strict neoclassical interpretation of trade flows affords a great deal of importance to human capital, as pointed out in Chapter Three. If comparative advantage can be engineered, it is through the provision of education and job skills, or the accumulation of human capital. High-skill industries will only be retained in those countries with highly skilled work forces.

In the Canadian context, the comparative advantage studies and fairly straightforward examination of historical trade data reveal a pattern of imports of high-skill goods and exports of low-skill and resource-intensive goods. Canadian incomes have been kept high, it is argued, by living off resource rents. As pointed out in Chapters Two and Three, there are good reasons why that particular pattern of trade may not be sustained in the longer term. The world shift in comparative advantage is going to place a number of the traditional industries with high-volume production and standardized products at a severe disadvantage in Canada relative to the low wage countries. This is happening already in steel, autos, rubber, heavy machinery, electrical equipment and assembly in electronics. There are reasons to believe Canada may lose these basic industries. The high technology alternative is thought by many to be the only hope. In some highly innovative Schumpeterian industries, this may well be the case. An educated labour force is a necessary prerequisite to producing in this type of industry, with high product turnover and flexible auto-mated production systems.

Within the non-traded goods sector, the move to automation has raised the possibility of substantial unemployment. Some economists argue that the employment-displacing effect of technological change could work much faster than the employment-creating effect. While most agree that in the long run technological innovation must lead to growth in real income, there is evidence that the short-run skill imbalances it creates lead to adjustment problems (Economic Council of Canada, 1982). Retraining displaced workers is an important mechanism by which those imbalances are alleviated.

In the industrial policy context, the emphasis is on policies which deal with these labour adjustment problems. While this study is concerned primarily with the trade side, there are some fairly obvious problems for policy to grapple with in the labour market. First, there is the recognition that demographics mean a bulge in the 30- to 40-year-old group within the population for the next ten years. To the extent that retraining is necessary for the emerging new industries, it will necessarily be of a form — adult retraining — in which the public education system has not played a great role to date. Second, the non-traded goods sector, or services, will have to deal with the bulk of the retraining because that is where better than 60 percent of the labour force is employed. Third, there is the general issue of the extent to which firms will undertake the retraining of workers without government encouragement. This has occurred in some sectors, such as in financial services, where the firm clearly sees the necessity and private benefits of providing training. But for reasons which are covered below, this is unlikely to be the case in most of the basic industries and the genuine losing industries. Job retraining programs are one of the most important aspects of a sensible industrial policy. Retraining will necessarily have to be targetted at certain occupations, although general training in microelectronic liter-acy should be useful. Manpower planning must be undertaken to some extent in order to provide coherence to the overall thrust of the retraining program.

In the education area, there will have to be greater emphasis on science and engineering. This is already happening to some extent. Years of no growth of the universities have produced a degree of stagnation in the whole system. Some radical changes will be necessary, although it is difficult to see how they will come about with the current financial situation.

The major problem with pursuing a policy of human capital accumulation within the economy, as with any saving policy, is finding the resources to carry it out. Generally, the economy must either borrow abroad to fund the accumulation, increase savings or divert existing investment funds from their present use to the human capital alternative. Given the relatively high savings rates of Canadians, diverting existing funds is probably the most sensible alternative. This could be done by creating special financial instruments to fund education and job retraining, such as a "technological initiative" bond which would carry tax-free interest. It might be necessary to reduce some of the incentives on existing savings instruments in order to encourage the substitution toward the new instruments as regular savings vehicles by households. The bonds, issued by federal and provincial governments, would be based on the ultimate ability of the future economy to generate additional tax revenue to pay them back.

Publicly funded retraining should be accompanied by policies to encourage the individuals who undertake job retraining and the firms who use the newly trained labour to bear some of the costs. The literature on job retraining includes a number of programs of this sort (Economic Council of Canada, 1982).

The effort to retrain the economy's work force will call for definite leadership on the part of government. The need is urgent and the potential social returns are probably greater here than in any other industrial policy area. The force of technological change, competition from low wage countries and the existence of a work force which is fairly young but about to become middle-aged are all compelling reasons to act soon.

Adjustment Policy and the Losing Industries

One arm of industrial policy is the programs to deal explicitly with the industries which are genuine losers due to shifts in the international division of labour. These industries have thus far been concentrated in the low-skill, labour-intensive industries located primarily in Quebec. They include certain parts of the clothing, knitting, textiles, leather and footwear industries and are likely to include others soon. Many would classify a large number of basic industries, such as steel, autos and rubber, as already on the list of genuine losers. I am not convinced of this, however, and discuss the "maybe" cases later in this chapter. In this section, the discussion is confined to those industries which are clearly identifiable as unsalvageable without fairly extensive protection.

In these industries, it is common to have a combination of protection and adjustment policies. The protection policies generally take the form of quotas and, in some cases, voluntary export restraints. The adjustment policies are of a wide variety, including explicit compensation and some job retraining allowances to those affected by import competition. Generally speaking, however, the protection side of the policy has been emphasized at the expense of the adjustment side of the policy.[18]

How should one deal with the losing industry problem? The Japanese model has been put forward as one alternative. Close government-business cooperation there produces a consensus on what the industry must do either to restructure and compete or to close down. If the former path is chosen, then temporary protection is provided, together with a coordinated reduction in capacity through a "government managed" if not outright government-run cartel. Closing down an industry means essentially finding employment for the workers laid off. One way the problem is handled is employee-sharing arrangements between large firms. There is, however, considerable evidence that the Japanese are really not better at solving the unemployment problem in a losing industry than anyone else.

Would such a model work for Canada? In the genuine losing industries, restructuring of the industry is not going to solve the unemployment problem. The only question is how long the protection is going to stay in place, and how adjustment of firms and workers will be promoted. It is clear that the workers are the victims of a shift in the world scheme of comparative advantage. The basic question is one of economic justice. Does society owe them their old jobs on the same terms or some compensation for the private economic losses they have incurred, or does it owe them nothing? This latter position is held by those who feel the government has no role in insuring citizens against every possible unforeseen event. It is clearly a political choice. The cost to society of maintaining everyone's current job indefinitely would be astronomical. The most sensible policy is to promote labour adjustment, even if the policy is likely to err on the side of promoting too much adjustment. Whatever compensation is politically necessary to remove the protection existing on these industries should be made. Compensation can take the form of cash settlements to older workers, mobility grants and job retraining for younger workers. The cost of making the adjustment, however large in the short run, is much less than the loss to society of maintaining workers indefinitely in an inefficient industry.

Policies to deal with firms in losing industries tend to be more controversial. The general view of many economists is that the death of firms imposes a calculated risk on equity owners and is part of the normal workings of the market system. To intervene in the process is bound to exacerbate inefficiency and possibly slow down the adjustment process. This is an interesting view but one that finds little support in economic theory. The one case which exists for firms undertaking an efficient adjustment to a decline in demand is that of competitive industries in which investment is non-industry-specific. Here the decline in industry capacity is carried out by a gradual decline in capacity and employment within each firm. As pointed out by Richardson (1960), if there is some degree of indivisibility in plant or firm size, so that efficient industry adjustment to a decline in demand requires that firms exit in some orderly temporal sequence, there are good reasons to believe the free market will not produce this type of outcome. This lack of market efficiency in managing declining industries becomes a defence for "recessionary cartels" and specific targetting of select firms as instruments of adjustment. Part of the emphasis on firms is fostered by the recognition that "industry restructuring" may actually involve a change in the firm's major product line in response to the competition, or adopting modern technology which makes the firm competitive. In Canada, the Department of Regional Industrial Expansion (DRIE) operates a number of these programs, although none go as far as full-scale organization of a recessionary cartel or even active promotion of mergers.[19] These policies are, for the most part, eminently sensible and should be explored further. To ignore the role the firm plays in the adjustment process is simply absurd. Careful coordination of labour and firm adjustment policies is required, and administrators of such a program must ensure that a program of positive adjustment does not turn into an implicit policy of long-term protection. Rigid timetables for adjustment might be one way to prevent such abuses. In general, policy makers should be more imaginative in their approach to declining industries.

The Problem in the Basic Industries

Much of the current policy concern is with de-industrialization through the decline of the basic manufacturing industries, defined as industries involving large-scale, standardized-production methods. The skill levels of labour required in these industries has been steadily decreasing, or at least not increasing. With the growth of the developing countries and the newly industrialized countries, it is argued that in the absence of intervention, natural forces of comparative advantage and global corporate strategies will dictate moving these industries abroad where labour is cheaper. The steel, auto, rubber, heavy machinery and electrical equipment industries are all targets for demise in North America, according to this theory.[20] Even the assembly of high tech goods is moving increasingly to the NICs. This is called the "Atari effect," after the move of production facilities of the video game maker Atari from California to Hong Kong.

There is nothing in the theory of comparative advantage or in market structure theories of trade which dictates that these industries should move to low wage countries. What forces this relocation is not a comparative advantage effect but a failure of wages to fall in the North American industry. Keynesian wage rigidities are the key factor here. If wages would fall in North America, the true forces of comparative advantage, including factor endowment and market structure determinants, would dictate that the plant actually stay right where it is. After all, the firm has a great deal of sunk capital in the form of existing productive capacity, supply and distribution networks. Transportation costs are another factor which would dictate that the production be located close to the market for which most of the product is destined. If its wage costs were in line with those in other countries, there would be no reason to abandon North American locations. The relocation decision is principally due to the fact that workers are unwilling to accept wage cuts which would make North America competitive with the NICs or other developing countries.

The social problem is that the wage cuts required to make these industries viable are so great that low-skill labour would generally receive something close to, if not below, the existing minimum wage. Given this fairly permanent wage rigidity, the outcome must be either protection to preserve the jobs of workers in these industries or substantial unemployment as firms close down plants and relocate elsewhere. Both types of responses have been observed in U.S. auto and steel industries, for example. A combination of plant shutdowns and temporary protection through such means as voluntary export restraints have become a routine occurrence in recent years.

At the same time, developments in technology are changing the nature of some of these industries. For example, the steel industry has become much less scale oriented and has shifted to a product differentiation strategy (Barnett and Schorsch, 1983). This change requires a location closer to the final market and a more skill-intensive work force. The other possibility is that the robotization of plants will reduce unskilled jobs to negligible proportions. As was pointed out in Chapter Two, protection could hasten the mechanization of the plant, as firms find it profitable to replace highly paid, low-skill workers with machines.[21]

The final outcome, though, will depend crucially on the dynamics of this process. The low wages in the less developed and newly industrialized countries, together with wage rigidity in North American labour markets, will hasten the departure of some industries from their present location. At the same time, the increasing sophistication of robotic technology reduces the necessary unskilled labour input for other industries. The robotic technology, however, is completely portable. If a plant moves to a low wage country, the low wages will slow down the competitive necessity to adopt the new technology but the technology can be adopted when it proves desirable. Because of the large-scale integrated natures of the production process, each plant will make a choice either to move to a low wage country and use existing technology with much lower cost labour, or to switch to a fully automated plant. The incentive to choose the former route increases with (a) intensity of the competition from abroad; (b) uncertainty in the suitability of the new technology; (c) higher capital costs; and (d) lower sunk costs in the existing production and distribution facilities.

From the point of view of the country losing the industry, the outcome is hardly a matter of indifference. Benefits in the form of support for local economies and the spin-offs from the supply and distribution networks will be lost if the industry moves. Whether the plant leaves or stays, the direct long-term employment consequences for the local unskilled labour are the same — they are out of a job.

If the industry goes the automation route, some additional benefits accrue to the economy. First, within the plant there will be increased demand for skilled workers capable of servicing and operating the new technology. Second, the switch to the automation process itself will increase the demand for new equipment, some of which may accrue to the domestic economy. While the total employment creation effects are not known, the return to capital, land and tax revenues accruing to the domestic economy could be substantial.

The policy choices are quite difficult. One extreme is simply to let the industry go, if that is what the market dictates. The other extreme is to put in place protection to keep the industry where it is. If plant automation is feasible, protection will hasten the rate at which this technology is adopted unless organized labour is successful in inhibiting its adoption. An alternative outcome could be had by refusing to protect but promoting the adoption of new technology. This would exacerbate the employment problem relative to the protection outcome, but not relative to complete loss of the industry. This policy would involve identifying those industries, among the class of basic industries, where automation could in the longer term provide a final product competitive in cost with that supplied from plants located in the low wage countries. If this were feasible, at least with some acceptable degree of risk attached, then the necessary instruments would be targetted subsidies or loan guarantees to the large-scale firms in these industries to encourage "premature automation." Complementary adjustment policies dealing with the displaced labour would also be required. This policy option deserves consideration as an alternative to the protection route, which is currently the most probable response to the problem in the basic industries.

Another approach, which is closer to the free market solution, would be not to intervene at all. In this case, only those industries or firms which succeed in getting wages down would remain. Those which do not would of necessity move offshore. The reluctance of workers in Canada to take wage cuts, some would point out, leads to the "socially just" outcome of transferring jobs to workers in the less developed and newly industrializing countries which are considerably lower on the income scale. While I have some sympathy with this approach, its political feasibility in Canada is probably slight. Because the industries are so large, the employment effects of even a single plant shutdown are substantial and the departure of the plant is highly visible in the economy. Organized labour in these industries, and probably the provinces where they are located, are not likely to let this happen.

The real choice is between protection and premature automation. Promoting automation through early advanced adoption of robotics prevents relocation offshore, although the labour problem will require adjustment and job retraining programs. The overall effect would be to push the economy in the direction of a technologically progressive economy at a faster rate than could be achieved under either a free market or protection.

Not all basic industries are suitable for this type of solution. It may be easier to shed some of the losers among the basic industries. Most of these industries are concentrated in Central Canada, particularly in southern Ontario. This regional concentration mitigates to some extent the problems of interregional adjustment.

An important part of industrial policy toward the basic industries involves multinationals. In the automotive sector, the Auto Pact covers the "Big Three" U.S. auto companies. There is every reason to believe the relationship between U.S. multinational parents and their subsidiaries will be particularly susceptible to the general problems of basic industry. If the competition from overseas production, either from non-U.S. multinationals or from foreign subsidiaries of U.S. multinationals, does not weaken, there is every reason to expect a fairly strong protectionist reaction to this competition in the United States. Indeed, this is already occurring. In this situation, there is a real danger that Canada could lose significantly in those industries not covered by an arrangement such as the Auto Pact. As U.S. MNEs begin to react defensively against the foreign competition and a reduced world market share, scale economies could provide a rationale for them to shut down Canadian plants in favour of production in the home market unless specialization within the Canadian plant, possibly through world product mandating, offsets this tendency.[22] The Canadian plant would thus stay viable by producing at a minimum for the North American market, and possibly for the world market. For an industry which is genuinely a loser on the world scale, though, this option might not be realistic.

A serious policy issue emerges for a basic domestic industry dominated by U.S. multinationals which is at the same time protected in the

U.S. market. Should Canada provide levels of protection comparable to those in the United States, or should it pursue some other policy? A policy of parallel protection would protect employment in that industry, but without Canadian–U.S. sectoral free trade in that industry, this policy would induce a miniature replica branch-plant effect. Thus, it might seem a sensible alternative to push for sectoral Canada–U.S. free trade in those industries with common trade barriers against overseas competition. However, the wisdom of this strategy should be seriously questioned in some basic industries.

If the North American market share of the world industry is inevitably going to shrink, hanging on to these industries within Canada through protection, bailouts and other forms of public support may be putting Canada at serious risk. There are two reasons for this. First, it could be argued that ultimately the industry must shift its locational base from North America. Even if Canada were to get access to the U.S. market in this industry, that at best might be a temporary solution. Second, as the pressure from the foreign competition builds up within these industries, the free trade arrangement might risk U.S. retaliatory action. Indeed, the initial basis for the free trade arrangement is dubious from the viewpoint of the U.S. labour force in these sectors. In these circumstances, the best policy for Canada might be to drop protection and either leave the industry to its own fortunes or push for premature automation within the industry. In either case, Canada would gain a longer term advantage over the United States by promoting faster structural change.

If Canada were to drop protection from these sectors while the United States raises or at least does not remove existing protection, U.S. multinationals would in all likelihood abandon production in Canada fairly quickly. The Canadian consumer would be the major beneficiary in the short run, as it would now be possible to import from abroad. The losers would be the Canadian employees of U.S. subsidiaries in these industries.

If the industry is on the list of those which might survive through technological revitalization, then the presence or absence of U.S. multinationals makes little difference to the mechanics of the industry policy. Foreign and domestic firms should be treated on equal grounds. Clearly, choosing industries for premature automation is in the policy category of "picking winners." Putting an industry on that list, as opposed to removing it, means a fairly dramatic difference in approach. However, in the absence of reducing the type of rigidities existing in labour markets, I see little way of avoiding this dilemma. From the politically feasible perspective, it is a simple choice between protection for all or some attempt to pick, if not winners, at least those industries which are not clear losers.

High Tech Industries, Industrial R&D and Technology Transfer

In the last chapter, the case was made that due to the nature of competition in the class of industries referred to as Schumpeterian, there is a strong case for offering some type of public support. In the small open economy, these industries offer a means of collecting quasi-rents in the form of profits and wages over the longer term. Furthermore, the technology transfer process is fairly efficient and works primarily to benefit the small open economy, while the industrial R&D process exhibits considerable evidence of market failure. The primary market failure is the presence of entry barriers in export markets which work against the export industries of small open economies. Within technologically progressive industries, a small open economy should have an advantage in those products where scale economies are not the primary entry barrier. Industries in which product differentiation is the most important structural feature of the innovation process offer the greatest chance for success for smaller firms from a small open economy to establish export market bases. It was further argued that capital markets provide absolute cost barriers to these industries. As world tariff walls come down, the incentive for all firms to compete through aggressive R&D pre-emption policies goes up. This tendency has been given impetus by the fact that all governments have given considerable aid to domestic firms in the industrial technology race. This section considers the appropriate stance toward these industries in light of an overall approach to industrial policy.

There are a number of issues to be kept in mind in designing a sensible policy toward high technology industries.[23] First is the question of public subsidy of industrial R&D versus other methods of dealing with the presence of entry barriers in export markets. Second is the extent to which other aspects of the economy, in particular the human resources problem, relate to the development of these types of industries. Finally, there is the extent to which defensive subsidization of R&D is justified in the small open economy.

As was argued in Chapters Six and Seven, the R&D performance of Canadian manufacturing in the past can be attributed in large part to either: (a) scale economies in the R&D process which naturally dictated a lower level of R&D by multinationals abroad than at home; or (b) the presence of entry barriers in export markets which prevented firms in small economies from establishing a post-innovation presence in the world industry sufficient to justify the initial R&D outlay. As a small open economy, Canada benefits naturally from the technology transfer by multinationals; it is not in Canadians' interest to hinder this process. Discriminatory treatment of foreign investment is a poor policy. If a small open economy wants to gain a base in the world's Schumpeterian industries, it must, however, overcome the entry barriers problem.

One way to deal with entry barriers in export markets directly is to subsidize exports of industries in which Canadian firms have a chance of success in the world market. Competitive export financing has become a fairly common method of export subsidy and one which attracted considerable attention within Canada with the Bombardier case. In Schumpeterian industries the export subsidy is supposed to provide the firm with a competitive advantage which allows it to establish a presence in the world market. The major problem with this type of policy is that government in the importing country can make use of contingent protection devices under existing GATT arrangements to prevent the successful capture of that market. A small country is at a competitive disadvantage in this "subsidy and protection" game because of its relatively small bargaining power. The major industrial players can divide up the world market in this type of game and the small countries can be effectively cut out.

An alternative class of strategies to promote these industries is to build up the domestic firm prior to entry to the world market such that, given an innovation of "average success" potential, it can effectively crack the entry barriers of the large firms already in the industry. Proposals for this type of policy include forced merger and rationalization of firms, joint ventures and even government ownership as an alternative, or at least prerequisite, to free trade strategy. Protection of the industry allows the domestic firms to mature into an efficient world class competitor by having sole access to the domestic market.

As should be clear by now, the presumed choice between the free trade and rationalization strategies is irrelevant. First, there are a number of inherent difficulties in attempting to foster such rationalization behind tariff walls. Some of these are legal problems having to do with possible violation of U.S. and Canadian antitrust law. The basic economic problem, though, is that protected firms serving the domestic market are not faced with the type of competition which they must deal with if they are to serve the world market. Protection at best delays the adoption of internationally competitive strategies, and at worst produces a firm incapable of competing internationally. Furthermore, even if Canada could undertake the sort of selective protection policy which is claimed to have worked for Japan, it would not be effective because of the small size of the Canadian market. In any case, Canada is committed under the GATT to not raising tariff barriers. Without access to a large market, participation by a small open economy in Schumpeterian industries is infeasible. If access to world markets can be secured, there remains the problem of how to promote the type of industry and firm structure which is likely to succeed.

A couple of observations are worth making. First, on average, it is unlikely that any small domestic firm is going to succeed in an industry where size and established presence in terms of world market share are necessary prerequisites. Industries which are already building on existing products and processes, or are part way through the product cycle, are clearly not those where a new entry is likely to be successful. Second, direct government intervention by forced merger and rationalization of industry is too political and relies too heavily on bureaucratic expertise to be reliable. Both the legal and political practicality of such a policy is highly suspect.

What then can be done? First, the policy should be targetted specifically at small to medium size domestic firms in technologically progressive industries where the benefits are likely to emerge and the barriers to entry in export markets are greatest.[24] Second, it should provide support to the firm in its early phase of development, either prior to getting in the export market or shortly thereafter. Third, programs should be targetted at firms rather than industries, or at individual R&D projects. The firm is the vehicle through which the economy earns quasi-rents. Firm success is, therefore, the appropriate measure of policy success. Within these general guidelines the policy should be as flexible as possible. Two types of policies seem like obvious candidates: support of R&D through tax, subsidy, loan guarantees or procurement policies; and explicit underwriting of lower cost loans in the capital market to foster the development of these types of firms. Policies of this sort, unlike export subsidies, get to the source of the problem. Export subsidies are subject to two additional problems in addition to those already mentioned. They are highly visible targets for countervail under the GATT arrangement and are inconsistent with a policy of securing access to larger world markets, particularly the U.S. market. They also give rise to a national welfare loss as domestic taxpayers directly subsidize foreign consumption. The policies described here focus on domestic factors of production and do not give rise to such an obvious transfer loss.

The policies must be designed with an explicit emphasis on firm and industry dynamics. Firms which do not grow or fail to penetrate export markets should be cut off from support. Also, once firms achieve success, they naturally cease to qualify for support. The whole emphasis should be on getting a base of potential domestic entrants to technologically progressive world industries. The resources available for this will be most effective if they are targetted on small and medium size firms in those industries where existing world market share is not a crucial prerequisite to success. By channelling resources to R&D and export market entry, the aspect of market failure motivating the policy is dealt with most effectively.

It has been argued throughout this study that the world technology race results in defensive and retaliatory subsidization of high technology industries by major industrial nations. Does this provide a legitimate case, different from the barriers-to-export argument, upon which to base the subsidy of R&D expenditures of industrial firms in the small open economy? If one accepts foreign subsidy as inevitable, it does provide an argument for the subsidization of Schumpeterian firms even in the absence of export barriers. The argument laid out in Chapter Six established that, given similar levels of risk to entry, the incentives to subsidize are greater for smaller countries than for larger countries. However, it must be recognized that the world as a whole may be worse off from this competitive subsidization of the technology race if the public good aspect of R&D spillover is minimal. Multilateral agreement to resist such subsidy would be the world's first-best alternative. To the extent that firms from a small country can overcome the barriers to export, this may actually lead to an improvement in world welfare by improving the state of international competition. Both arguments provide a case for intervention in the national interest, but intervention toward overcoming export barriers may also be in the world interest. In the case in which R&D spillovers are significant, from the world point of view the competitive subsidization of the technology race is a good thing. In this situation, however, the national case for defensive subsidization of R&D by a small open economy is weaker. The case for overcoming export barriers remains intact, however, even under these circumstances.

An important class of Schumpeterian industries are those where the post-innovation entry barriers are due to static scale economies with large capital requirements. The small open economies face the biggest disadvantage in these industries. Nevertheless, in many countries there seems to be a political commitment to have such industries. Canadian participation in the aerospace industry is one example. If such an industry already exists and is successful, there is little in the export barriers argument to justify support by special measures. If the industry does not yet exist but government is contemplating creating a firm within such an industry on the grounds that it is a potential Schumpeterian winner, the risks are great indeed. If the private sector will not do so on its own initiative, government should attempt to only if there is good reason to enter such an industry.

The most favourable case I can imagine is the following conjunction of circumstances. First, the "industry" must not be new but rather based on a product which builds on some significant base of sunk costs, putting the firm on a strategic base similar to, or preferably better than, competing firms in other countries. Second, competing firms in other countries should be receiving R&D support or other forms of subsidy. If the small country does not face undue risk, the optimal policy response is to provide a similar level of support. It is conceivable that in the world technological competition, a small country will have some industries of this sort, although the number will probably be small. In Canada, R&D –

intensive industries with close ties to the resource base or other peculiarly Canadian features may be candidates for this type of strategy.

It is important to provide some kind of assessment of the future relative importance of Schumpeterian industries in terms of their share of world industrial products. Any judgment here is at best an educated guess. The shift to knowledge-intensive industries is an increasing trend worldwide.[25] The basic industries and resource industries within the industrialized countries are under a great deal of competitive pressure at present. At least in the near term, there seems little chance of a recovery in primary commodity prices. Basic manufacturing is certainly destined in part for relocation to the NICs and LDCs. Hence, in terms of traded goods, technologically progressive industries are bound to be of increasing importance. The significance to Canada of this worldwide shift must not be understated.

The target level of R&D proposed by the Ministry of State for Science and Technology was 1.5 percent of GNP by 1983. This type of aggregate targetting is often criticized on economic grounds as being relatively meaningless. On the other hand, it can also be regarded as a useful means of focussing attention on the problem and mobilizing bureaucratic and political resources. In general, I agree with this assessment. The 1.5 percent figure is, if anything, probably too low. If Canada is to have its share of the technologically progressive industries, it will have to devote resources closer to the proportion spent in the major industrial countries. In 1977, this share within the manufacturing sector was closer to 5 and 6 percent (Palda and Pazderka, 1982). The difficulty is deciding how such targets should be met: through government intervention directly at the R&D level, or through incentives for firms to raise their R&D expenditures by changing market structure. The ministry's responsibility for these policies will require good judgment and a sense of what is practical. Economic policy as a complete package, however, should focus considerable attention on these types of firms and industries.

An important aspect of the emphasis on technologically progressive industries is the relationship between this type of structural change in industry and labour markets. If the labour skills are not available to foster high tech industry, any other policies which attempt to encourage their development are doomed to failure. These include not only the scientific skills necessary in the R&D process, but also the skills needed in the production phase. The crucial thing to recognize is the dynamic nature of the whole process. At the level of the individual firm, dynamic pre-emption through innovative success is the cornerstone on which Schumpeterian rents are earned. These rents, in turn, accrue to labour through payments to skilled scientific and production personnel. There is a large infant-industry component to the whole story, though. A successful Schumpeterian sector builds a base of technological expertise and skill in the domestic economy upon which other firms can build. The "success breeds success" hypothesis implies there are significant dynamic external benefits to individual firm activity to foster investment in the Schumpeterian sector as a whole.[26] The skill mix in the labour force, on the other hand, is the basis on which the industry begins. If you start from a labour force which lacks the necessary skills, the probability of successful innovation and marketing is lower. On the other hand, having created a base of skilled labour, little in the way of rents will be earned on that investment unless some Schumpeterian industries are established. The whole process is highly interdependent. Industrial policy and labour market policy will necessarily have to be coordinated to some extent.

The technology transfer process, particularly through the multinational enterprise, will continue to work in favour of the small open economy. Defensive industrial policies by the large countries, including possible control of foreign direct investment, may attempt to slow down the technology transfer to some extent. There is little a small open economy can do to affect these developments. However, it is crucial to create a favourable environment for multinationals through the treatment of foreign investment and trade. Canada benefits significantly from the invisible transfers of technology from these firms. Spillovers from these transfers into the establishment of the base upon which Schumpeterian industries are built make the benefits even greater. The parallel to effective protection is striking. The intermediate inputs used by the export industries are more efficient or cheaper to the extent that they use the best technology available. Export industries can be given negative-effect protection if supplying industries do not have the best technology available.

Free trade and non-discriminatory policies against foreign investment are the most effective ways to deal with the technology transfer problem. Deliberate subsidization of technology transfer does not seem warranted on economic criteria. The market failure here clearly works in favour of the importer — thus, Canada benefits from the investment in R&D by other countries. Through both domestic and foreign competition, import-competing and non-traded goods industries have the incentive to adopt the most efficient technology when it is economically sensible. Limited public resources for industrial policy are better channelled to export industries and to promoting adjustment out of losing industries.

Industry Location and Policy Coordination

A basic question which comes up in the design of industrial policy is the relationship between declining and expanding industries on a locational basis. Briefly, is there a case for promoting the growth industries to locate in the same regions as the declining industries? The case *for* rests on the fairly obvious proposition that this would mitigate both the social and economic costs of adjustment. The case *against* is that any form of intervention to affect location decisions might induce inefficiencies which would be detrimental to the long-run objectives of adjustment. In Canada, the question of industrial location is intertwined with regional economic policy and is therefore distinctly political.

Ignoring the political argument, the case for influencing the location decision of new plants in the direction of mitigating the adjustment costs of labour seems eminently sensible. Each case must be considered on its own merits in order to avoid obviously inefficient location decisions. Infrastructure, material supplies, transport costs and labour force requirements all figure in the firm's location decision. But to the extent that the plant is genuinely footloose, the efficiency cost of having it in one location versus another is likely to be small.

In dealing with plant location decisions, an important role for the federal government is to mitigate competitive bidding for the firm by lower level governments. This type of competition is especially pernicious when an industry is genuinely footloose. The resource loss can be measured almost exactly by the cost of the winning bid. Hopefully, instances of this type of competition can be kept to a minimum.

The other important aspect of plant location policy is in dealing with multinationals' decisions to locate new plants in one country versus another. The general rule of thumb should be to assist the MNEs in a positive way toward preferred locations, but to avoid competitive bidding with other countries for the plant location. International competitive bidding, in general, can be very costly to the winner — the "winner's curse", as it is referred to in formal bidding theory. In dealing with multinationals, policy should rely on forces of comparative advantage and market structure in determining location. Location assistance policy should be geared toward firms that are more or less committed to locating within Canada and only concerned with deciding where in Canada. This means an emphasis on the location of domestic firms and those multinationals which are already committed to a location decision within Canada. To put it in another way, plant location policy should have as its primary goal the assistance of the adjustment process by affecting location within Canada, rather than by attracting industry into Canada in the first place. Plant location policy should focus on the firm's location decision per se, rather than other decisions. In general, this means a subsidy geared towards the location-specific costs of the firm, which become genuinely sunk costs once the location decision has been made. Subsidizing these costs means providing temporary assistance in the early phase of the plant's life. Obvious kinds of effective assistance would be providing local infrastructure and subsidizing capital expenditure items which are location and industry specific. Subsidizing operating costs or mobile capital goods would clearly be less effective.

Promises of favourable future tax treatment are particularly costly. Because such promises have a genuine lack of credibility, the level of the ongoing tax subsidy must be very high in order to influence the location decision of the firm.

In summary, a sensible plant location policy designed to match contracting and expanding sectors can be a sensible way to mitigate social and economic adjustment costs. It has the obvious additional benefit of reducing domestic political pressures for protectionism.

Non-traded Goods Sector

A final part of industrial policy is the programs for the non-traded goods sector. This section often gets little attention because of the outward-looking nature of the small open economy and because it is often the focus of employment policies, since the services sector employs the largest proportion of the labour force. In addition, many people regard this sector as passively responding to external development, and thus not crucial as a "leading sector."

Some of these perspectives on services can be misleading. First, as economic integration occurs, what was previously non-traded can gradually become a traded good. Thus, as economic integration occurs on a worldwide level, trade in services will become increasingly important. Trade in information flows will be of particular importance. At the moment, the best policy toward trade in services would be to seek extension of existing trade arrangements to cover services trade as well.

The employment potential of the services sector means that any policies which are taken there may impact in important ways on the traded goods sectors. The ability of the economy to deal with the problem of unemployment stemming from technological change will be dealt with primarily in the non-traded goods sector. While this problem lies largely outside the scope of this study, the ability to deal with technological unemployment in the services sectors will ultimately spill over into the traded goods sectors. In particular, if the technological unemployment argument is used to inhibit adjustment within the non-traded goods sector, the same argument will be used by those affected by technological change in the traded goods sector. The long-run consequences for Canada of failing to meet the employment needs of changing external circumstances could be drastic. The distinction between adjustment in the traded and non-traded sectors is at best blurred, and in many cases does not warrant emphasis.

Conclusion

This chapter has outlined the design of industrial policy and the general options for Canada and discussed central questions of trade policy and industrial assistance. The specific issues of losing industries, basic industries and the emerging high technology industries have been covered. In all cases, the policy of free trade is seen as essential to a sensible overall policy. However, in the general area of adjustment to structural change, there is clear room for additional policy measures to promote positive adjustment. A strong case exists for active promotion of the emerging high technology growth industries within the Canadian industrial structure, and for active disinvestment in those industries which are clear losers.

Chapter 8

Conclusion and Summary

This study has outlined the concerns of trade and industrial policy in the traded goods sector of the Canadian economy. The emphasis has been on particular problems posed by structural change, and principally the concerns raised by fears of de-industrialization. The question many Canadians have asked themselves in recent times is what type of jobs they are likely to be doing in the next ten to twenty years. On the one hand, manufacturing is under intense competitive pressure. At the same time, the resource sectors are not proving to be the source of income they once were. There are real fears these trends may continue. As resources and manufacturing are the two most important tradable goods sectors, a decline in both could bring about a serious reduction in the real incomes of Canadians. The industrial policy debate in advanced industrial countries is a manifestation of some of these concerns. It revolves around two sets of substantives issues. First, what are the causes of structural change, what changes are likely in the near future, and how will the economy respond? Second, given an analysis of these changes, what is an appropriate policy response? This study is concerned with these questions as they pertain to trade and the relationship of Canadian industry with the rest of the world.

There are four broad developments in the world economy which give rise to the type of concerns discussed above. The first of these is the rapid and extensive technological revolution which is occurring throughout all industries as the result of advances in microelectronic technology. This includes automated manufacturing, robotics, computer-aided design and the revolution in information technology. The impact of this technological change is felt immediately in terms of increased productivity in selected industries and loss of jobs in a broad range of industries. The longer run effects of these changes are not known. There is a real worry that technological change has resulted in a shift in the international division of labour in a manner which will create severe problems for traditional industries in the industrialized countries.

The second development is the emergence of industrial competition from the lesser developed and the newly industrializing countries. While this has been occurring for some time in industries such as textiles and clothing, it has now shifted to more highly skilled industries such as electronics and large-scale basic industries such as steel, autos and rubber. The large pool of cheap labour in these countries has raised the spectre of intense competition as these nations advance in their economic development. This development is viewed incorrectly by many as a negative or zero-sum conflict, in which income in the developing countries expands but only at the expense of jobs in the industrialized countries.

The third development involves protection among the industrialized countries, where trade barriers have been reduced throughout the post-war period under the auspices of the General Agreement on Tariffs and Trade. In recent years, however, there has been a worldwide increase in protection as countries seek to reduce the impact of international competition on their own economies. For a small country such as Canada, this rise in protectionism is particularly worrisome.

The fourth development, which is intimately connected with the last three, is the increasing resort by the industrialized countries to non-traditional forms of government intervention in industrial markets. The most negative aspect of this development is implicit or explicit subsidization of export industries by a large number of countries. These aggressive industrial policies are viewed as a threat to the stability of the world trading system and a retreat from the utilization of the market system as the normal channel through which international trade is conducted. They pose a major problem for the small countries. It is possible that in the fight for world market share among the multinationals of the major industrial countries, the small countries could be effectively cut out of many world markets. Collectively and individually, these developments are bound to put considerable strain on the Canadian economy and the institutions through which economic policy is conducted in Canada.

The policy response to these problems can take a wide variety of forms. One extreme is simply for governments to do nothing. This would mean letting the free market dictate resource allocation and refraining from any planning or intervention whatsoever. The other extreme would be for government to plan in a very deliberate sense, with the adoption of the explicit industrial strategy which would govern the allocation of human and non-human resources for the purposes of economic development within the nation.

The adherents of non-intervention point to the problems of undertaking economic planning, given the large amount of uncertainty as to developments in the world economy, and highlight the virtues of markets as resource allocation methods. Adherents of industrial strategy take the view that conscious policy determinism toward economic development is preferred to subjecting the nation to the whims of the free market; moreover, the existence of the uncertainty is precisely why planning and strategy are necessary. For Canada this debate so far has tended to be conducted along the lines of the old debate about free trade versus protection, or nationalism versus continentalism. Proponents of an industrial strategy are often identified with those who resist a movement toward free trade and economic integration with the United States in particular. Industrial strategy, which usually includes protection as part of the total policy package, is viewed as an alternative to free trade. The free market position, of course, is adhered to by those who favour free trade and resist pressures for government intervention in the economic development process.

A major conclusion of this study is that it is a serious mistake to view the policy perspective given by the industrial policy as an alternative to free trade. In order to conduct rational economic policy in Canada, it is essential to dismiss the perceived incompatibility of free trade and industrial policy as approaches to dealing with structural change and external shocks.

A major problem in dealing with these issues is the "paradigm" problem. Economic theory plays a very important role in these discussions because it provides the intellectual position for various policy positions. Within Canada and most of the industrialized OECD countries, the dominant paradigm for dealing with trade and resource allocation or structural economic issues is the neoclassical theory of competitive markets. This is the orthodox economic theory in Western countries, and one which governs the most serious economic policy discussion. A major emphasis within this study is that some of the general assumptions of orthodox theory are seriously in error, especially when analyzing the allocation of resources in world industrial markets. In particular, the maintained assumptions of static and perfect competition in product and factor markets overlook the important ways in which dynamic oligopolistic firms in international industries impinge on trade and industrial structure. The point of adopting the alternative paradigm is not to throw out the insights provided by the theory of comparative advantage, but to integrate a more realistic view of market structure within the comparative advantage framework. Much of this study has been concerned with tracing the implications of this integration for trade and industrial policy within the small open economy. The policy perspective provided by this paradigm is quite different to that provided by the simple neoclassical model, and is more relevant to current problems.

Part of the study examined the implications and evidence for the traditional comparative advantage theory, which seeks to explain trade and industrial structure across countries by reference to international differences in relative supplies of the factors of production. In general, the conclusion was that comparative advantage, while perfectly adequate in its ability to explain trade in primary products, is inadequate in its ability to explain trade in manufactured products. This recognition leads to a further conclusion that it is a mistake to assume the traditional emphasis on primary resources as the sector in which Canada has a comparative advantage, and manufacturing as the sector in which it has a comparative disadvantage. Manufacturing is more properly viewed as a collection of industries with no factor abundance base. Therefore the economic connections between manufacturing and resources are not determined by references to difference in factor use in the two sectors. Trade in manufactures is more properly viewed within the context of world market competition and the structural variables determining competition in those markets. The comparative advantage approach, for example, suggests that Canada is at a disadvantage in high-skill, capital-intensive goods. For numerous reasons the study argues that this view is based on fallacious theoretical and empirical argument.

Comparative advantage theory does offer some sensible conclusions, though, about possible developments in the resource sectors. It is clear that the Canadian share of world resource supplies is becoming notably smaller in some areas, particularly forests and conventional supplies of oil and gas. Aggressive exporting by Third World producers is another problem for the Canadian resource sector, particularly in the mining industries. The combination of these problems and continued uncertainty in world commodity prices will render planning and economic development in the resource sector difficult. While this sector should continue to be a source of income and employment, it may not play the significant role it has in the past. Careful management of long-term resource supplies will be crucial to long-term viability of this sector.

Trade in manufactured goods can be explained more adequately by recognizing the determinants of world market structure. The entry barriers approach to market structure offers the most adequate theoretical structure for the analysis of these markets. While this approach has not been the dominant theory of trade, there have fortunately been a number of empirical studies exploring the implications of market structure for trade. One of the virtues of this theory is that it accommodates the multinational firm quite naturally as an important economic actor whose behaviour affects the patterns of world trade in important ways. The major entry barriers which are encountered by firms are scale economies, product differentiation, absolute capital requirements and dynamic economies which create advantages to firms that succeed in getting into a market first. Trade between countries is explained by determining why firms in some countries are successful in some industries and not in others. Two-way trade is a natural feature of trade in manufactured goods because an industry is located in more than one country. Firms in all countries ship to each other's domestic market.

The major policy implications of the entry barriers approach to trade for small open economies is twofold. One is recognition of the crucial importance to the manufacturing sector of a small industrial economy in gaining access to a large market. Canada is one of the few industrialized countries which is not guaranteed access under a common market or free trade arrangement to an industrial market of more than a 100 million people. There are a couple of immediate corollaries which follow from this observation. First, in industrial markets in which competition is among large oligopolistic firms, there are large real income gains in getting access to a large market, such as the U.S. market, and large costs in being denied access. Second, protection of the domestic market in these industries has first and foremost a negative effect on industry productivity, because of the anti-competitive effect of protection on the domestic market structure. In short, both foreign and domestic protection in these sectors can cost the small open industrial economy dearly.

The second implication of entry barriers for the small open economy is the recognition that in a dynamic situation the development of new export markets by entry of domestic firms into a concentrated world industry is bound to be difficult, even in the absence of trade barriers. There exist not only industry entry barriers in the form of high advertising or large capital requirements, but also genuine fixed costs to entering an export market which puts the smaller firms based in a small economy at a competitive disadvantage. Public policy to deal with this transitional difficulty should be an important concern for Canada.

Multinational enterprises are major participants in the world industrial markets. Their importance to the Canadian economy in the past is likely to continue into the future. They provide two major benefits to the Canadian economy. First, they allow Canada to participate in concentrated world markets, particularly where firm-level scale economies are an important entry barrier and where otherwise a domestic firm could not survive. Second, they serve as a major mechanism by which technology is transferred to the Canadian economy. The principal policy issue for Canada with respect to multinationals is to decide the appropriate response to their natural tendency to relocate production to low cost countries. By integrating the world market, the location decisions of multinationals have an important impact on world trade patterns. The ability of multinationals to shift economic activity around the world relatively quickly will bring them increasingly into conflict with governments and is likely to accentuate attempts by government to control foreign investment. There is little to recommend for Canada in discriminating policies toward foreign investment. The principal policy toward multinationals should be to treat them on equitable ground with domestic firms. This is dictated by the importance of our trade relations with the United States and by the growing importance of Canadian multinationals within the U.S. and world markets.

The microelectronics revolution has led to an explosion in the growth of high technology industry worldwide. The major industrial countries, through a variety of policies, have subsidized their domestic firms in the international competition within these industries. Technologically progressive industries are often characterized by high levels of market concentration, an observation attributed to Schumpeter. Consequently, these industries are often referred to as Schumpeterian. The question of whether or not a small open economy should encourage development of domestic Schumpeterian firms and industries was examined in Chapter Six. There have been numerous critics of the support of this type of economic development. The general conclusion of this study was that small industrial economies have a strong incentive to develop such industries, provided access to world markets can be assured. With this proviso, industrial development in Canada can occur in this direction with appropriate government policy. The dynamic nature of entry barriers in these industries would mean that failure to develop domestic firms that could enter the world industry relatively soon would effectively ensure the decline of the Canadian manufacturing sector over the long run, or reduce this sector to one serving the domestic market only — a highly inefficient alternative.

The longer term benefit of fostering high technology industry would be in the form of higher wages to skilled research and production workers. The existence of extensive external economies in these industries lends support for the general goal of raising the share of GNP devoted to industrial research. Equally important, however, are policies which focus on the development of small and medium size firms, and aid them in overcoming export barriers.

The final part of the study examined the general role for industrial policy and some specific problems in dealing with import competition and export promotion. The major conclusion as to industrial policy is that it should be properly viewed as complementary to a general policy of promoting free trade. Large-scale economic planning as in a full-blown strategy does not seem either feasible or desirable. However, the collection of policies which impinge on industrial economic development should be designed and managed with some consistent overall goals in mind. What should these goals be? Absolutely crucial to the long-run success of Canadian industrial development is access to large external markets. This is needed now, not at some date in the distant future. While the GATT has provided some degree of access to world markets, the rising trend in protectionism presents a significant problem for Canadians. A Canada–U.S. free trade arrangement is the next logical alternative. Efforts to negotiate such an arrangement should be the most important item on the industrial policy agenda.

At the same time, access to large world markets is not enough. An industrial policy which emphasizes positive adjustment in the face of world competition and technological change should be actively pursued. The rationale for such a policy is grounded in three propositions. First, there are some significant market failures, or failures of competition, which for dynamic reasons lead to industrial market structures that put the small economy's firms at a competitive disadvantage in world markets. Second, the political imperative of actively fostering adjustment, as opposed to the alternative of protection, is overwhelming. The policy of non-intervention is simply not politically relevant in existing circumstances, whatever its economic merits might be. Third, an active industrial policy is the optimal policy for a small country in response to the imposition of similar policies by other industrial nations. Bilateral and multilateral negotiation will have to work consciously at ensuring that market access on agreed-upon terms is guaranteed to all countries. Clearly defined distinctions must be drawn between industrial adjustment policies and protection policy. This is the area in which further trade policy negotiations are urgently required. Canada should actively promote such negotiation within the GATT. Given that the structural problems facing Canada and the United States are similar, a free trade arrangement with the United States should explicitly cover the legitimacy of alternative industrial policy instruments in both countries.

The discussion of industrial policy covered the general issue of targetting firms and sectors. The conclusion was that the emphasis on picking winners has been, for the most part, misdirected. It has been sensible in the past and will continue to be sensible in the future for industrial policy in Canada to be targetted in many instances at specific firms and occupations. The small market size of the Canadian economy, its large geographic size, the large size of the modern corporation within concentrated industrial markets, and the dynamics of individual firm development all dictate that the individual firm will be the natural focus of certain industrial policies. To claim otherwise is simply to be unrealistic as to the relevant importance of individual firms within the economy. Industrial policy, therefore, will in many circumstances take on the form of business-government-labour negotiation at the micro level, with less unilateral imposition by government of broadly based policies. In general terms, industrial policy should be pragmatic and flexible, with safeguards against unnecessary political abuse of the procedure.

Industrial policy within Canada must include a focus on three major, specific problems. First, it should attempt to mitigate the adjustment problem in those industries which are genuine losers in the changing international division of labour. This will involve a variety of labour adjustment policies including compensation, mobility grants and job retraining. It may also involve helping firms in the industry to restructure and rationalize if this is a sensible alternative. Positive adjustment out of losers, as quickly as possible is the best option. Protection of the industry is *not* the optimal response.

Second, there is the problem of competition facing large-scale basic industries such as autos, rubber and other traditional manufacturing industries. Labour market rigidities which keep wages high in these industries will dictate that production move offshore in the absence of protection. In some of these industries the possibility of plant automation means that in the longer term they may be competitive in their present North American location. Premature plant automation, encouraged through specific subsidy programs, may be one policy response which is warranted. This will keep the industry in its present location and continue to provide jobs for skilled labour and spillovers to the economy. It will not save jobs for unskilled workers. The premature automation route should be seriously considered, with the recognition that protection is probably the only realistic political alternative. In the event that the United States undertakes to protect its domestic industries, it is evident that if the premature automation policy is not feasible, Canada should refrain from adopting a parallel protection policy even if a Canada–U.S. free trade area is established. Eventually, foreign competition in these industries would seriously risk the Canadian access to the U.S. market. A more sensible strategy would be simply to let the industry stand or fall on its own and put public resources elsewhere.

The third focus of industrial policy should be on the development of high technology Schumpeterian industries. The problems of policies toward these industries have already been discussed and will not be repeated here.

The fact that industrial policy is often targetted, and in most instances focusses, on transition problems with a limited time dimension, means that two particular problems must be faced squarely. First, there will inevitably be both losers and winners from targetted and broad-based policies. Policies must be designed with specific provision so that as soon as losers are identified they cease to receive public support. Second, winners must be assured of only temporary support, however given. Thus, while targetted industrial assistance can be expected to be in place for some time, any specific firm would receive assistance for a short term only.

It is worth emphasizing that job retraining, education and labour market policies must be complementary with industrial policy if the long-run viability of manufacturing industries is to be assured. The necessary human resources in scientific, managerial-entrepreneurial, and skilled craft areas are absolutely essential. While not covered explicitly in this study, the general problems of manpower must be recognized as the ultimate constraint on any industrial policy.

Canada's policy toward trade and industrial development will be absolutely crucial in determining where the long-term future of the economy lies. In the current period of rapid and extensive structural change, government can provide active leadership in the public discussion of alternative courses of future economic development and in the provision of policies which direct the course of economic development. The world economy will change rapidly in the next few decades. Technological development and economic growth in the less developed and newly industrializing countries will create both new competition and new markets. The response of the industrialized countries to these developments is uncertain. For Canada, they create both great opportunities and some legitimate risks.

The conclusion of this study is that active promotion of free trade together with an active industrial policy which promotes positive adjustment is the policy mix most likely to succeed in promoting the best course of long-term development in the traded goods sectors. Other aspects of structural change, for example in the services sector, will hinge crucially on the type of traded goods sector Canada develops. Through appropriate policy, Canadian governments can provide the basis for private sector initiative which will ensure that Canada continues to be a major industrial country involved in the development, production and export of commodities on the leading edge of the world product cycle. This in turn will create income and provide jobs in the emerging world industries. Inevitably, this course of economic development will necessitate the integration of the Canadian economy within the world economy even further than has been the case thus far. It will also call upon Canadians to take some very deliberate risks. There is simply no way this can be avoided; such is the nature of the current world market. A policy which deliberately fails to promote development in the direction of new internationally competitive industry, either by doing nothing or by returning to a general policy of protectionism will be less risky in the short run. In the long run, however, it will guarantee the relative decline of the Canadian industrial sector. This is not an outcome many Canadians would find desirable.

Notes

1. Williamson (1983, chap.1) provides a useful summary on world economic developments.
2. Quoted in "G.M. Shift: Outside Suppliers," *New York Times*, October 14, 1981.
3. The results of the Carnegie study are reported in part in Ayres and Miller (1982a, 1982b).
4. Bliss (1982) provides a convenient summary of the historical literature. French (1980) gives an interesting summary of economic development policy in the 1970s.
5. These studies will be reviewed in Chapter Five.
6. See Government of Canada, White Paper on *Economic Development for Canada in the 1980s* (November 1981).
7. A summary of Arrow's work on market failures can be found in Arrow (1968). Since then, there has been considerable work on informational failures in markets.
8. The Chicago school of economics is the best known group associated with this position. In some instances, they deny the relevance of market failure completely, arguing that efficient cooperative agreement among individuals, subject to transactions costs, will always emerge. See Demsetz (1967).

CHAPTER 2

1. See Caves and Jones (1973, chap. 7) for an exposition of the Ricardian theory of comparative advantage.
2. The factor proportions model was first expounded in the case of two factors of production by Heckscher (1919) and Ohlin (1933). Caves and Jones (1973, chaps. 8 and 9), give an excellent exposition. The problems of extending the theory to more than two factors are covered in Chapter Three.
3. The original article is by Leontief (1954). The Leontief paradox is discussed further in Chapter Three.
4. Empirical tests of the factor proportions model are discussed in the second section of Chapter Three.
5. There are many sources on descriptive and statistical patterns of world trade in addition to primary statistical sources, such as the United Nations, the International Monetary Fund, and the Organisation for Economic Co-operation and Development. Some recent studies of particular interest to Canada include Balassa (1979) and Wilkinson (1980).
6. The development of the postwar international financial system, beginning with the Bretton Woods Agreement of 1944, is described in Triffin (1964).
7. The first major work on human capital theory was that of Becker (1964).
8. These trade studies which focus on the technology factor are discussed in the third section of Chapter Three.
9. One of the early studies was by Dunning (1958). The literature since that time has grown enormously. Caves (1983) provides a survey.
10. For documentation on the growth of the NICs and their relative importance in world trade, see Balassa (1978).
11. Previous statistical documentation on industrial support across countries is difficult to compile because of both differences in reporting conventions and institutional differences between the price setting mechanisms. Evidence in support of fairly extensive use of industrial subsidies in a number of countries is provided in Schwartz (1983), Warnecke (1978), and OECD (1975).
12. Cooper (1975) provides an excellent discussion of the British textile industry's attempt to prevent the technology transfer.

13. Amsden (1983) contains an interesting discussion of the growth of skilled labour in the NICs.

14. See "Labour Shortage Crimps Economy's Rise," *Wall Street Journal*, January 12, 1984.

CHAPTER 3

1. See Ricardo (1911), Heckscher (1919), and Ohlin (1933).

2. Strictly speaking, tastes must be not only identical but also "homothetic," i.e., all goods must have an income elasticity of demand equal to one.

3. This is the Heckscher-Ohlin theorem (see Caves and Jones, 1973, chap. 9).

4. Vanek (1968) was one of the first to explicitly identify this concept when there are many goods and factors.

5. Recent studies on U.S. data include Harkness (1978) and Leamer (1980).

6. The only recent and theoretically consistent study I am aware of is Kohli (1975).

7. See Postner (1975) and Harkness (1983).

8. Some of the early studies in the FP tradition, which included human capital disaggregated by skill category, include Kenen (1965), Keesing (1966), Baldwin (1971) and Branson (1971).

9. Branson (1971) is probably the strongest statement supporting such a view.

10. A partial list of studies in the "neo-technology" tradition include Hufbauer (1966, 1970); Gruber, et al. (1967); Keesing (1967); Vernon (1966); and the papers contained in the volume edited by Vernon (1970).

11. The debate and evidence for factor proportions and neo-technology theories is surveyed by Stern (1975).

12. Wells (1972) contains a number of case studies on the product cycle model.

13. These propositions are reviewed in any textbook on international trade. For example, see Caves and Jones (1973, chap. 12).

14. The "second-best" argument for a policy hinges on the proposition that the main purpose of the policy is to correct for distortions or inefficiencies created by other policies. Corden (1974) surveys the second-best argument for promoting export industries.

15. Wilkinson (1980) raises serious questions about the comparative advantage of a number of Canadian resource sectors. He is carrying out further work in this area for this Commission (Wilkinson, 1985).

16. The intellectual defence of this position is grounded in what has come to be known as the "market failures" doctrine. An early statement of market failures is Bator (1958). Kenneth Arrow has often been described as one of the proponents of market failure theory (see Arrow, 1968, for one statement). The major critics of this approach are the Chicago school of economists, and the Buchanan-Tullock public choice criticism. It is not my intention to review this debate. Boadway (1981) gives a summary of the various positions and references.

17. Wilkinson (1980) is a recent survey of the historical export performance of the resource sectors and their future potential.

18. Scott (1973) is a classic Canadian reference on resource management problems.

19. In the economics literature, there is remarkably little econometric evidence on capital versus goods mobility over short time horizons. In a long-run perspective, which is perhaps how FP theory ought to be interpreted, capital *services* are necessarily mobile because the capital *goods* generating the services are traded.

20. The market structure and tariff effects on foreign direct investment are reviewed in Chapter Five.

21. Boothe et al. (1984) provide direct evidence on the mobility of financial assets between Canada and the rest of the world. In economics, the word "capital" has many meanings. In the present discussion, it is important to keep clear the distinction

between physical capital (buildings, machines) and financial capital assets (bonds, common stocks, bank credit).

22. Usher (1982) is relatively pessimistic about the ability of investment incentives actually to induce private investment which otherwise would not have taken place. McFetridge and Warda (1983) express a similar pessimism on the part of R&D investment incentives. DRIE (1984), however, is somewhat more optimistic about the effectiveness of investment incentives. The industrial policy literature, as in Warnecke (1978) or Reich (1983), for example, is largely premised on the assumption that sectoral investment incentives "work."

23. It is not my intention to survey the broad literature on human capital, job training and education. For an early systematic statement of the basic theory, see Becker (1964). For a survey, see Fleisher and Kneisher (1980, chap. 8). For a broad perspective on the education issue, encompassing economic growth and technological change, see T.W. Schultze (1981).

24. The classic statement of this problem is due to Akerlof (1970). Much of the recent theoretical literature has been concerned with this problem.

25. C.L. Schultze (1983) makes precisely this statement.

26. I ignore here the problem of accumulating intangible assets such as firm-specific good will and a stock of technology through R&D. This will be dealt with in subsequent chapters.

27. The reason for this is that economic theory for the most part works within a metastatic *equilibrium* framework in which all decisions are taken simultaneously. While this has long been recognized as a problem, no one has offered a plausible theory of "leading" or "first moves," as game theoreticians refer to the problem.

28. For a brief summary of pattern in interprovincial trade statistics, see Whalley (1983).

CHAPTER 4

1. Williamson (1975) is an excellent exposition of this approach. See also Arrow (1974). Both contain extensive references to the literature.

2. Caves (1982) surveys the literature on multinational enterprises (MNEs). The approach of some economic geographers to regional economics is related to the approach pursued in the MNE literature.

3. See Richardson (1978, chap. 3) for the determinants of agglomeration economics.

4. A classic exposition of this type of interregional trade is Losch (1954), first published in German in 1941.

5. A similar description of traded and non-traded goods is offered by Vernon (1963).

6. See Britton (1978). Wonnacott and Wonnacott (1982) grant some of their points, but maintain that their earlier conclusions are qualitatively correct.

7. The decline in transport-cost oriented industry reflects improvements in transportation technology, the emergence of new technologies and products in which the bulk-to-value ratio is very low, and the more efficient processing and use of material inputs, which reduce bulk material input requirements for a given level of output. Steel, for example, is an industry which was once very transport-cost oriented but is considerably less so today. See Hogan (1971).

8. Vernon (1979) and Porter (1980, chap. 13) classify firms on a similar basis.

9. See Williamson (1971) on organizational efficiency gains to vertical integration.

10. Rumelt (1974) provides evidence on the response of corporate organization to various exogenous change.

11. Caves (1983, chap. 2) reviews the basic literature.

12. Dreze (1960) used this argument to explain why Belgian industry in the 1950s was concentrated in the production of standardized commodities. With the emergence of low wage competition in the 1980s, the argument seems of little relevance today.

13. A Statistics Canada study found that in 1978, 72 percent of total imports were to foreign-controlled firms. Most of these imports were estimated to be intrafirm trade.

14. For a formal analysis and evidence, see Horst (1972).

15. A study by the Ministry of State for Science and Technology (1978) estimated that in 1975, there were $500 million worth of "invisible" R&D transfers to Canada by multinationals. This is better than 50 percent of the total R&D expenditures in Canada for the same year.

16. Industrial policy will be covered in greater detail in Chapter Seven.

CHAPTER 5

1. The literature on scale economies and Canadian trade is so vast as to preclude any comprehensive citation. Eastman and Stykolt (1967) and Wonnacott and Wonnacott (1967) are the two major early pieces. A survey can be found in Harris (1984b, chap. 3).

2. Relative to the well-developed neoclassical theory of trade, the industrial organization theory of trade is both small and relatively new. Wonnacott (1983) and Caves (1983) are recent surveys.

3. The productivity evidence used in this debate is surveyed in Daly (1979).

4. Caves (1982, pp. 40–45) surveys the relevant evidence.

5. The Canadian literature is surveyed in Harris (1984b, chap. 3), and references are provided to the international literature.

6. See Scherer (1980, chap. 3) and Khemani (1980) for Canada.

7. Blair (1972) reviews the evidence on the scale bias of firm-level technical change and generally finds scale economies increasing over the period he surveys.

8. Gold (1981) agrees that scale economies are declining in significance, and descriptions of flexible-based CAD/CAM manufacturing systems support this position. See "The Next Industrial Revolution," *Fortune*, October 5, 1981.

9. This work is surveyed and improved upon by Caves et al. (1980).

10. The Economic Council of Canada has undertaken a good deal of research on this question. See Economic Council of Canada (1983, chaps. 8 and 9).

11. Krugman's (1980) work is the best theoretical statement of this position.

12. Scherer (1980, chap. 14) surveys the entry barriers literature on product differentiation and advertising.

13. Scherer (1980, pp. 104–108) surveys the evidence on capital market imperfections related to firm size. He also cites studies pertaining to the risk of entry.

14. Two of the better studies on this question are Hanel and Palda (1980) and Glejser et al. (1980). Evidence is also provided in Caves et al. (1980, chap. 4) on the characteristics of export industries.

15. The literature on intra-industry trade is surveyed in Harris (1984b, chap. 3). Balassa (1975) contains a summary of his position on intra-industry trade. In the case of the economic integration of the European common market, he ascribes the largest portion of adjustment to intra-industry trade adjustments.

16. Hanel and Palda (1980) provide evidence supporting the existence of set-up costs to export.

17. The argument is reviewed in Boadway (1981, chap. 20).

18. Basic contributions to the dynamic theory of pre-emptive entry barriers include Eaton and Lipsey (1979), Dixit (1980) and Spence (1977).

19. Brander and Spencer (1983) provide a formal model illustrating the effects referred to in this paragraph.

20. Welle (1979) provides a survey of the literature on the learning curve. Porter (1980, pp. 15–17) provides a concise summary of the strategic possibilities a learning curve presents to a firm, as does Scherer (1980, pp. 251–52).

21. See, for example, the popular *Theory Z*, by Ouchi (1981).

22. Corden (1974) reviews the infant-industry argument.

CHAPTER 6

1. An excellent survey of the empirical literature on market structure and innovation is Kamien and Schwartz (1982, chaps. 2 and 3). Unfortunately, virtually all of this literature deals with the closed economy.
2. Scherer (1980, chap. 18) provides an account of the public good perspective on innovation.
3. Subject to the qualification that technology is not transferred abroad. See the Economic Council of Canada (1983, chap. 4).
4. The views of the Science Council of Canada seemed to have changed on the exact nature of the support, but continue to push for an activist approach by government to technology policy. See, for example, Britton and Gilmour (1978) and Science Council of Canada (1981).
5. International technology transfer is surveyed by Caves (1982, chap. 7) and by the Economic Council of Canada (1983, chap. 5).
6. This list comes from my own reading of the market structure R&D literature. See Kamien and Schwartz (1982, chap. 3), for example. I will not attempt to provide a listing of the more than two hundred studies on the subject.
7. For a discussion of methodology, see Griliches (1979) and Fisher and Temin (1973).
8. For example, see Safarian (1969).
9. For a survey, see Caves (1982, pp. 197–200). The Canadian evidence is covered in the Economic Council of Canada (1983, pp. 40–43).
10. See Kamien and Schwartz (1982, pp. 100–102), and Economic Council of Canada (1983, chap. 5) for evidence on diffusion. Indirect evidence on slow imitation is provided by the high estimates of private returns to R&D. See Griliches (1980), for example. Why imitation rates are slow remains to be answered.
11. These transactions are studied intensively in the context of MNEs. Market transactions are predominantly licensing arrangements. Non-market transactions are predominantly internal transfers of technology between a parent and its subsidiary. Caves (1982, pp. 204–207) surveys the evidence on the factors influencing the choices between these forms of technology transfer.
12. This theoretical literature is surveyed by Dasgupta (1982). Two of the fundamental papers in the area are Loury (1979) and Futia (1980).
13. The "success breeds success" hypothesis is due to Phillips (1966). Kamien and Schwartz (1982, pp. 72–75) review the evidence on this hypothesis.
14. The theoretical models of Posner (1961) and Vernon (1966) are particularly relevant.
15. See the discussion in Chapter Three.
16. One study of 17 industrial innovations estimated the average social rate of return to be 50 percent. See Mansfield et al. (1977).
17. The evidence is summarized by Scherer (1980, pp. 258–62).
18. See Hufbauer (1970), Baumann (1976), Glejser et al. (1980) and Aquino (1981).
19. The one exception which stands out is Sweden; numerous studies have noted its revealed comparative advantage in high technology industrial goods.
20. Hanel and Palda (1980) find exports and R&D intensity at the firm level positively connected. Caves et al.(1980, chap. 4) find that technological intensity has a positive influence on both Canadian exports and imports. However, they find that the only R&D done efficiently in Canada was that which adapted foreign technology to the home market, and furthermore, that domestic R&D had a negative effect on the profitability of Canadian industry (Caves et al., 1980, chap. 9). Daly and Globerman (1979) present a very positive view on Canadian innovation and its effect on economic performance.
21. There is a fair amount of evidence on private risk to R&D in the closed economy. This evidence is at least partially relevant as an indicator of social risk to industrial R&D in the small open economy. Scherer (1980, pp. 415–18) surveys this evidence and finds that generally the risk is not as high as is commonly thought. Success rates on industrial R&D projects are on the order of 70 percent to 80 percent.

CHAPTER 7

1. The industrial policy debate has been going on in the U.S. press for close to four years now. One of the more popular pro-industrial policy books is by Reich (1983). In Canada, the Science Council has been a leader in promoting industrial strategy. For a recent statement, see its 1981 publication, *Hard Times, Hard Choices*. French (1980) gives an interesting review of the Canadian debate up to 1980. A more recent survey is Davenport et al. (1982).

2. For example, see Schultze (1983) and Watson (1983).

3. Some literature which deals specifically with the small open economy can be found in Warnecke (1978). See also *Canadian Business* (January 1983), Richardson (1983), and Thurow (1983a).

4. Thurow (1983b) argues this point persuasively.

5. See Jenkin (1983) and the literature cited therein.

6. Cooper (1968) provides an excellent discussion of these issues.

7. The arguments are reviewed by Schultze (1983) and Watson (1983).

8. For a criticism of targetting criteria, see Krugman (1983).

9. See Bliss (1982) for an historical perspective on Canada. In the European community, targetting at the firm level has a long tradition. See Warnecke (1978), for example.

10. Lazar (1981) surveys these developments.

11. See the collection of articles in the special supplement to *Canadian Public Policy* (1982) on Canada–U.S. trade for a review of the debate.

12. For an elaboration of these arguments, see Harris (1983).

13. See "The Rising Winds of Trade War," *Business Week*, January 9, 1984.

14. It is difficult to find a proposal for industrial policy which is entirely motivated by defensive concerns. Most proposals, though, are at least partially defensive in nature.

15. The parallel approach clearly is related to the continentalist position on Canadian economic development. It does not, however, presume that free markets combined with tariff protection are the only mechanisms for resource allocation.

16. Thurow (1983a) proposes that Canada follow such a model based on an analogy between Canada–United States and Austria–Germany.

17. Including agriculture seems unrealistic because of the extreme difference in agricultural policy between the two countries.

18. The Canadian literature on labour adjustment and protection policies for these industries is summarized in Pearson and Salembier (1983). Harris et al. (1984) provide an economic analysis of the adjustment problem due to a shift in the terms of trade. The literature on the adjustment of firms is much less extensive. This Commission held a symposium on these problems in January 1984 and a summary of the papers presented there will be forthcoming.

19. For a description of some of these programs, see Canada, Department of Regional Industrial Expansion (1984).

20. Bluestone and Harrison (1982) present a strong case for de-industrialization of U.S. industry. Many of their arguments (some of which I do not agree with) could be made equally well for Canada.

21. See "The Race to the Automatic Factory," *Fortune*, February 21, 1983.

22. For an analysis of world product mandating focussing on R&D relevant to Canada, see Rugman and Bennett (1982) and Poynter and Rugman (1982). These studies conclude that encouraging world product mandates may not be successful because of conflicts with overall corporate policy. Baldwin and Gorecki (1983), however, provide evidence that increased product specialization within plants occurred over the 1970s.

23. Existing systematic Canadian policy programs toward high technology industries are summarized by the Economic Council of Canada (1983, chaps. 6 and 7). There is also a good deal of piecemeal, non-systematic policy. This occurs in a variety of ways: bailouts, Crown corporations, policies of Investment Canada (formerly the Foreign Investment Review Agency), and trade policy. All of these impact in a variety of ways on high technology industries.

24. A very interesting study precisely on this class of questions, done through survey methods, was carried out by Guy Steed (1982) for the Science Council. In general, the broad thrust of his recommendations (Steed, 1982, chap. 7) toward what he calls "threshold firms" seems sensible and concurs with my own analysis.

25. Numerous presentations to the Commission's hearings stressed the importance of the high technology industries in future economic development. For example, see Canadian Manufacturers Association (1983).

26. See the argument in Chapter Six.

Bibliography

Akerlof, G.A. 1970. "The Market for 'Lemons': Quality Uncertainty and the Market Mechanism." *Quarterly Journal of Economics* 84: 488–500.

Amsden, A.H. 1983. "De-skilling, Skilled Commodities and the NIC's Emerging Comparative Advantage." *American Economic Review* 73 (2) (May).

Aquino, A. 1981. "Changes Over Time in the Pattern of Comparative Advantage in Manufactured Goals: An Empirical Analysis for the Period 1962–1974." *European Economic Review* 15: 41–62.

Arrow, K.J. 1968. "The Organization of Economic Activity: Issues Pertinent to the Choice of Market Versus Nonmarket Allocation." *In Analysis and Evaluation of Public Expenditures: The PPB System.* Washington, D.C: Government Printing Office.

———. 1974. *The Limits of Organization.* New York: Norton.

Ayres, Robert, and Steven Miller. 1982a. "Industrial Robots on the Line." *Technology Review* 85 (4) (May/June).

———. 1982b. "Robotics and Conservation of Human Resources." *Technology in Society* 4: 181–97.

Bain, J.S. 1956. *Barriers to New Competition.* Cambridge, Mass.: Harvard University Press.

Balassa, B., ed. 1975. *European Economic Integration.* Amsterdam: North-Holland.

———. 1978. "The Changing International Division of Labour in Manufactured Goods." Staff Working Paper no. 239. Washington, D.C.: World Bank.

Baldwin, J., and P. Gorecki. 1983. "A Test of the Eastman-Stykolt Hypothesis of Plant Scale Inefficiency." Working Paper. Ottawa: Economic Council of Canada.

Baldwin, R.E. 1971. "Determinants of the Commodity Structure of U.S. Trade." *American Economic Review* 61: 126–46.

Barnett, D.F., and L. Schorsch. 1983. Steel: *Upheaval in a Basic Industry.* New York: Ballinger.

Bator, R. 1958. "The Anatomy of Market Failure." *Quarterly Journal of Economics* 72: 351–79.

Baumann, H. 1976. "Structural Characteristics of Canada's Pattern of Trade." *Canadian Journal of Economics* 9: 408–24.

Becker, G.S. 1964. *Human Capital.* New York: National Bureau of Economic Research.

Blair, J.M. 1972. *Economic Concentration: Structures, Behavior and Public Policy.* New York: Harcourt Brace Jovanovich.

Bliss, M. 1982. "The Evolution of Industrial Policies in Canada: An Historical Survey." Discussion Paper 128. Ottawa: Economic Council of Canada.

Bluestone, B., and B. Harrison. 1982. *The Deindustrialization of America.* New York: Basic Books.

Boadway, R. 1981. *Public Sector Economics.* Boston: Little, Brown.

Boothe, P., K. Clinton, A. Côté, and D. Longworth. 1984. "International Asset Substitutability: Theory and Evidence for Canada." Ottawa: Bank of Canada. Mimeo.

Brander, J., and B. Spencer. 1983. "International R&D Rivalry and Industrial Strategy." Discussion Paper 518. Kingston: Queen's University.

Branson, W.H. 1971. "U.S. Comparative Advantage: Some Further Results." *Brookings Papers on Economic Activity* 3: 754–59.

Breton, A. 1974. *A Conceptual Basis for an Industrial Strategy.* Study prepared for the Economic Council of Canada. Ottawa: Information Canada.

Britton, J.H.N. 1978. "Locational Prospectives on Free Trade for Canada." *Canadian Public Policy* 4 (Winter): 4–19.

Britton, J.N.H., and J.M. Gilmour. 1978. *The Weakest Link: A Technological Perspective on Canadian Industrial Underdevelopment.* Science Council of Canada Background Study 43. Ottawa: Minister of Supply and Services Canada.

Canada. 1981. *Economic Development for Canada in the 1980s*. A white paper. Ottawa: Minister of Supply and Services Canada.

Canada. Department of External Affairs. 1983. *A Review of Canadian Trade Policy*. Ottawa: Minister of Supply and Services Canada.

Canada. Department of Finance. 1983. *Economic Review, April 1983*. Ottawa: Minister of Supply and Services Canada.

Canada. Department of Regional and Industrial Expansion. 1984. "Canada's Industrial Adjustment to Trade Policy Change and External Shocks."Study prepared for the Royal Commission on the Economic Union and Development Prospects for Canada, Research Symposium, Ottawa.

Canada. Ministry of State for Science and Technology. 1978. "Importation of Invisible Research and Development, 1974–1976." Background Paper 3. Ottawa: The Ministry.

Canadian Manufacturers' Association. 1983. "Future Making: The Era of Human Resources," Brief submitted to the Royal Commission on the Economic Union and Development Prospects for Canada. Ottawa.

Caves, R.E. 1982. *Multinational Enterprise and Economic Analysis*. Cambridge: Cambridge University Press.

_____. 1983. "A Survey of Recent Developments in Trade and Industrial Organization." Lectures delivered at Bergen, Norway.

Caves, R.E., and R.W. Jones. 1973. *World Trade and Payments*. Boston: Little, Brown.

Caves, R., M.E. Porter, and M. Spence, with J.T. Scott. 1980. *Competition in the Open Economy: A Model Applied to Canada*. Cambridge, Mass.: Harvard University Press.

Cooper, R.N. 1968. *The Economics of Interdependence: Economic Policy in the Atlantic Community*. New York: McGraw-Hill.

_____. 1975. "Technology and U.S. Trade: A Historical Review." In *Technology and International Trade*. Proceedings of the symposium sponsored by the Academy of Engineering. Washington, D.C.: National Technical Information Service.

Corden, W.M. 1974. *Trade Policy and Economic Welfare*. Oxford: Oxford University Press.

Cox, D., and R. Harris. 1985. "Trade Liberalization and Industrial Organization: Some Estimates for Canada." Forthcoming article for the *Journal of Political Economy*.

Daly, D.J. 1979 "Canada's Comparative Advantage." Discussion Paper 135. Ottawa: Economic Council of Canada.

_____. 1980. "Mineral Resources in the Canadian Economy: Macro-economic Implications." *In Natural Resources in U.S.– Canadian Relations: The Evolution of Policies and Issues*, vol.1, edited by C.E. Beigie and A.O. Hero, Jr. Boulder, Colo.: Westview Press.

Daly, D.J., and S. Globerman. 1976. *Tariff and Science Policies: Applications of a Model of Nationalism*. Toronto: Ontario Economic Council.

Dasgupta, P. 1982. "The Theory of Technological Competition." Paper presented to the International Economic Association Conference on New Developments in the Theory of Market Structures, Ottawa.

Davenport, P., C. Green, W.S. Milne, R. Saunders, and W. Watson. 1982. *Industrial Policy in Ontario and Quebec*. Toronto: Ontario Economic Council.

Demsetz, H. 1967. "Towards a Theory of Property Rights." *American Economic Review* 62: 347–59.

Denison, E.F. 1962. *The Sources of Economic Growth in the United States*. New York: Committee for Economic Development.

Dixit, A. 1980. "The Role of Investment in Entry Deterrence." *Economic Journal* 90: 95–106.

Dreze, J. 1960. "Quelques réflexions séreines sur l'adaptation de l'industrie belge en Marché Commun." In *Comptes rendus des travaux de laSociété Royale d'Économie Politique de Belgique*, no. 275.

Dunning, J.H. 1958. *American Investment in British Manufacturing Industry*. London: Allen and Unwin.

Eastman, H., and S. Stykolt. 1967. *The Tariff and Competition in Canada*. Toronto: Macmillan.

Eaton, C., and R.G. Lipsey. 1979. "The Theory of Market Pre-emption: The Persistence of Excess Capacity and Monopoly in Growing Spatial Markets." *Economica* 46: 148–58.

Economic Council of Canada. 1975. *Looking Outward: A New Trade Strategy for Canada*. Ottawa: Information Canada.

————. 1982. *In Short Supply: Jobs and Skills in the 1980's*. Ottawa: Minister of Supply and Services Canada.

————. 1983. *The Bottom Line*. Ottawa: Minister of Supply and Services Canada.

Fisher, F.M., and P. Temin. 1973. "Returns to Scale in Research and Development: What Does the Schumpeterian Hypothesis Imply?" *Journal of Political Economy* 81: 56–70.

Fleisher, B.M., and T.J. Kneisher. 1980. *Labor Economics*. 2d ed. Englewood Cliffs, N.J.: Prentice-Hall.

French, Richard D. 1980. *How Ottawa Decides: Planning and Industrial Policy-Making 1968–1980*. Ottawa: Canadian Institute for Economic Policy.

Futia, C. 1980. "Schumpeterian Competition." *Quarterly Journal of Economics* 94: 675–95.

Galbraith, J. 1952. *American Capitalism*. Boston: Houghton Mifflin.

Glejser, H., A. Jacquemin, and J. Petit. 1980. "Exports in an Imperfect Competition Framework: An Analysis of 1,446 Exporters." *Quarterly Journal of Economics* 20: 508–24.

Globerman, S. 1974. "Technological Diffusion in Canadian Manufacturing Industries." Technological Innovation Studies Program Research Report 17. Ottawa: Department of Industry, Trade and Commerce.

————. 1979. "Foreign Direct Investment and 'Spillover' Efficiency Benefits in Canadian Manufacturing Industries." *Canadian Journal of Economics* 12: 42–50.

Gold, B. 1981. "Changing Perspectives on Size, Scale and Returns: An Interpretive Survey." *Journal of Economic Literature* 19: 5–34.

Goreckl, P. 1980. *Economics of Scale and Efficient Plant Size in Canadian Manufacturing Industries*. Ottawa: Department of Consumer and Corporate Affairs, Bureau of Competition Policy.

Griliches, Z. 1979. "Issues in Assessing the Contribution of Research and Development to Productivity Growth." *Bell Journal of Economics* 10: 92–116.

————. 1980. "Return to Research and Development Expenditures in the Private Sector." *In New Developments in Productivity Measurement and Analysis*, edited by J.W. Kendrick and B.N. Vaccara. Chicago: University of Chicago Press.

Gruber, W., D. Mehta, and R. Vernon. 1967. "The R&D Factor in International Trade and International Investment of United States Industries." *Journal of Political Economy* 75: 20–37.

Hanel, P., and K. Palda. 1980. "Innovation and Export Performance in Canadian Manufacturing." Discussion Paper 209. Ottawa: Economic Council of Canada.

Harkness, J. 1978. "Factor Abundance and Comparative Advantage." *American Economic Review* 68: 784–800.

————. 1983. "The Factor Proportions Model with Many Nations, Goods and Factors: Theory and Evidence." *Review of Economics and Statistics* 65: 298–305.

Harris, R.G. 1983. "Comment on a Paper by Professor Stern." Paper delivered at a conference on Canada–U.S. economic relations, London, Ontario.

————. 1984a. "Applied General Equilibrium Analysis of Small Open Economies with Scale Economics and Imperfect Competition." *American Economic Review* 74: 1016–32.

————. 1984b. *Trade, Industrial Policy and Canadian Manufacturing*. Toronto: Ontario Economic Council.

Harris, R.G., F. Lewis, and D. Purvis. 1984. "Adjustment: Theory and Policy." In *John Deutsch Round Table Conference on Economic Policy*, edited by D.Purvis. John

Deutsch Memorial for the Study of Economic Policy, 1982. Kingston: Queen's University.

Heckscher, E. 1919. "The Effect of Foreign Trade on the Distribution of Income." *Ekonomisk Tidskrift* 21: 497–512.

Hogan, W.T. 1971. *Economic History of the Iron and Steel Industry in the United States.* Lexington, Mass.: D. C. Heath.

Horst, T. 1972. "The Industrial Composition of U.S. Exports and Subsidiary Sales to the Canadian Market." *American Economic Review* 62: 35–37.

Hufbauer, G.C. 1966. *Synthetic Materials and the Theory of International Trade.* Cambridge, Mass.: Harvard University Press.

————. 1970. "The Impact of National Characteristics and Technology on the Commodity Composition of Trade in Manufactured Goods." In *The Technology Factor in International Trade*, edited by R.Vernon. New York: National Bureau of Economic Research.

Jenkin, M. 1983. *The Challenge of Diversity: Industrial Policy in the Canadian Federation.* Science Council of Canada Background Study 50. Ottawa: Minister of Supply and Services Canada.

Johnson, C. 1982. *MITI and the Japanese Miracle.* Stanford, Calif.: Stanford University Press.

Johnston, Hon. D.J. 1983. Brief Submitted by the Minister of State for Economic and Regional Development for Science and Technology, Government of Canada, to the Royal Commission on the Economic Union and Development Prospects for Canada (September).

Kamien, M.I., and N.L. Schwartz. 1982. *Market Structure and Innovation.* Cambridge: Cambridge University Press.

Keesing, D.B. 1966. "Labour Skills and Comparative Advantage." *American Economic Review* 5 (2): 249–58.

————. 1967. "The Impact of Research and Development on United States Trade." *Journal of Political Economy* 75: 38–44.

Kenen, P.B. 1965. "Nature, Capital and Trade." *Journal of Political Economy* 73: 437–60.

Khemani, R. 1980. *Concentration in the Manufacturing Industries of Canada: Analysis of Post-war Changes.* Ottawa: Department of Consumer and Corporate Affairs.

Kohli, U. 1975. "Canadian Technology and Derived Import Demand and Export Supply Functions." Ph.D. diss., University of British Columbia.

Krugman, P. 1980. "Scale Economics, Product Differentiation, and the Patterns of Trade." *American Economic Review* 70: 950–59.

————. 1983. "Targeted Industrial Policies: Theory and Evidence." Cambridge, Mass.: Massachusetts Institute of Technology. Mimeo.

Lazar, F. 1981. *The New Protectionism, Non-tariff Barriers and their Effects on Canada.* Toronto: James Lorimer.

Leamer, E. 1980. "The Leontief Paradox Reconsidered." *Journal of Political Economy* 88: 495–503.

Leontief, W.W. 1954. "Domestic Productions and Foreign Trade: The American Capital Position Re-examined." *Economia Internazionale* 7: 3–32.

————. 1956. "Factor Proportions and the Structure of American Trade: Further Theoretical and Empirical Analysis." *Review of Economics and Statistics* 38: 392–97.

Longworth, David. 1985. "Some Exchange Rate Policy Considerations when Trade is Liberalized." *In Domestic Policies and the International Economic Environment*, volume 12 of the research studies prepared for the Royal Commission on the Economic Union and Development Prospects for Canada. Toronto: University of Toronto Press.

Losch, A. 1954. *The Economics of Location.* New Haven: Yale University Press.

Loury, G. 1979. "Market Structure and Innovation." *Quarterly Journal of Economics* 93: 395–410.

Mansfield, E., J. Rapoport, A. Romeo, S. Wagner, and G. Beardsley. 1977. "Social and

Private Rates of Return from Industrial Innovations." *Quarterly Journal of Economics* 91: 221–40.

McFetridge, D.G., and J.P. Warda. 1983. *Canadian R&D Incentives: Their Adequacy and Impact*. Canadian Tax Paper no.70. Toronto: Canadian Tax Foundation.

Mundell, R.A. 1957. "International Trade and Factor Mobility." *American Economic Review* 47: 321–35.

Mundell, R.A., and J.J. Polak. 1957. *The New International Monetary System.*(Reprinted 1977.) New York: Columbia University Press.

Organisation for Economic Co-operation and Development. 1975. *The Aims and Instruments of Industrial Policy: A Comparative Study*. Paris: OECD.

Ohlin, B. 1933. *Interregional and International Trade*. Cambridge, Mass.: Harvard University Press.

Ouchi, W.G. 1981. *Theory Z: How American Business Can Meet the Japanese Challenge*. Reading, Mass.: Addison-Wesley.

Palda, K.S., and B. Pazderka. 1982. *Approaches to an International Comparison of Canada's R&D Expenditures*. Study prepared for the Economic Council of Canada. Ottawa: Minister of Supply and Services Canada.

Pearson, C., and G. Salembier. 1983. *Trade, Employment and Adjustment.*Montreal: Institute for Research on Public Policy.

Phillips, A. 1966. "Patents, Potential Competition, and Technical Progress." *American Economic Review* 56: 301–10.

Porter, M.E. 1980. *Competitive Strategy: Techniques for Analyzing Industries and Competitors*. New York: Macmillan.

Posner, M.V. 1961. "International Trade and Technical Change." *Oxford Economic Papers* 21: 323–41.

Postner, H.H. 1975. *Factor Content of Canadian International Trade: An Input-Output Analysis*. Study prepared for the Economic Council of Canada. Ottawa: Information Canada.

Poynter, T.A., and A. Rugman. 1982. "World Product Mandates: How Will Multinationals Respond?" *Business Quarterly* (Fall).

Reich, Robert B. 1983. *The Next American Frontier*. New York: Times Bank.

Ricardo, David. 1911. *The Principles of Political Economy and Taxation*. London: J.M. Dent and Sons.

Richardson, G.B. 1960. *Information and Investment*. Oxford: Oxford University Press.

Richardson, H.W. 1978. *Urban Economics*. Hinden, Ill.: Dryden Press.

Richardson, J.D. 1983. "The New Nexus Among Trade, Industrial and Exchange-Rate Policies." Working Paper 1099. Cambridge, Mass.: National Bureau of Economic Research.

Rugman, A., and J. Bennett. 1982. "Technology Transfer and World Product Mandating." *Columbia Journal of World Business* (Winter): 58–62.

Rumelt, R.P. 1974. *Strategy, Structure and Economic Performance*. Boston: Harvard Business School, Division of Research.

Safarian, A.E. 1969. *The Performance of Foreign Owned Firms in Canada*. Montreal: Canadian-American Committee.

Scherer, F.M. 1980. *Industrial Market Structure and Economic Performance*. 2d ed. Boston: Houghton Mifflin.

Schultze, C.L. 1983. "Industrial Policy: A Dissent." *Brookings Review* 2 (1): 3–12.

Schultze, T.W. 1981. *Investing in People*. Berkeley: University of California Press.

Schumpeter, J. 1934. *Theory of Economic Development*. London: Oxford University Press.

Schwartz, W.F. 1983. "Regulation of Industrial Subsidies in the EEC, the United States and GATT." *In Federalism and the Canadian Economic Union*, edited by M.J. Trebilcock et al. Toronto: University of Toronto for the Ontario Economic Council.

Science Council of Canada. 1981. *Hard Times, Hard Choices*. Ottawa: Minister of Supply and Services Canada.

Scott, A.D. 1973. *Natural Resources: The Economics of Conservation*. Carleton Library Series no. 68. Toronto: McClelland and Stewart.

Sharma, B.L. 1982. "International Flow of Manufacturing." *European Economic Review*: 382–94.

Solow, R. 1957. "Technical Change and the Aggregate Production Functions." *Review of Economics and Statistics* 34: 312–20.

Spence, A.M. 1977. "Entry, Investment and Oligopolistic Pricing." *Bell Journal of Economics* 8: 534–44.

Steed, G.P.F. 1982. *Threshold Firms, Backing Canada's Winners*. Science Council of Canada Background Study 48. Ottawa: Minister of Supply and Services Canada.

Stern, R.M. 1975. "Testing Trade Theories." *In International Trade and Finance*, edited by P.B. Kenen. Cambridge: Cambridge University Press.

Teece, D.J. 1977. "Technology Transfer by Multinational Firms: The Resource Cost of Transferring Technological Knowhow." *Economic Journal* 87: 242–61.

Thurow, L. 1983a. "An Immodest Proposal for Canada." *Canadian Business* (April).

_____. 1983b. "A Case for Industrial Policy." Cambridge, Mass.: Massachusetts Institute of Technology. Mimeo.

Trebilcock, M.J., J.R.S. Prichard, T.J. Courchene, and J. Whalley, eds. 1983. *Federalism and the Canadian Economic Union*. Toronto: University of Toronto Press for the Ontario Economic Council.

Triffin, R. 1964. *The Evolution of the International Monetary System: Historical Reappraisal and Future Perspectives*. Princeton Studies in International Finance no.12. Princeton: Princeton University, International Finance Section.

Usher, D. 1982. "The Benefits and Costs of Firm Specific Investment Grants: A Study of Five Federal Programs." Kingston: Queen's University. Mimeo.

Vanek, J. 1968. "The Factor Proportions Theory: The n-Factor Case." *Kyklos* 21: 749–56.

Vernon, R. 1963. *Metropolis, 1985*. New York: Doubleday.

_____. 1966. "International Investment and International Trade in the Product Cycle." *Quarterly Journal of Economics* 80: 190–207.

_____, ed. 1970. *The Technology Factor in International Trade*. New York: National Bureau of Economic Research.

_____. 1979. "The Product Cycle Hypothesis in a New International Economic Environment." *Oxford Bulletin of Economic Statistics* 41: 255–67.

Wahl, D.F. 1961. "Capital and Labour Requirements for Canada's Foreign Trade." *Canadian Journal of Economics and Political Science* 27: 394–58.

Walters, D. 1970. *Canadian Growth Revisited, 1950–1967*. Ottawa: Queen's Printer.

Warnecke, S.J., ed. 1978. *International Trade and Industrial Policies: Government Intervention and an Open World Economy*. London: Macmillan.

Watson, W. 1983. *A Primer on Industrial Policy*. Toronto: Ontario Economic Council.

Welle, L.E. 1979. "The Learning Curve: Historical Review and Comprehensive Survey." *Decision Sciences* 10: 302–28.

Wells, L.T., ed. 1972. *The Product Cycle and International Trade*. Cambridge, Mass.: Harvard University, Graduate School of Business Administration.

Whalley, J. 1983. "Induced Distortions of Interprovincial Activity: An Overview of the Issues." *In Federalism and the Canadian Economic Union*, edited by M.J. Trebilcock et al. Toronto: University of Toronto Press for the Ontario Economic Council.

Wilkinson, B.W. 1968. *Canada's International Trade: An Analysis of Recent Trends and Patterns*. Montreal: Private Planning Association of Canada.

_____. 1980. *Canada in the Changing World Economy*. Montreal: C.D. Howe Research Institute.

_____. 1985. "Canada's Resource Industries: A Survey." In *Canada's Resource Industries and Water Export Policy*, volume 14 of the research studies prepared for the Royal

Commission on the Economic Union and Development Prospects for Canada. Toronto: University of Toronto Press.

Williamson, J. 1983. *The Open Economy and the World Economy*. New York: Basic Books.

Williamson, O.E. 1971. "The Vertical Integration of Production: Market Failure Considerations." *American Economic Review* 61: 112–23.

―――――. 1975. *Markets and Hierarchies: Analysis and Anti-trust Implications*. New York: Free Press.

Wonnacott, Paul, and R.J. Wonnacott. 1967. *Free Trade Between the United States and Canada*: The Potential Economic Effects. Cambridge, Mass.: Harvard University Press.

―――――. 1982. "Free Trade Between the United States and Canada: Fifteen Years Later." *Canadian Public Policy* 8, Special Supplement (October).

Wonnacott, R.J. 1975. "Industrial Strategy: A Canadian Substitute for Trade Liberalization." *Canadian Journal of Economics* 8: 536–47.

―――――. 1983. "A Survey of Some Recent Developments in Trade Theory and Policy." Ottawa: Institute for Research on Public Policy. Mimeo.

THE COLLECTED RESEARCH STUDIES
Royal Commission on the Economic Union
and Development Prospects for Canada

ECONOMICS

Income Distribution and Economic Security in Canada (Vol.1), *François Vaillancourt, Research Coordinator*

Vol. 1   Income Distribution and Economic Security in Canada, *F. Vaillancourt* (C)*

Industrial Structure (Vols. 2-8), *Donald G. McFetridge, Research Coordinator*

Vol. 2   Canadian Industry in Transition, *D.G. McFetridge* (C)
Vol. 3   Technological Change in Canadian Industry, *D.G. McFetridge* (C)
Vol. 4   Canadian Industrial Policy in Action, *D.G. McFetridge* (C)
Vol. 5   Economics of Industrial Policy and Strategy, *D.G. McFetridge* (C)
Vol. 6   The Role of Scale in Canada–US Productivity Differences, *J.R. Baldwin and P.K. Gorecki* (M)
Vol. 7   Competition Policy and Vertical Exchange, *F. Mathewson and R. Winter* (M)
Vol. 8   The Political Economy of Economic Adjustment, *M. Trebilcock* (M)

International Trade (Vols. 9-14), *John Whalley, Research Coordinator*

Vol. 9   Canadian Trade Policies and the World Economy, *J. Whalley with C. Hamilton and R. Hill* (M)
Vol. 10   Canada and the Multilateral Trading System, *J. Whalley* (M)
Vol. 11   Canada–United States Free Trade, *J. Whalley* (C)
Vol. 12   Domestic Policies and the International Economic Environment, *J. Whalley* (C)
Vol. 13   Trade, Industrial Policy and International Competition, *R. Harris* (M)
Vol. 14   Canada's Resource Industries and Water Export Policy, *J. Whalley* (C)

Labour Markets and Labour Relations (Vols. 15-18), *Craig Riddell, Research Coordinator*

Vol. 15   Labour-Management Cooperation in Canada, *C. Riddell* (C)
Vol. 16   Canadian Labour Relations, *C. Riddell* (C)
Vol. 17   Work and Pay: The Canadian Labour Market, *C. Riddell* (C)
Vol. 18   Adapting to Change: Labour Market Adjustment in Canada, *C. Riddell* (C)

Macroeconomics (Vols. 19-25), *John Sargent, Research Coordinator*

Vol. 19   Macroeconomic Performance and Policy Issues: Overviews, *J. Sargent* (M)
Vol. 20   Post-War Macroeconomic Developments, *J. Sargent* (C)
Vol. 21   Fiscal and Monetary Policy, *J. Sargent* (C)
Vol. 22   Economic Growth: Prospects and Determinants, *J. Sargent* (C)
Vol. 23   Long-Term Economic Prospects for Canada: A Symposium, *J. Sargent* (C)
Vol. 24   Foreign Macroeconomic Experience: A Symposium, *J. Sargent* (C)
Vol. 25   Dealing with Inflation and Unemployment in Canada, *C. Riddell* (M)

Economic Ideas and Social Issues (Vols. 26 and 27), *David Laidler, Research Coordinator*

Vol. 26   Approaches to Economic Well-Being, *D. Laidler* (C)
Vol. 27   Responses to Economic Change, *D. Laidler* (C)

* (C) denotes a Collection of studies by various authors coordinated by the person named.
  (M) denotes a Monograph.

POLITICS AND INSTITUTIONS OF GOVERNMENT

Canada and the International Political Economy (Vols. 28-30), *Denis Stairs and Gilbert R. Winham, Research Coordinators*

Vol. 28 Canada and the International Political/Economic Environment, *D. Stairs and G.R. Winham* (C)

Vol. 29 The Politics of Canada's Economic Relationship with the United States, *D. Stairs and G.R. Winham* (C)

Vol. 30 Selected Problems in Formulating Foreign Economic Policy, *D. Stairs and G.R. Winham* (C)

State and Society in the Modern Era (Vols. 31 and 32), *Keith Banting, Research Coordinator*

Vol. 31 State and Society: Canada in Comparative Perspective, *K. Banting* (C)

Vol. 32 The State and Economic Interests, *K. Banting* (C)

Constitutionalism, Citizenship and Society (Vols. 33-35), *Alan Cairns and Cynthia Williams, Research Coordinators*

Vol. 33 Constitutionalism, Citizenship and Society in Canada, *A. Cairns and C. Williams* (C)

Vol. 34 The Politics of Gender, Ethnicity and Language in Canada, *A. Cairns and C. Williams* (C)

Vol. 35 Public Opinion and Public Policy in Canada, *R. Johnston* (M)

Representative Institutions (Vols. 36-39), *Peter Aucoin, Research Coordinator*

Vol. 36 Party Government and Regional Representation in Canada, *P. Aucoin* (C)

Vol. 37 Regional Responsiveness and the National Administrative State, *P. Aucoin* (C)

Vol. 38 Institutional Reforms for Representative Government, *P. Aucoin* (C)

Vol. 39 Intrastate Federalism in Canada, *D.V. Smiley and R.L. Watts* (M)

The Politics of Economic Policy (Vols. 40-43), *G. Bruce Doern, Research Coordinator*

Vol. 40 The Politics of Economic Policy, *G.B. Doern* (C)

Vol. 41 Federal and Provincial Budgeting, *A.M. Maslove, M.J. Prince and G.B. Doern* (M)

Vol. 42 Economic Regulation and the Federal System, *R. Schultz and A. Alexandroff* (M)

Vol. 43 Bureaucracy in Canada: Control and Reform, *S.L. Sutherland and G.B. Doern* (M)

Industrial Policy (Vols. 44 and 45), *André Blais, Research Coordinator*

Vol. 44 Canadian Industrial Policy, *A. Blais* (C)

Vol. 45 The Political Sociology of Industrial Policy, *A. Blais* (M)

LAW AND CONSTITUTIONAL ISSUES

Law, Society and the Economy (Vols. 46-51), *Ivan Bernier and Andrée Lajoie, Research Coordinators*

Vol. 46 Law, Society and the Economy, *I. Bernier and A. Lajoie* (C)

Vol. 47 The Supreme Court of Canada as an Instrument of Political Change, *I. Bernier and A. Lajoie* (C)

Vol. 48 Regulations, Crown Corporations and Administrative Tribunals, *I. Bernier and A. Lajoie* (C)

Vol. 49 Family Law and Social Welfare Legislation in Canada, *I. Bernier and A. Lajoie* (C)

Vol. 50 Consumer Protection, Environmental Law and Corporate Power, *I. Bernier and A. Lajoie* (C)

Vol. 51 Labour Law and Urban Law in Canada, *I. Bernier and A. Lajoie* (C)

The International Legal Environment (Vols. 52-54), *John Quinn, Research Coordinator*

Vol. 52 The International Legal Environment, *J. Quinn* (C)
Vol. 53 Canadian Economic Development and the International Trading System, *M.M. Hart* (M)
Vol. 54 Canada and the New International Law of the Sea, *D.M. Johnston* (M)

Harmonization of Laws in Canada (Vols. 55 and 56), *Ronald C.C. Cuming, Research Coordinator*

Vol. 55 Perspectives on the Harmonization of Law in Canada, *R. Cuming* (C)
Vol. 56 Harmonization of Business Law in Canada, *R. Cuming* (C)

Institutional and Constitutional Arrangements (Vols. 57 and 58), *Clare F. Beckton and A. Wayne MacKay, Research Coordinators*

Vol. 57 Recurring Issues in Canadian Federalism, *C.F. Beckton and A.W. MacKay* (C)
Vol. 58 The Courts and The Charter, *C.F. Beckton and A.W. MacKay* (C)

FEDERALISM AND THE ECONOMIC UNION

Federalism and The Economic Union (Vols. 58-72), *Mark Krasnick, Kenneth Norrie and Richard Simeon, Research Coordinators*

Vol. 59 Federalism and Economic Union in Canada, *K. Norrie, R. Simeon and M. Krasnick* (M)
Vol. 60 Perspectives on the Canadian Economic Union, *M. Krasnick* (C)
Vol. 61 Division of Powers and Public Policy, *R. Simeon* (C)
Vol. 62 Case Studies in the Division of Powers, *M. Krasnick* (C)
Vol. 63 Intergovernmental Relations, *R. Simeon* (C)
Vol. 64 Disparities and Interregional Adjustment, *K. Norrie* (C)
Vol. 65 Fiscal Federalism, *M. Krasnick* (C)
Vol. 66 Mobility of Capital in the Canadian Economic Union, *N. Roy* (M)
Vol. 67 Economic Management and the Division of Powers, *T.J. Courchene* (M)
Vol. 68 Regional Aspects of Confederation, *J. Whalley* (M)
Vol. 69 Interest Groups in the Canadian Federal System, *H.G. Thorburn* (M)
Vol. 70 Canada and Quebec, Past and Future: An Essay, *D. Latouche* (M)
Vol. 71 The Political Economy of Canadian Federalism: 1940–1984, *R. Simeon and I. Robinson* (M)

THE NORTH

Vol. 72 The North, *Michael S. Whittington, Coordinator* (C)

COMMISSION ORGANIZATION

Chairman

Donald S. Macdonald

Commissioners

Clarence L. Barber	William M. Hamilton	Daryl K. Seaman
Albert Breton	John R. Messer	Thomas K. Shoyama
M. Angela Cantwell Peters	Laurent Picard	Jean Casselman-Wadds
E. Gérard Docquier	Michel Robert	Catherine T. Wallace

Senior Officers

Executive Director
J. Gerald Godsoe

Director of Policy	*Senior Advisors*	*Directors of Research*
Alan Nymark	David Ablett	Ivan Bernier
	Victor Clarke	Alan Cairns
Secretary	Carl Goldenberg	David C. Smith
Michel Rochon	Harry Stewart	
Director of Administration	*Director of Publishing*	*Co-Directors of Research*
Sheila-Marie Cook	Ed Matheson	Kenneth Norrie
		John Sargent

Research Program Organization

Economics	**Politics and the Institutions of Government**	**Law and Constitutional Issues**
Research Director	*Research Director*	*Research Director*
David C. Smith	Alan Cairns	Ivan Bernier
Executive Assistant & Assistant Director (Research Services)	*Executive Assistant*	*Executive Assistant & Research Program Administrator*
I. Lilla Connidis	Karen Jackson	Jacques J.M. Shore
Coordinators	*Coordinators*	*Coordinators*
David Laidler	Peter Aucoin	Clare F. Beckton
Donald G. McFetridge	Keith Banting	Ronald C.C. Cuming
Kenneth Norrie*	André Blais	Mark Krasnick
Craig Riddell	Bruce Doern	Andrée Lajoie
John Sargent*	Richard Simeon	A. Wayne MacKay
François Vaillancourt	Denis Stairs	John J. Quinn
John Whalley	Cynthia Williams	
	Gilbert R. Winham	
Research Analysts	*Research Analysts*	*Administrative and Research Assistant*
Caroline Digby	Claude Desranleau	Nicolas Roy
Mireille Ethier	Ian Robinson	
Judith Gold		
Douglas S. Green	*Office Administration*	*Research Analyst*
Colleen Hamilton	Donna Stebbing	Nola Silzer
Roderick Hill		
Joyce Martin		

*Kenneth Norrie and John Sargent co-directed the final phase of Economics Research with David Smith